THE FAMILY

CHRIS JOHNSTON & ROSIE JONES

SCRIBE

Melbourne • London

Scribe Publications
18–20 Edward St, Brunswick, Victoria 3056, Australia
2 John St, Clerkenwell, London, WC1N 2ES, United Kingdom

First published by Scribe 2016
Copyright © Big Stories Co Pty Ltd 2016

Typeset in 11.75 / 17 pt Sabon by the publishers
Printed and bound in the UK by CPI Group (UK) Ltd, Croydon, CR0 4YY

Scribe Publications is committed to the sustainable use of natural resources
and the use of paper products made responsibly from those resources.

9781925321678 (Australian edition)
9781925228687 (UK edition)
9781925307597 (e-book)

CiP data records for this title are available from the
National Library of Australia and the British Library.

scribepublications.com.au
scribepublications.co.uk

For all the people who had the courage to speak out

CONTENTS

WALK ON

She is skeletal and pale, 95 years old and living in a nursing home in the outer suburbs of Melbourne, Australia. There are dense layers of secrecy surrounding her, as there have always been. Her followers have been told since the beginning to protect her, and never to betray her.

To these followers, Anne Hamilton-Byrne is a reincarnation of Jesus, a living god. But her story is one of betrayal upon bitter betrayal. Outsiders — 'left-hand forces', according to Anne — are never to be trusted.

We have been allowed to visit her in the nursing home: Rosie Jones, a documentary filmmaker, and me, Chris Johnston, a newspaper journalist. I had been writing stories on The Family, the group which Anne led, for *The Age* in Melbourne — mainly about behind-the-scenes shuffling of assets in her vast property portfolio as she edges closer to death — when I heard that Rosie was making a film. She had amassed a lot of information over two years of research and was gradually developing relationships

1

with key people from the cult. We started comparing notes, and then decided to collaborate on a book in conjunction with the film.

The story of Anne Hamilton-Byrne and The Family is a tragic, sensational one about power, money, love, hope, and ultimately abuse — and the extent to which everyday people are prepared to believe the most extraordinary things. As we continued to find our way into the story and piece the book and documentary film together, we both desperately wanted to meet the woman at the centre of it, to understand, if possible, the source of her power. Now, in this most humble of settings, we are here with her.

Anne has dementia and uses a wheelchair. The nursing home is within view of the forested hills on Melbourne's fringe, where she formed her cult more than 50 years ago. But she will not return to the sanctuary of those hills now. She lies here in the final throes of her life even though she said she could transcend death. Her hair is long and silver and tied back very tightly, and she is dressed beautifully in blue, her cult's most totemic colour, with delicate white slip-on shoes on her withered feet. Her eyes dart around the room. A cult member told us it was always, always in the eyes: 'If you could look into her eyes,' he said, 'you would understand.' Those eyes are piercing but somehow also vacant, as if the mystery, hope, fantasy, and lies inside them from decades past have flickered away, the focus lost.

Anne's cult was at first called The Great White Brotherhood. Then it became known as The Family, and it seemed that's what she wanted: a family. She was glamorous and, of course, charismatic — a Kim Novak blonde who wore red to the parties the cult had in the 1970s. But she was cruel and ordered others to be cruel for her. She was able to make well-educated, 'ordinary' people do immoral things. The children she accumulated as her own allege they were abused and drugged.

Now Anne's dementia means she can never again be challenged in court over her actions. It also means she cannot tell us or anyone else anything of real value. During her life as a self-proclaimed spiritual Master, her every word was taken as a glimmering truth, a light, a pathway. But now she talks only in dementia's loop of echoes. 'Mummy really goes me,' she says, as we sit in front of her. 'I just get along.' Then, in a glimmer of clarity: 'Altogether we had four, five ... we had seven or eight children, Bill and I.' Bill was her third husband and co-conspirator; photographs of him, distinguished and handsome, adorn her room. The pictures of the two of them show an immaculately dressed and confident pair.

So the dilemma for Rosie and me is this: Anne cannot answer our questions. She can't talk about Bill, her grand intentions for The Family, her unusual relationship with her mother. We can only gather glimpses of her, as filtered through the memories of others, or from photographs and the recordings she created over a lifetime. What is true and what is false in this complex, often contradictory story of the cult? Many, many people crossed Anne's path, and among them many victims. Most of those caught up in this story are scarred in some way, and the testimonies they give are confronting. Whose version is closest to the truth?

In unpacking this extraordinary story, we wanted to understand the circumstances — societal and personal — that led this woman to operate at the edges of human belief. How did she convince people to trust her and take a leap of faith?

It was Michael, one of Anne's most devoted followers, who brought us to meet her. This was against the wishes of other cult members. A rumpled man in his sixties, from one of Melbourne's most eminent families, Michael loves Anne, and has done with extraordinary loyalty and deference for almost 50 years. At her peak she had perhaps 500 followers like him, but now they are few. Michael has been helpful — we've had lunch together and been to his home. He is prepared to trust us, perhaps because he believes Anne has been persecuted and he wants to defend her. By defending her, he validates his own choice to belong to what he still calls The Brotherhood. Anne is introverted now, focused on her internal world. Michael says she doesn't need to speak or be cogent because her spirit as the Master is as powerful as ever.

Anne is wheeled from the common room back to her room, and we follow. There is a bib discarded on the bed. She sits in a chair sucking a protein drink from a straw.

'Have you got a doggie down there?' She rests her head on a tea tray in front of her. 'Mummy really goes me and I just get along. That's what I am and that's all I am.' Even today, a regular Thursday in the nursing home, she is wearing pearls. She struggles to itch her ankle with long, finely boned fingers heavy with gold rings. A story went around that she also had diamond earrings but one day they suddenly disappeared, after a visit by a cult member left her with bleeding earlobes.

There's a plastic doll under a crocheted blanket on her bed, and she picks it up and cradles it tenderly. On the walls there are photographs of the children she acquired and dressed up. Who were they, where did they come from? We want to hear her perspective, but she cannot tell us why.

There is another photograph, of Anne playing the harp, beside a print of da Vinci's *The Last Supper*. In her younger days she wore Chanel perfume and loved to sing soprano. She also gave out a mantra to all her cult members, spelling out the order never to betray. She offered hope but would ultimately be double-crossed by some who had been so loyal. Is the da Vinci print a coincidence, or a reminder?

Anne hid herself and her adult followers in the forested hills near Melbourne, the Dandenong Ranges, an hour by car now and even further through the 1960s, 1970s, and 1980s, when The

Family was most active. The roads are steep, through mountain ash trees and national parks. The houses are concealed.

Anne hid the children two hours away in another direction, beside Lake Eildon, in the foothills of the High Country. The artificial lake is surrounded by mountains and has partly submerged trees dotted throughout it, as if there is a secret life under the surface. Entire living plains were flooded to make the lake; it's a very pretty place, but the trees rising up from the water give an air of menace.

Anne offered her followers a message of eternal life and hope. She took it all from many sources — Christianity, Hinduism, hatha yoga, and New Age journeys into crystals, auras, light, colour, LSD and magic mushrooms, and even extraterrestrial life. She used to always say it was a warning when the flying saucers came in spring.

One of Anne's signature sayings was *walk on*. Michael told us what she meant was *walk on, into the oneness*; it seemed to us what she meant was *follow me; I am the light. Nothing or no one can offer more.* The phrase gave her followers further permission to do her will.

And so, confused, rambling, and very old — but, it must be said, quite radiant — Anne fields visitors from dwindling cult ranks in her tiny room but can never properly know what has happened in her past or what might be in her future.

She pushes her protein drink away, across her tray, and rests her head again on her arms. She drifts in and out of sleep. When she wakes, those eyes dart around the room. There are crystals on a table, and a newspaper.

'What's that woman with children done?' she says. 'Done a bunk?'

PART ONE

1

THE SEEKERS

Anne was born Evelyn Grace Victoria Edwards in an Australian country town called Sale, two hours east of Melbourne, in 1921. Sale was so small then that it wasn't even classified as a town — just a farming settlement with a main street.

Birth records show that her mother, Florence Hoile, was from Wandsworth, in South London. She spent 27 years in mental hospitals in Australia, and eventually died in one. Florence was rumoured to have set her hair on fire in the street in Sale in the 1920s. She claimed to be a medium and psychic who could speak to the dead.

Anne's father, Ralph Edwards, was born in an inner-Melbourne factory suburb in 1892. He went to Europe to fight in World War I, and while he was there his first wife died giving birth to their child. He married Florence upon his return from the front.

The couple had seven children, with Anne the oldest. Records show that Anne was at the Old Melbourne Orphanage for some time as a child, with her father classified as 'whereabouts unknown' after running away from an unpaid war veteran's debt. When Anne was three, he turned up in a small Victorian fishing port a long way from Sale.

In 1929, at age eight, Anne was enrolled at Sunshine Primary School in the working-class suburbs of Melbourne's west. Then things become obscured. Most of Anne's life was documented, but there is a gap in the 1930s, the period when she entered her teens. It is as if she disappeared, and maybe in some ways she did. With her mother already showing signs of mental illness and her father itinerant, perhaps she became the stand-in mother for her siblings. It's tempting to fill the void with speculation and think that these were the lost years that changed her, or made her, or unmade her.

Anne's mother was first put into an asylum around 1941, while her husband was in the army, and just as Anne, aged 20, married a man called Lionel Harris. He came from a tiny place on the state's northern border and worked on fruit farms. Anne seemed to have had a magnetic power over him because after the army posted him interstate, he went AWOL for nearly eight months and was arrested by military police after being found with Anne back in Victoria. He served another year before being discharged on compassionate grounds.

When World War II began, Anne's father again enlisted, describing his religion on his army forms as Methodist. He was stationed in and around Melbourne as an officer and an engineer, but developed health problems — both his heart and lungs were poor — and was discharged in 1944. By that time, he gave his religion as 'spiritualist' and his number of children as none. Anne later said she considered her father to be a Buddhist. Ralph worked as a railway clerk in Melbourne after the war, moved to Brisbane in 1955 and died there, in hospital, in 1966.

Almost half of Florence's life was spent in asylums in and

around Melbourne: the Royal Park mental hospital, Mont Park, Ararat, and Sunbury. Florence died in 1971, just as her daughter's strange cult was booming.

It seems clear from this history that Anne's parents were distant and troubled. Yet according to Anne, her parents were worldly and enlightened. They went to India on a spiritual journey after the war, she has claimed, visiting an ashram opened by Nobel Prize winner Rabindranath Tagore. She often told cult members that her father was friends with Lord Nuffield — Sir William Morris, the famous British Morris cars millionaire and philanthropist.

There were also stranger claims. In a sermon to her followers — or a 'discourse', as she called them — Anne said that her mother wrote dead people's stories after channelling their spirits, and this was why she had been classed as mentally ill. Yet Anne claimed her mother was 'quite happy, she didn't mind. She taught us a great deal … to show others how to be quiet and how to live and how to stop mocking the divine life.'

Anne also said her entire family could astral travel out of their bodies and into the spirit world. She claimed she was three when she realised that 'Mummy was different' and started seeing her not only as her mother but also as a spiritual teacher. And 'Mummy' had her own teacher: a Tibetan guru who was instructing her in yoga. 'There was no doubt about it: my mum was with a guru at the time. A lot of spiritual polishing had to be done … to gain the necessary and deeper understanding of this thing called yoga.'

However, Florence's death certificate gives her religion as Church of England, and there is little documentary evidence to support claims that she had a Tibetan guru.

Yoga was important to Anne: to her, it was a form of 'soul travelling'. Yoga — and the search for inner peace and majesty and stillness that underlies it — kickstarted her cult. But she brought untold baggage and esoterica to it, and her practice of yoga quickly transformed into something dangerous. 'The conclusion I finally reached is that anyone can practise this whether they are under a spiritual teacher or not, although it is always better to have a guru,' she noted in a recorded sermon.

Anne said she met her mother's guru at age 14. 'Some students follow the inner master who never shows himself on this plane, Mother said, and in the physical form others will find a guru in the earthly body who spends a lot of time on all planes teaching their disciples how to leave the body and helping them if they become entangled in a morass of psychic difficulties.'

From this, she said, 'Freedom, wisdom, kindness, lovingness and caring — what they call charity in the churches' would follow. Her promise was to be liberated from 'matter'. The Jesus in the Bible tried his best but the world wasn't ready. So he had come again, this time to Melbourne in the 1970s, through her. 'Christ did say "Come follow me!" but very few knew what he was saying, and he wanted them to go with him into the worlds beyond. And they were not prepared to take the journey. So he turned away from them, leaving an eternal message, and you all know it,' she told her followers.

Anne started teaching yoga in Melbourne and in Geelong, a satellite city close by, in the late 1950s. This was just as yoga was emerging in the post-war west. The Gita School of Yoga was opened in 1960 in Melbourne by Margrit Segesman, under whom Anne trained and with whom she worked. Segesman was the daughter of a Swiss banker; she lived in Indian ashrams and followed a Tibetan guru. She also claimed to have lived in an Indian cave for five years. Anne's story was that she met Segesman in the street on a windy, rainy day in Melbourne and helped her pull some awnings down outside her school; Anne introduced herself as a physiotherapist and nurse.

According to Barbara Kibby, who, like many, would become a cult member through Anne's early yoga classes, Anne was an excellent teacher. Many who crossed Anne's path say this; that in the very early days, she was wonderful. She gravitated towards teaching middle-aged women in wealthy suburbs. These women were going through a mid-life crisis, Kibby said: 'Children grown up, husbands having affairs, but it was in the days when divorce was not as normal as it is today. Divorce was a very big deal. There were a certain number of Jewish women and she targeted them, mainly because they were very vulnerable due to their situation in society at that time and because they came from wealthy families.

'She knew if she could get them to leave their husbands, their families would disown them — she'd have them for life,' says Barbara. 'There was nowhere for them to go.'

Anne encouraged such women — and men, though in fewer numbers — to turn their backs on their previous lives. 'There's no own family,' she would say. 'Only love. Great love.'

Middle-age was the perfect time, she said, to begin their real journeys. 'It is very important and rather advisable for any individual who is midway through their physical incarnation to sever their ties with old things that they do by erecting a new home which will contain new facilities and furnishings which are symbolic of new life powers and blessings and beauties into which you have consciously entered.'

'There's no ifs or buts in that at all,' Anne told her followers. 'Also remember making changes like that are going to involve human and financial sacrifice, but it is a small price to pay, remember, for the fullness of the benefit to be gained by living in agreement with that you know. What must come to you before everything else are the imperishable gifts of the divine spirit through your training.

'I know a tremendous effort has to be made to break the old habits of fear and all the holding back of the self and false economies,' she said. 'Where you are now is like a season. It is a season of your unfoldment.'

Yoga, all kinds of yoga, was a booming craze. It was the thing to do in Melbourne through the 1960s for wealthy women who had raised children. But Anne and her aggressively spiritual — almost occult — approach was gaining attention in the yoga community. At Segesman's school, she cast a spell on a young man in a class who disagreed with her. The incident caused Segesman to break all ties with Anne. 'Anne went into the kitchen when they were clearing up,' says a former cult member, 'and she muttered, "He's not going to be here tomorrow, he's going to be very sick." And of course the next day the man was. Now you can say that's coincidence, it probably is coincidence, but she already was gaining that intention and that reputation of having influence over people's wellbeing, for good or for bad. It made you pretty wary. You stood back. You were careful.'

Three days before Christmas 1962, a Saturday, Dr Raynor Johnson heard the doorbell ring. He was in his study, at his home in the grounds of the University of Melbourne — the academic heart of the city's establishment.

'A day of destiny for me,' Johnson wrote later in a strange, unfinished manuscript that has become a sort of hidden manifesto for the cult.

Johnson, who was 61 in 1962, was the English-born head of the university's Queen's College, a brilliant physicist but a most peculiar man. He was something of a marquee signing for the university: a venerable and very liberal English academic with impeccable pedigree. By the early 1960s, however, he was on the tail-end of his career and had moved in his mind from physics into metaphysics. He was the archetypal seeker.

'A young lady of perhaps 30 to 35 years of age, of fair hair and complexion, of medium to slender build, of clear grey sparkling eyes and a quiet attractive voice, addressed me,' he recorded.

In fact Anne was nearly 41, but may have looked younger as she had begun what was to be a long regime of facelifts.

'I don't think you know me,' she said, addressing Johnson by name, 'but I know you well. My name is Anne —.'

She called herself Anne Hamilton, but Johnson's diary is very coy about names; he either doesn't give them, doesn't give them in full, or uses just initials. For many years to come in speeches and writings, he referred to Anne as an anonymous male.

He invited her in, leading her into his study and showing her to an easy chair. 'She said, "I understand you are shortly going on a visit to India?"'

He was indeed to embark, with his wife, Mary, on a six-week trip involving a lecture on 'science and spirituality' at a conference, followed by some travel. 'I think I felt a little surprised that this was known.'

This was one of Anne's main ploys: to find out about people surreptitiously and then dazzle them with her insight. Two men she was said to know well were in and around Queen's College at the time and were likely feeding her information about Johnson. One was John Champness, a Melbourne psychologist who had studied at Queen's. He was a friend, possibly boyfriend, of Anne's before she first married, and he knew Johnson. Later, she told followers she met Champness while singing at the British Empire Society in Melbourne. The other was Michael Riley, her soon-to-be second husband, a South African ex-navyman who would marry Anne for a year, in 1965. He was in charge of catering and then gardening at Queen's. He was very keen on Johnson's increasingly esoteric mysticism, and the two were friendly. Riley later claimed to have awoken Anne sexually, and the two were said to be in a relationship of some sort when he initially told her about Johnson.

It was Anne's first masterstroke — to court and recruit a man of influence in Melbourne. By 1962, as shown in his academic writings, Johnson was so deep into transcendence, the paranormal, and the promise of bliss that he wanted a teacher — a guru, in the Eastern sense — to guide him. She wanted to be that guru.

Johnson was from Leeds, and he went to university in Oxford and London. His specialty in physics was spectroscopy: the science of radiation and light. He worked in London with Ernest Rutherford, who split the atom and discovered the proton during World War I. In 1934, he came to Melbourne with Mary. He was looking for more, more, more, always more to the physical dimensions of life. In the United Kingdom, he had been involved with the Society for Psychical Research, exploring things such as telepathy, poltergeists, and mediums. He was also a poet and had begun to publish arcane books on mysticism. Former student Ian Weeks remembers him as a mischievous, impish man with constantly twinkling eyes, large ears, and buck teeth: 'Perfectly cast for the role of the Mad Hatter in *Alice in Wonderland*. He had a disproportionately large head. His head was somewhat like an egg turned upside down.'

But he was very open. He was a friend to his students, many of whom he invited back to his home on the university grounds for late-night discussions on philosophy and religion. He was known as having very liberal beliefs, and the students called him Sam. 'Raynor was always very gentle to human beings, to others,' says Weeks, a Melbourne academic specialising in the history of religions, himself from a family of noted Methodists.

'Very thoughtful, and always took you seriously, even if you were speaking utter rubbish. He was extremely polite.'

Anne dazzled Johnson that Christmas of 1962 in his study. He found that both he and Anne — this wonderful, attractive woman who appeared on his doorstep and knew the future — were enamoured with Helena Blavatsky, a Russian medium who co-formed the Theosophical Society in New York in 1875. 'Madam' Blavatsky said she was taught esoteric wisdom by a spiritual teacher in Tibet: she was interested in cosmology, transcendental meditation, and the paranormal, but her main message to followers, who included Rudolph Steiner and Thomas Edison, was of a single ancient wisdom in the form of an energy. Her star pupil, Annie Besant, helped set up the first World's Parliament of Religions an organisation aimed at cultivating harmony among members of the world's different religious and spiritual communities.

Anne had in fact hosted homeopath Thomas Maughan, the head of Britain's The Druid Order, in her home a couple of years earlier. Maughan quoted Blavatsky in his books. He said he could talk to the dead. The link was so direct that Maughan married a Family cult member, briefly.

This mysticism aligned entirely with Raynor Johnson's headspace. Anne also told him that she was making her early followers read a Greek-Armenian guru called George Gurdjieff, who, with help from wealthy patrons, set up an institute in a French chateau. He preached that the universe was created by cosmic matter called Etherokilno, and referred to the god within it as 'Our Almighty Omni-Loving Common Father Uni-Being Creator Endlessness'. Followers said that he gave off a strong blue light, which could be used to cure mental and physical illnesses.

Then she talked to him about India. 'There will be many on this side — and elsewhere — who will be interested in your visit.'

Johnson later wrote that he suspected right away she had extrasensory perception; that she knew things other people could not. He failed to recognise that all she had likely done was ask around about him and what he was up to. He seized on her use of the word 'elsewhere'. 'I formed the idea that "elsewhere" might be conveying something of "beyond this plane of existence,"' he wrote.

Anne told him that he would need to be careful of his wife's health on the trip. 'I can see there is danger here,' she said.

She had pushed three crucial buttons in just a few minutes: she apparently knew the future, she knew how important India was to him, and she sensed that his wife was in danger. Johnson asked if Mary could join them in the study. Anne told them that Mary would get so sick on their trip they would have to come back to Melbourne early.

'I asked Mrs Johnson if she believed in clairvoyants,' said Anne in a recorded sermon, 'and she said, "Oh yes!" and I said, "Well, look, it comes to me clairvoyantly" — it came to me as a shock in my solar plexus — that she would die, when she got there, of eating fish. I said, "It will weaken you for a long time to come even if you stay alive, so if you don't eat it you won't get the tummy poisoning."'

They took the trip, and Mary got acute dysentery.

'She was in a very bad way,' said Anne later. 'It was very, very close. She had to come home and she was very ill. She was not quite herself for a long, long time, as prophesised.'

This event was an important marker in Anne's power over Johnson. He was her first believer, and he was crucial in building the cult she would head, based in part on the strength of his name.

'It is scarcely necessary to say that upon our return in February 1963 the person we were most looking forward to seeing again was Anne,' he wrote in his diary. 'It was for us the beginning of a friendship in which weekly visits were interchanged between our homes — and wonder deepened.'

She returned to the university several times to see Johnson. Ian Weeks saw her one day walking in a quadrangle, waving flowers around at the entrances of buildings, in a ritual. He says that she was clearly grooming Johnson. 'She was a very attractive woman. He was naïve. He did not have a very strong sense of the real nature of evil in the world. I think he was misled by her. She was very capable, very intelligent, with a spiritually active and interested persona, and the combination of those two people came to have considerable force.'

Johnson's spiritualism, says Weeks, led him to believe he had been invited by a 'college of spirits' to widen spiritual beliefs in the world. He thought that he could 'speak to his generation', and the fact that he was scientist would make him more influential. Johnson was an Edwardian liberal who questioned organised religion, societal convention, and the aristocracy; his was a generation looking for meaning, even in the arcane. 'Spiritualism was very widely held at the time,' says Weeks. 'People like Conan Doyle, who wrote the Sherlock Holmes stories, were interested in it. A number of playwrights and writers, and authors of various kinds, used to go to spiritualist places, and in many homes if you had a dinner party, after you'd had coffee and port you'd have a ouija board, and you'd try and connect with spirits beyond. This was really surprisingly widespread in the upper middle-classes particularly.'

By early 1963, Australian troops were in Vietnam but none had yet been killed. The Beatles were about to make their first album. In Australia, there were more suicides that year than ever recorded. It was a time of seeking and questioning. And Johnson was bewitched. Anne had been telling him all about her first husband — Lionel, who had died in a car crash in 1955 — and how sad and tragic her life had been. She told him she had lost three children and had contemplated suicide.

Anne also started to tell him a lot more about her own guru, or at least the one she said she had. Johnson was the only person she ever gave his name to: Sri Yugananda. She said he had been in Australia but was now able to 'prototype' to her — in other words, to duplicate himself and be in two places at once. When Lionel died, she said, the guru sent Anne a cable saying *Walk on*.

She told Johnson that he was part of her grand design and that what she really wanted for him was what she already had — eternal life, to live and die outside of the restraints of humanity. She had travelled with her guru through the cosmos, she said, and she made it sound beautiful and assured: 'Once you have a glimpse of these superior ones just with your old eyes it will completely change your life. You could look at them for years and years and not know them, then all of a sudden through your training you see them. You find that the supreme ruler god has manifested and given enlightenment and divine wisdom for all creatures.'

It was time for her first miracle.

Anne had a biological daughter called Judith with Lionel Harris. Judith later came to be known as Natasha and now lives in the United Kingdom, but is no longer involved with The Family and doesn't speak to her mother. In May of 1963, she was 19, and she rolled her car on the outskirts of Melbourne, fracturing her skull and wounding an eye. Doctors told her she might lose her sight. 'Her mother immediately organised spirit help,' Johnson wrote, and a week later Judy left hospital much earlier than expected and in good shape. Johnson told his wife: 'I think this is the most Christ-like person I have ever met.'

Anne quickly proclaimed herself Johnson's post-retirement 'teacher'; she told him to slow down his activities, sit quietly for an hour a day, reduce thinking to a 'vanishing point', and not eat for two days a week. She told him she often fasted for three-week stints.

A group of like-minded seekers would be formed around him, she said. They would receive revelations and the 'joy and peace of being really on The Path'. The first seven of her followers were soon to be consecrated, and he was one of them.

Johnson was primed to believe Anne when she entered his life: he had already been drawn in by a succession of odd mentors over the years, which in many ways set him up for Anne's audacious courtship. As soon as he moved to Melbourne in 1934, he had met one of these: Ambrose Pratt, a journalist, author, and businessman who helped form the modern Liberal Party in Australia.

They had met at Pratt's 60th birthday party. Pratt was a handsome, goateed man with a twirled moustache. He had retired after an extraordinary multi-tasked career. He had been a lawyer in the Supreme Court in Sydney; he described his younger self as an 'insufferable coxcomb' with a monocle. He moonlighted writing left-wing articles for *Australian Worker*, before moving to England to write novels and work for the *Daily Mail*. Then he came back and took a job in Melbourne at *The Age* newspaper.

Just before World War I, Pratt went to South Africa on assignment with the Australian prime minister, Andrew Fischer, a left-wing former coal-miner from Scotland. Pratt ended up writing a book critical of apartheid. He was also heavily into the early thinking on tariff protection, where a country taxes imports to encourage buying local goods — and he became still more politically involved when he joined 'The Group', which included future prime minister Bob Menzies, to form what is now called the Liberal Party.

Pratt was also friendly with Sir Reginald Ansett, who would go on to own an Australian airline and a television channel. Pratt introduced Johnson to Ansett.

Pratt and Johnson, like Anne, loved mediums and the paranormal, and all the quasi-science these things entailed. None of it was quasi then, though, because it hadn't been tested. It now seems odd that Pratt was front and centre in 'The Group': a man who said he could see auras in humans, animals, and trees and considered the human aura a shape-shifting 'quasi-physical luminescence'.

They only knew each other for ten years; Pratt died in 1944. He was much older than Johnson, but Johnson adored him and was greatly influenced by him.

But it was in death that Pratt spoke loudest to Johnson. The academic became convinced he was still communicating with his dead friend through a series of bizarre series of letters from an infamous Irish medium who claimed to be channelling Pratt. These letters, perhaps more than anything else, told Johnson that a spiritual Master — who materialised for him with uncanny timing in Anne — was what he needed.

The Irish medium was Geraldine Cummins. Johnson had met her in 1953 in London, just after he had published *The Imprisoned Splendour*, a book that argues science has room for the mystical. Cummins asked him to give her a sample of his handwriting. A few months later, back in Melbourne, he got a letter from Cummins with what she said was a letter to him from Pratt, nine years dead. He had written his name from the afterlife in code. Many more letters followed. Around the same time, Cummins claimed to have found the missing British explorer Percy Fawcett, who had disappeared in Brazil. He was alive but sick, she said, and had discovered the lost undersea city of Atlantis in the jungle.

Johnson treasured the letters. He said his dead friend — who he wrote as '[deceased]' — was intimate and authoritive still, and was instructing him to get a Master. He was advised to look for someone with 'schooling in the spirituality of the Himalayas' and special powers, such as the ability to 'dematerialise' their physical bodies and then pop them up in another place.

One particular letter in 1958 was about death and real love and the promise of the eternal. It asked if a man's wife died 50 years before, could he be reunited with her as a young woman, in the beyond?

The answer, Johnson read, was yes — if she was 'evolved'. Except that someone else, nearer to 'earth-level', had taken her personality. If the man loved the woman's 'real self', when he died she would come back down to earth and take back the personality he once knew. Then the pair would be able to renew and relive the 'ecstasy' of their love affair because the man would be reborn to live again as a child and she would teach him how it was done.

This was Johnson's eureka moment. This seemed to him to be the answer to everything he sought. But everything was dependent on the right teacher. Coincidentally, that was when Anne appeared, and it was also her primary message.

By winter in 1963, with the hills in the Dandenong Ranges verdant and wet, the unsealed roads often impassable through the season's mud and flooding, Johnson was about to be initiated as one of the first seven members of Anne's new cult.

Aldous Huxley's *Island*, a groundbreaking novel in which an enlightened future race live in a paradise with children and psychedelics, had just been published. Pratt had also written about similar subject matter: his novel *Lift Up Your Eyes* came out in the 1930s, just after Johnson met him. It was about a man who wanted to re-form the world with orphaned children, so he built a compound (called 'Manuka') to educate them among the hills and fern gullies. They would be taught to 'subdue their appetites' in an atmosphere of spartan, holy living in order to become mentally stronger. In the novel, Manuka was attacked by newspapers for being a privately run asylum educating orphaned children in an un-holy way. The government did not investigate.

Johnson's moment of promise arrived. Anne told him she had been visited by the prototyping Sri Yugananda, who announced that her star pupil was ready. Yugananda came to her and spoke to her, she said, and then she said she went outside her house in the hills, into the winter night, and experienced ecstasy. She encountered clouds and raindrops containing spirits. A tree spoke to her: 'We never die: only our mortal shell can perish.'

Yugananda had decreed that Johnson and his wife should be given hallucinogenic drugs — 'sacred manna' — because he considered these 'a divine gift to man imprisoned in this dense physical level'. The group they would join through this induction would be called The Great White Brotherhood of Initiates and Masters. Johnson would begin as a lowly member.

What wasn't clear from our research was how much Johnson led Anne on. Who preyed on whom? We know she seduced him spiritually, but did his leap of faith mean that he encouraged her to go further too? It's not clear from his journal, which is in essence a propaganda piece. Ian Weeks thinks he probably did knowingly influence Anne. Johnson was a man very sure of his own pedigree in both science and religion. 'Raynor would have thought of himself as more knowledgeable than the clergy, the professors of the New Testament or Old Testament or theology or church history. He would have believed deeply that he himself was close to the real spiritual world. This would have played into what some might call a God complex.' After all, he was already viewed as a kind of guru himself within the university. 'My first reaction,' says Weeks, 'was that this was just an extension of the sort of nuttiness that I'd seen at the university. But it soon became clear it was more than that.'

Whether naïvely or with some degree of knowingness, Johnson agreed. He considered Anne by now a 'mystic of a high order ... unquestionably the wisest, the serenest, and the most gracious and generous soul I had ever met.'

'I had met my Master,' he wrote.

When he was initiated, Raynor saw grand visions. 'The screen of my mind unfolded its panorama,' he wrote. He saw 'prison cells passing rapidly before the eye like hundreds of pages of a living picture book allowed to turn over between fingers and a thumb'. He took the prison cells to mean 'eons of time and oceans of suffering'. Anne presented herself to Johnson — and his daughter Maureen, who was also being inducted — as Jesus. 'Anne decided to rise into that high state of consciousness known to Masters and God-conscious souls as "Samadhi" — one form of God-consciousness,' he wrote. 'Her face became, to my human eyes, supernaturally beautiful and She spoke with authority and divine power as one might imagine the Christ would do if speaking in the first person to each person there. Looking around slowly from one person to another, and then at each of us individually, She said, "Do you know who I am? I and my Father are one. My peace I leave with you. You will be my gurus, all of you."'

Johnson knelt at her feet. Anne said her own Master had already told her that she should die — 'last Thursday' — but she had decided to stay alive to help him and others, that she needed to stay for the 'needy, sad and distressed souls'. She said to him that he would never again experience such a visitation from her as Jesus, but to know that she was Him, 'the Master of Masters Himself'.

Johnson was awestruck. 'I shall never, never forget the look on Anne's face — the power and challenge of Her eyes as Christ spoke through Her. I feel it was the supreme experience of all my incarnations,' he wrote. Johnson believed at this point that he had already lived seven times. 'I thank God for so unspeakable a privilege.'

Anne told Johnson about the Biblical Jesus's life '1900 years ago'. He had come to Earth then as a revered figure with a beard, and, according to Johnson, she said that if he had come with a beard again he might have been recognised and persecuted once more. So he had come as her.

Anne named Johnson 'John The Baptist'. She told him the world would end in 1983, and that he needed to stay silent about everything that had happened between them. To do otherwise — to betray — may kill her. 'To disclose her Mastership to others outside The Path might do irreparable harm and might even lead to her death,' he wrote. 'The forces of evil were always looking for ways to frustrate the work. The plan for Her was to work unseen, unheard and unknown.'

After his induction, Johnson started taking drugs in Anne's presence. He would kneel at her feet high on either LSD or psilocybin. 'How can I describe these sacred hours with Anne? Her face became divinely beautiful with sublime authority, always loving and radiant, but at times stern, and sometimes anguished and sorrowful.' Yet privately, he confessed 'spiritual shock'. He couldn't quite believe that 'a turning point in history' — Jesus in the Melbourne hills in Anne's body — was taking place before his eyes. He had doubts. 'Was I being fooled by a "delusional?" Was the incredible setting and its story true — or was I led "up the garden path" by someone, however good and admirable, who had a gift for making the incredible credible?'

He convinced himself that it was all true. He said Jesus's disciples in the Middle East must have also been confused and doubtful. Also, if Jesus were to come back, it would have to be incognito. 'We must therefore go forward,' he wrote. 'Walk ON.'

2

UPTOP

'A better bunch of kids you couldn't wish for,' says Syd Savage, the handyman at The Family lakehouse in Eildon. 'So pleasant, so tidy. They had them very well controlled.'

Almost ten years after Anne first swayed Raynor Johnson and set the cult's wheels in motion, children started arriving at the lakehouse — Uptop, or Kai Lama — in 1971.

Kai Lama was the realisation of a vision Anne had long held: the monastery, her Manuka. The house itself was a classic split-level timber Australian holiday home behind tall trees. Anne gave the name Kai Lama as a tribute to the Tibetan Buddhism to which she said she adhered.

At first seven children were moved, in stages, from one of Anne's homes in the hills. This first group of kids were all aged around three. Through the 1970s, the numbers would grow to 14. In 1978, Anne married William Byrne — Bill — her third husband. She added her surname, Hamilton (which was not her real surname), to his, and thus the children took the surname

Hamilton-Byrne. Another group of 14 or so children were subsequently acquired and called 'fosters' because they did not take Anne's name.

The Hamilton-Byrne children all thought they were brothers and sisters as they were growing up, but of course they were not. Some had been scouted for adoption by cult insiders at Melbourne hospitals and taken for Anne with fake paperwork. Or they were gifted to Anne by parents who were involved with the cult. These parents felt it was an honour to give over a child: their son or daughter would be raised by the hand of God.

Johnson wrote about the children. He began keeping his diary in a deed-box at a bank near the hills, for security. In a section headed 'Suffer the Little Children to Come Unto Me', he claimed that the gathering and educating of them was 'the most amazing' aspect of Anne's life. 'Viewed as a piece of organisation, with devoted and sacrificial help, it is staggering in its outlook, yet it was planned with consciousness of its magnitude and the great responsibility of this undertaking. It had to cover say 10–15 years before it could lead to success. Only a great Master, equally at home in this world and the next, could have hoped to carry it through to a conclusion.'

'It amounted to this,' he continued. 'A group of children, some already born here, some yet to be born, were brought together, fostered and adopted and trained from the beginning of their lives in as perfect conditions as could be provided. Their health was meticulously supervised and all aspects of their welfare and education were considered and provided for. Before they came, it was known by the Master when and where and to what parents they were coming and what qualities potentially they brought with them from past lives ... It is safe to say the future age will see them, unknown though they are, as custodians and continuers of the work their Master has set going in many parts of the world

29

Ian Weeks, Johnson's former student, believes Johnson would never have entertained the idea that anything was wrong at Uptop. 'He might have thought, *Well, it's very nice that these people are looking after a lot of children, who might be orphans.* My guess, and it has to be a guess, is that perhaps you could say that he shut his eyes to some things that he ought not to have shut his eyes to.'

And for many years, hardly anyone did know something was wrong. Barely anyone from the outside was allowed into Uptop. Through the 1970s and 1980s, it became an increasingly paranoid enclosure: the cult motto of 'unseen, unheard, unknown' was paramount. Syd Savage was allowed in because he didn't ask questions, despite seeing what were probably some very odd things. He posed no threat. Syd kept the place running: the power, the water, the cars, the plumbing, the gas (he owned the nearest petrol station). The cult bought a white Toyota minivan, which they named Jupiter, and he kept Jupiter humming along too.

'As far as we were concerned,' says Christine, his wife, 'it was just a private school with children that were being home-schooled.'

Syd sometimes suspected unusual things were happening, but he thought it couldn't have been anything too serious because the children were so polite, and so well turned out. 'They certainly had a brilliant education,' he says. 'They presented well, they were dressed immaculately, extremely clean and tidy and extremely well mannered.'

When he walked into the house, the children would stop what they were doing and greet him. If he ate there, which he sometimes did — despite many of the children often going hungry or being punished by having meals taken away — they would wait until he had picked up his knife and fork before doing so themselves. 'Typical extreme boarding house rules,' he says.

Anne was always 'dripping in expense ... she looked good by

the time she was all painted up. A bit rough early in the morning, but she was much older than everybody believes. You don't get facelifts for nothing. And I think she wore wigs.'

Most of the kids eventually had the same sinister dyed-blonde hair, and Syd saw that too, though it didn't strike him as strange at the time. The dressy clothes they wore were old-fashioned, but he never asked why. Both Syd and his wife insist that the children were happy and healthy. 'I never had any kid come up to me and say "get me out of here," he says. 'We aren't going to put up with seeing someone hurt their children, no matter whose they are. Cats and dogs and kids — they looked after the lot.'

Once he saw an old cult dog called Dinky lying dead in state inside the house, surrounded by candles. The place was full of cats and dogs, which, unbeknown to Syd, were often fed better than the children. One Uptop child's favourite dog — Girly, a blue heeler — had been rescued by Bill, from the lake at the foot of the house, and given to the child, but when it got sick it wasn't taken to the vet but instead put on a home-made drip, and it died. A white sheet was put on the bed, and the dog lay on it for three days before being buried in the garden.

The cult's business was split between Lake Eildon, where most of the kids lived, and the Dandenong Ranges, home to most of the adults. Bill and Anne mainly lived together in the hills, their home shaded by eucalypts, when they were in Australia. Anne had encouraged her adult followers to move into the same street — a steep grove in the suburb of Ferny Creek — because she said they should be near her, and according to our sources, because she thought that if the authorities or the unbelievers tried to kill her she would be protected.

There had also been cult meditation sessions and prayer meetings in a house in Melbourne's blue-ribbon suburb of

Brighton, next to Port Phillip Bay. But there were too many neighbours in the area; it wasn't covert enough. The landlord started asking cult members about the strange noises — the *om* chant — being heard coming from the house, and the neighbours did too. Then the police came. On one of her taped sermons, which she would make while she was travelling overseas and send to her followers on cassette, Anne said, 'The police sergeant — his name was Les — asked us what went on. I said, "We are meditating." Then he came again with another constable and said, "All those cars up and down here have only been here since you have been here." He said, "Not only that, my bank manager comes to see you." I said, "What do you want us to do?" So he gave the names of the streets to park our cars in.'

The cult then built themselves a brown-brick temple in the hills: the Santiniketan Lodge, pronounced *shan-tin-ik-et-an*, and meaning 'abode of peace', named after an ashram in Tagore, India. It sits on three green and ferny hectares next to protected forest, with high, padlocked gates. Days of worship — which involved listening to Anne speak, either in person or on a taped discourse — were Thursdays and Sundays. When Anne was present, she delivered her message from a purple chair up the front of the Lodge: her throne.

However, Anne and Bill's time in Australia was also split with time spent at their overseas homes: the couple had begun to use cult money and 'loans' from followers to accumulate lavish properties in Kent, near London, and in Hurleyville, in the Catskill Mountains near New York. This was at Anne's say-so. Bill Hamilton-Byrne was an ex-RAF Englishman who had found wealth in Australia as a rural earthmoving contractor and held positions on the shire council. One of the former cult children told us he was nothing more than a handsome handbag: compliant, rich, and willing.

Ben arrived at Uptop as a child. He is now a member of an evangelical Christian community in Western Australia, a devout family man who has been writing online about his experiences as a child of The Family. As with all the survivors of the cult that we met, we approached him cautiously because of the magnitude of what he had been through. But Ben was happy to tell his story.

He was born in a country town close to Lake Eildon in 1972, but his paperwork was faked to make him a twin born to Anne and Bill in another state. His biological mother was a cult member; both she and Ben's grandmother had practised yoga with Anne in the 1960s.

When Ben's mother became crippled with severe cervical degenerative disc disease and was bedridden, Anne contacted her. This was before Ben was born, but he has heard the story many times: Anne, at his mother's bedside, told her that she could heal her and give her a reason to live. Within six weeks, Ben's mother was out of bed and, after a year was walking, rusted onto the cult.

'Anne pulled her back from death and gave her a future,' Ben says. 'From that moment, Anne was, as far as my mother was concerned, exactly who she claimed to be: the reincarnation of Jesus. With the power to prove it.'

From the outside, Uptop would have seemed idyllic. There were two playgrounds, a sandpit, a basketball ring, a badminton net, monkey bars, and six vegetable gardens. It was a messy, sprawling compound, with lots of places for children to explore and play. In one of Bill's home movies, he filmed the children in matching red shorts and tops exercising in unison, doing star-jumps and running on the spot.

The house itself had wood-panelled walls and chintzy furniture, with soft toys and china figurines lining the shelves. There were beds and trundles everywhere, and images of Jesus and Anne in most rooms, alongside posters of koalas and cats.

A telescope was covered in plastic sheets; there was a piano. Propped up near the fireplace in the main living room was a corkboard of photographs of the Uptop kids in matching blue tracksuits, holding on to one another.

The lake glimmered at the bottom of their sloping property, the partially submerged trees twisting and rising towards the sky, but the children were rarely allowed near it. Uptop was all they knew.

By the time Ben was at Uptop in 1972, Anne and Bill were becoming visibly wealthier. Cult members were donating money to them as a kind of membership fee, and the couple were also benefitting from property and estates donated by cult members. They were travelling regularly overseas and said to enjoy luxury cars: Daimlers and Jaguars. When not in Britain or New York State, they were in Hawaii, in a home donated by a wealthy American property developer who was married to a cult member.

Anne and Bill would visit Uptop from afar like dignitaries — a holy pair coming back to the doomed fairytale they were creating. 'She would appear, like a magic queen,' says Sarah Moore, one of the first to be adopted and go to Uptop, where she was christened with a new name: Andree.

Ben's earliest memory is lying in his bed at Uptop looking at all the schoolbooks in a cupboard. He also remembers a car either approaching or driving away from the house. 'We'd wait outside for them to arrive, the car coming down. It was normally a very much looked-forward-to event. Very special, a lot of hype, this was a wonderful thing. They would leave on Sunday night often, saying good night to us, putting us to bed, and they'd leave. It was sad to see them go. We'd hear them calling down from the steps, "Good night, everyone!"'

They could be away from Australia for months at a time; 18 months was the longest absence.

Anne delegated the task of looking after the children at Uptop to a group of women she dubbed 'the Aunties'. Inside the house, with Anne away, discipline was strict, and the punishments meted out by the Aunties soon became abusive and cruel. They were under enormous pressure to keep Anne happy and keep their cool in a house full of children who were not theirs. They would work two weeks on and then two weeks off. Most were made to become nurses if they weren't already, and donated their nurses' wages — earned during the fortnights away from Uptop — to the cult.

'They were chronically overtired,' says Michael, the cult member who broke the rules to take us to see Anne in her nursing home. His own son Jerome spent time up there. 'And young kids being young kids, they lost it sometimes, I'm sure they did.'

Uptop had two senior Aunties, who held rank over the others. Elizabeth 'Liz' Whitaker was a large, frumpy dark-haired woman, the ex-wife of a psychiatrist who helped Raynor Johnson and Anne to form the cult. Patricia 'Trish' MacFarlane was a chain-smoking cricket fan with a broad Australian accent who enjoyed a drink and drove a Leyland P76, a 1970s Australian muscle car. Margot McLellan, their deputy, was born Peggy Warren, and started doing yoga in the 1960s with Anne. At Uptop, she slept on a trundle mattress in a bathroom, next to the toilet. She was also made to sleep on a stair landing, and she kept her belongings in her car. The Aunties were made to submit to Anne too, like the children. Anne described this treatment of her enablers as part of their 'training'.

All three Aunties are now dead, but Rosie and I met Margot not long before she died, in 2014. Her line was that Uptop was overwhelmingly positive for the children but the discipline was at times overdone. There's a strong thread of denial in these kinds of memories. 'There were so many children, unwanted children, and

Anne took them on,' she told us. 'It was such a unique situation that you don't have anything to go by. We were inventing it, and you learnt not to be shocked at anything.'

She said the children were always dressed beautifully and went on overseas trips, remembering them riding double-decker buses in London. 'We had games — we'd get down on the floor with them and play card games. I used to take them shopping with me and we'd go to the local coffee shop and we'd sit down. Their table manners were lovely — very proud of them, I was.'

She said she distanced herself from the cruelty at Uptop and accepted that which she did encounter as part of their 'pioneer' spiritual life there. 'A couple of the other Aunties used to put the boot in. We'd ring Anne and she'd mete out the punishment. I mostly had feelings about the shy ones, the ones that were a bit on the frightened side. I wanted to encourage them. But I didn't believe in physical punishment at all.'

She told us that the discipline was for the children as well as the Aunties. 'It's a spiritual path. A tough one. And we were sometimes told to do things we didn't really like doing.' Anne continually told Margot that she needed to be more humble, and that Anne could do that for her — change her personality. And Margot believed her. 'Spiritually, I think she had it.'

Margot took many of Uptop's secrets to her deathbed. A few weeks before she died, she confided to an elderly friend in a suburban nursing home that she wanted to talk in detail about The Family, but she never got the opportunity. Instead, all we have of her are impressions from one conversation.

Trish MacFarlane grew up in an affluent bayside suburb in Melbourne. Her father worked for a bank. She went to a private Anglican girls' school and became a nurse during World War II, then married a former airforce pilot called Don Webb, a lapsed Methodist and the son of missionaries.

Don and Trish were both were interested in broadening their ideas around religion, and before they were married, they had started looking into non-mainstream churches and spiritualities. After they married, they would go to bookshops together to encounter new ideas.

In the early 1960s, Don, by then an architect, was moved to country Victoria for work. He met Bill Byrne, Anne's future husband, through a local Rotary Club. Bill had his earthmoving business based there, and both men were ex-airmen. They soon struck up a friendship.

Meanwhile, back in Melbourne in the mid-1960s, Trish, now a mother, went to listen to Raynor Johnson give a Council of Adult Education talk at a high-school hall, and was so taken with his lecture that she introduced herself afterwards. Johnson set about luring her in to the cult, first by telling Trish he wanted her to meet his wife — which happened soon after, over afternoon tea at Trish's house — and then by telling her all about Anne, the special one. The Master.

Trish went twice to Johnson's office at the university, telling him all about her marriage troubles with Don, who was unfaithful. 'He [Johnson] was an extremely kindly man and I was very fond of him,' Trish later said, according to police sources. Johnson befriended her — and kept telling her about the charismatic Anne.

Then, in 1967, Trish and Don's son Adrian died in a car crash; he collided with a milkman's horse and cart in the middle of the night. Two days later, Anne knocked on her door. 'I could only assume that Raynor had told her of Adrian's death. I was so beside myself with grief that I didn't even question her presence at my home.'

Anne knew — also through Johnson — that Don was having an affair with a woman called Brenda. That day at Trish's house,

Anne ordered Don, who she had just met, to go and get Brenda and bring her over. 'Anne talked with her alone,' Trish said.

There was a funeral for Adrian, and then Anne summoned Don to the hills and told him that he and his dead son had an afterlife connection. Trish and Don were soon initiated into the cult. Anne then allegedly summoned Trish and Liz Whitaker, whom she had already earmarked, to her bedside at a private Melbourne clinic, the Cotham, where she had just had one of her facelifts. Her head was covered in bandages and she was heavily bruised. Don and Dr John Mackay — a stalwart cult member and Anne's GP to this day — turned up as well.

Anne reportedly decreed the first marriage swap in The Family to take place immediately. Trish and Don split, and Don moved in with Liz. Anne told John Mackay to divorce his wife and move in with Trish, and that's what happened. Anne was directing adult cult members' movements as if they were marionettes, creating a complex shadowland of strange loyalties and odd cult couplings.

'It honestly never crossed my mind to argue with any of Anne's instructions,' Trish said.

Trish's extended family stepped in, worried. Anne told her not to talk to them anymore. 'She used to say, "I'm your family now, you have a whole family."'

A house was chosen in Ferny Creek for Trish and John, which they bought and started paying off. John, who was a psychiatrist at a private hospital at the time, still lives there today. Liz Whitaker and Don Webb moved into a house over the road from Anne, in the grove in Ferny Creek.

Anne was drumming into her new and increasingly loyal disciples that she was the Master who had been put on Earth at that exact time to be with them and guide them, but that her training came with non-negotiable requirements. It was the only way. As she noted on a taped discourse: 'It is a call to that which is very noble in us. Nobody wants to be in anything they haven't earned. My mother's Teacher was a great friend who led her to become the person she was, and Mother always said her Teacher always said that those who are in earnest, fixed upon God, will go forward. Find the kingdom and help every other living thing. We have the great adventure open before us with the life itself as our initiator. We don't know the divine until we find it. Remain humble, true, strong, loving, gentle. All the mystics down the ages and all the modern mystics tell the same story. Strong, sure and silent.'

By now Trish was wrangling eight kids at her Ferny Creek home: two of hers, five of John Mackay's, and one 'adopted' boy who ostensibly belonged to Raynor Johnson's daughter Maureen and her husband, Barry Ashcroft, a dentist. Anne had apparently procured the child for them from the Royal Women's Hospital. Ashcroft wasn't happy with the scenario and left Maureen, saying, according to police, that secrecy was considered spiritual in the cult and that the only loyalty a member must have was towards Anne.

Around the same time, Trish also adopted a child for Anne. Trish was told one day to hotstep it to the Royal Women's Hospital from the hills to collect a baby. A doctor who addressed her as 'Mrs Webb' brought the baby out to her and explained she had a malformed jaw. Trish said she handed the baby to Anne while still inside the hospital. 'I left the hospital alone,' Trish recounted.

The child was given the name Anna (many of the girls had some variation of 'Anne' in their new cult names), but her real name is Leeanne. We met her, like all of the former Family children who have spoken to us, as an adult. She cried when telling us about her relationship with the man she knew as her father, Bill Hamilton-Byrne, and her difficulties in leaving the cult and trying — like the others she grew up with — to find and live a new life.

Leeanne became Bill's favourite. 'He was my father,' she told us. 'I was always Daddy's girl, always. To me, he was amazing. I idolised him. We looked alike. We both had black curly hair, except mine was dyed blonde. We both had blue eyes. I did feel loved by him when I was a child, when I was a lot younger. I did feel loved by my father that I grew up with my whole life.'

Yet Bill did awful things, she saw. He hit children and was complicit in dozens of other crimes. If anyone was mesmerised by Anne, and compromised in his morality by her influence, it was him. Initially Anne had said she could cure, or at least look after, Bill's son from another marriage, who had mental-health issues. But as Leeanne sees it, Bill became a puppet. 'Some of the things he did were just horrific,' says Leeanne. 'When he lost his temper and he beat people, he was savage and he was horrible. He never did that to me, and the one time he did beat me, only one time I remember, I didn't speak to him for a week, and he didn't like that so he never did it again. I adored him.'

Because of the faked paperwork showing her as Leeanne's mother, Trish got a government child-support benefit payment. When she received the cheques, she would cash them and give the money to Anne, she said. Trish got these cheques for 16 years.

Her partnership with John Mackay soon ended. Trish didn't want to live in the same house as him anymore — she hadn't wanted to live in the same house as him in the first place. She bought her own house in the hills. Then Anne told her to get her face and hair done. Many of the cult women received this order from Anne, and most had to use Anne's surgery of choice, the Cotham. Next, Trish was told to go to an orthodontist to get her front teeth fixed. There was nothing wrong with her teeth, and the orthodontist told her so, but the work went ahead. The tops of four front teeth were drilled away and crowned, and her hair was dyed blonde.

Some of the other cult women had begun wearing blonde wigs, as Anne did. Appearances were everything; everything must be seen to be of a certain standard and status. Anne gave Trish a wig too, but Trish said she never wore it. Anne's natural hair was quite lovely, with a coppery colour. Trish always wondered why Anne wore wigs when she didn't really need to. They were masks, these new heads of hair, new faces, new noses, new teeth. New names.

Then, in 1971, Trish was dispatched to Uptop as 'Aunty Trish'.

The regime of punishments, as the 1970s ticked through, became horrific. According to the children's own accounts to the police and, 30 years later, to us, it extended into wilful neglect and chronic, endemic abuse. This happened as the children got older and less compliant, and as numbers grew, particularly as the 'fosters' — those without the Hamilton-Byrne surname — arrived.

'There's a hairline,' a cult member told police, 'between heaven and a heap of shit.'

A violin rest went missing, for example. It belonged to an adult cult member who lived in the hills but visited Uptop to give music and singing lessons. She stayed in a caravan outside. One of the children was accused of stealing the violin rest and was taken upstairs and hit repeatedly with a three-cornered black plastic cane.

Ben remembers hearing the beating and the whistling of the cane as it was being swung. He heard yelling — adults trying to get a confession out of the boy — heard him fighting back, and saw the cane as it flew down from a window above. 'The Aunties tramped outside, yelling at him — bring it back up, keep doing it — and then it was on. He refused to confess.'

That's because he didn't do it. The missing violin rest was found on the ground outside the caravan — the music teacher had dropped it herself. There was no apology.

By this stage, the boy had already been dunked. This was when an errant child's head was forced repeatedly, to the brink of drowning, into a bucket of water. During the violin-rest fracas, other children were similarly beaten with the cane on bared bottoms, leaving bruising, according to Ben, and then dunked, one by one. If one kid transgressed, many could cop it. Fear and secrecy sat among them, and also skewed notions of loyalty and friendship. Some 'betrayed' their siblings. Some chose not to, which in itself was a betrayal.

The dunkings were frightening. 'You could hear each of the girls screaming in pain. It was terrifying, thinking of what their next torture method would be in order to obtain their confession,' says Ben. 'As each returned, you could see their clothes were wet. They were still gasping for air and their faces looked a bluey colour, extremely pale and absolutely distraught.'

The children's arms and feet were held behind them, and their heads were held down in the bucket by their hair. 'They'd pull it back out, gasping for breath, asking, "Did you do it?" Ten seconds, 20 seconds to answer and straight back in again, to the point where you are asphyxiated, you're close on blacking out. I just remember my head being put in there, trying to hold your breath as long as possible. You'd begin bobbling, you can't hold it any longer, you're pulled up gasping for air.'

Ben once made the mistake of not lining up his shoes outside the front door properly, when he was about 11. He says Trish beat him with a hairbrush, bruising his head. Then there was an incident after a hot Australian summer night when a portable fan in a boys' bedroom was left on overnight. Liz Whitaker took to the five boys in the room with a metre-long wooden ruler.

'She wielded it above her head like a ninja,' says Ben. One boy suffered abrasions to the ribs and bruised legs and back.

At Uptop, says Sarah Moore, Anne treated the girls much more harshly than the boys. A lot of it was to do with sexuality and her notions of purity. Yet as with everything she did to her captives, it was also about control and fear. 'She would go into these incredible rages and psychotic outbursts towards us girls,' says Sarah, 'where she'd talk about cancerous tumors coming out of female genitals, and she would accuse us of walking in a way that would be trying to attract men. This was at age five.'

She says Anne hit her with the head of a broom. Another time, she had her hand held in a candle flame after she was caught playing with the wax. She stashed some food away in a hiding place and was hit 50 times with a round stick by Liz Whitaker. One former Uptop child's foremost memory is the sensation of a stinging face.

Anne could be 'a magic queen or a wicked witch depending on the mood she was in,' Sarah tells us. 'You never knew, and it could flip at any second.' This was part of her 'psychosis', according to Sarah, who became a doctor after leaving the cult. 'She might give us gifts, be nice to us. We might get good food or something when she was there, or she might start screaming abuse at us and beating us.' Anne's favourite weapon was a stiletto heel, Sarah told us. 'You knew there was always going to be some kind of excitement or horror when she was there.'

Sarah's real mother had her at 16 and was disowned by her family, but during her pregnancy was seen by a female doctor, who happened to be one of Raynor Johnson's daughters and a cult member. When Sarah was born, her mother was reportedly drugged and a pillow was put over her face so she never saw her child. She was forced to give Sarah up.

Sarah wrote a book about her time in the cult, called *Unseen, Unheard, Unknown*, in 1995. In it, she writes that the children developed intense self-loathing, to the point where they would hurt themselves by picking scabs and making them infected or holding their breath until they fainted. Sarah says she cut herself with pins and scissors rubbed in dirt and fantasised about killing herself by drowning in the lake or poisoning herself with Dettol.

Anne would throw things at the children; she once threw a bowl of pears, we were told. One morning, Ben blew on a spoonful of porridge to cool it and some flew off. She hit him in the head and then threw a chair at him, he says.

The children were isolated not only from society but also from one another in their own bizarre community, the only place they knew. They didn't know who they were. They thought, and would continue to think until their teens, that Anne and Bill were their biological parents, but they weren't. Their ultimate mother figure was Anne, and she was for them a totem of all that could be good, or all that they knew as good, even though it was frequently very bad. So they craved her attention and affection.

The Aunties, meanwhile, beat the children and trod them down but also nurtured them in a perfunctory, distant, and inconsistent way. It was all the nurturing many had.

The Family's teachings to the children in the Uptop monastery were about guiding them towards being able to see and access other spiritual dimensions, and then show other chosen ones how to do the same. Ben says the children were taught to try and access the divine consciousness. This was through hours of hatha yoga, meditation, and Hindu readings.

Anne said she could free others from the cycle of life and death. This is what Ben and Sarah and all the others believed as children. Only those on the inside could know the answer; it was only they who belonged properly to the world. Outsiders, and especially police, were dangerous: the children were told police would put them in bags to torture and rape them.

'Anne was the filter for everything,' Ben says. 'Take a young child and train them up and control their inputs ... I guess like Hitler did.'

Anne also said the world would end in an apocalypse. She was paranoid about nuclear war. This was post–Cuban Missile Crisis, when fear of another war involving the nuclear-capable superpowers was widespread. She said the chosen ones — the children, and the adults who were loyal — would survive and re-educate other survivors on how to transcend earthly realms. The children were to be a new race. They were bestowed with this responsibility: they were 'perfect children who would save the world,' as one former Uptop child puts it.

'When the holocaust happened, we would come out as world leaders,' Ben says.

In one of her taped discourses, Anne proclaimed that cruelty — ironically, such as that happening at Uptop — was a sin: 'If anyone can be cruel, they are better off to ask God almighty to take them now. Don't let us hurt or cause suffering in any way or any level ... death is preferable, of course it is. Start again. There's always more growth in whatever happens in the knowledge of God and his ways. Nothing else matters, all else is superficial, and the Earth is seen merely to be a training school for that soul.'

This notion of the tension between reality and appearance took on an especially curious dimension at Uptop. While still young, the children were made to star in home movies and photoshoots. This idealisation of what was happening beside the lake was aimed at persuading cult members that Uptop was as promised.

In these videos, the children look happy and relaxed. The girls wear pretty dresses and clutch Easter Eggs. They dance, and cuddle Anne and Bill, in scenes that were often orchestrated. These were 'special days', says Sarah, 'where we would have to get dressed up in, actually, very fine clothes. We'd all be lined up in order of age and photographed ... her fantasy of these perfect children all lined up in a row.'

The Aunties acted as crew, set dressers, and costume designers for the home movies, which were shot on Super 66 film. They were depicted as benign carers.

Occasionally the kids would be shown the footage back on a screen inside. The image projected was of 'perfect children in perfect array having fun,' says Sarah.

3

THE HOLE

The kitchen cupboards at Uptop were padlocked; the Aunties had sets of keys dangling from their waists. There was a chain and padlock around the fridge, and an Aunty would often be on guard duty in the kitchen.

The children ate a Spartan vegetarian diet at Uptop that was very low in protein. Breakfast was usually two or three segments of fruit. Lunch was always steamed vegetables, and dinner was salad or soup and sometimes raisins and nuts; perhaps yoghurt. But a child could go up to three days without eating, as a punishment for even little things such as not screwing the toothpaste cap back on or getting their clothes dirty while outside. The withdrawal of food became a form of disciplinary leverage for the Aunties.

The children would scavenge like animals. They'd look under the dining table, in the rubbish bins and compost bins. Sarah says she ate leaves and grass. Another went for the bacon bones that were fed to the dogs. They ate the stale bread that was thrown outside for the birds; they would eat birdseed too.

A young girl called Anouree came to Uptop in 1973. Her father was Bill Hamilton-Byrne's son Michael, her mother a vulnerable young woman caught up in the cult. Anouree spent her first three years living between them and Winbirra, Anne's house in Ferny Creek. Her mother was back and forth between the hills and psychiatric hospitals and had tried to keep Anouree, but Anne reportedly stood between them. Then Michael handed her over to Anne and Bill. Anouree says she was driven halfway to Lake Eildon and exchanged for $AU7,000 with an Auntie on the side of the road.

As she got older, the only way she found she could escape was in her mind. She imagined she was on a deserted planet, based on her concept of Mars. It was people who caused her harm; in her imagination there were creatures that she said were much friendlier: '… probably more like cats than humans … furry and very cuddly'.

'I wanted to hide. Sometimes I would hide under my bed — that was my place to be. I would just sit on my bed, frozen as a statue, just staring out the window. I'd just shut down. Which is why I uselessly dreamed of going to Mars and living there. There were no humans, just little creatures that would be getting about in an industrial way making their civilisation work.'

When the children were taken on outings to the local town of Eildon, she remembers not understanding what was going on around her, what shops were for, what people meant when they used conversational language. If someone in the street spoke to her, she didn't know what to say. 'For example, if someone said, "Good day, how's your day been?" I would find it difficult to respond. What's "good day", for example?'

The children were also regularly weighed, under orders from Anne. If they were deemed too heavy, they would be denied food. The children, especially the girls, purged like bulimics before weigh-ins to drop their weight. 'It was a very desperate time for a lot of my siblings.'

When the girls approached puberty, it was drummed into them that their changing bodies were ugly. 'The message we'd been given was that our body was really a disgusting thing to think about,' says Anouree. One of her 'sisters' had an anatomy book, from which they learned, but Anouree couldn't even look at herself. She didn't recognise her body as the body in the book. 'I didn't really use a mirror even to look at my face when I was up at Eildon, I don't think. I don't remember looking at myself much at all.'

She calls it a denial, on Anne's part and administered through the Aunties, of their bodies. A refusal to believe they were growing up and might harbour independent thought or physical strength. Or strength of mind. When the girls started getting their periods, it was made hard for them because pads were rationed.

'There was always this underlying feeling or theme that girls were dirty and sexual,' says Sarah. 'It was an insidious sort of thing that made us feel yucky and bad and evil for no reason, and it was obviously something that preoccupied her a lot.'

Sarah says the effect on some of the girls, who are now women, is an enduring sense of shame around their bodies. At Uptop, they were taught or shown nothing about adolescence or sexuality. Girls were accused of being lesbians if they were perceived to be being sexual in the way they dressed or walked. 'It was this weird sort of coyness and recoil from anything that had to with sex or sexuality, so we were very naïve, very innocent, but we also had that feeling of dirtiness they had projected onto us.'

Anne had hang-ups in this regard, according to interviews with those who knew her. She was known to be extremely modest, in terms of not letting anyone see her get dressed or in a state of undress. As Sarah says, it appears she transmitted this

phobia to the girls at Uptop; it was an idea of modesty combined
with a sense of fright at being anything other than chaste. The
girls were unfamiliar, almost, with the way their bodies worked.
The contradiction was that Anne also had a dirty mouth at
times. She used the word 'pussy'. She also commonly referred
to sex in her discourses as one of the universe's great powers.
'Sex, baby!' she once told followers. 'That's all there is.' And
of course although she only ever gave birth to one child, by
her first husband, she pretended to have many, and even faked
pregnancies.

The girls were also getting the message that they were not
perfect enough, despite trying, for Anne, to be so. Consequently,
they strived to be more 'ideal' — and thin.

Food was always the ultimate battleground. The Aunties ate
better-quality food, and while the children were sometimes given
such treats as salmon mornay or macaroni cheese, this was a
rarity. Survival instincts kicked in, and as the situation worsened
they started to steal food both from Uptop and from empty
holiday houses nearby. There was a shed near the house where
canned food and fresh fruit and vegetables were kept. One of the
kids figured out how to unscrew the hinges on the locked door.
Anouree went in one night with some others and couldn't get the
bread and canned fish into her mouth fast enough. They were
in a hurry, trying to be quiet while eating as quickly as possible.
They were overwhelmed and confused and happy in the moment.
'One of my siblings said, "Come on, come on, Boo, hurry up."
I said, "I can't, I can't."'

Sarah was the most adventurous of the Uptop children. She
was the bravest, others thought, and the wisest. She discovered
she could get into an Aunty's empty caravan at night and make
toast and vegemite. But one night she wiped a knife on a tea
towel and left a telltale smear of vegemite behind. Anne hit her

with a shoe and threw her down a staircase, she tells us, and she had a chair thrown at her.

Sarah began walking further away at night, leaving the property, and saw all the other houses, the holiday houses, empty. One night there was an open window, and she scrambled in and found things she had never seen: lollies, cakes. She showed Anouree, but the food confused her. She didn't know what it was. They found some Nutri-Grain — 'little things with holes in them, and we wondered among ourselves, "I wonder what you do with these?" So we just ate them without any milk, we just ate them by themselves, and we thought they were really good. And another thing we ate was raw pizza. We didn't know that you cooked it, for example. And we didn't really know it was called pizza.'

Stolen food would be hidden in piles of leaves. Only Sarah and Anouree knew at first, but then word leaked out. Ben joined them on a mission to find more one night, and they broke into a house and took a pack of cards. But Trish caught them. Ben was contrite, frightened: 'I said, "I'd rather be dead." She said, "I bet you do, you little shit, look what trouble you've caused us all."'

The great contradiction of Uptop was the regimentation coupled with the unpredictability. The monotony would suddenly be broken by wild outbursts of punishment and violent anger. The children never knew exactly how to escape punishment because the rules changed all the time. They were not allowed to say they were unhappy. The children became hyper-vigilant, traumatised, anxious: scared of being punished but not sure how to prevent it. Compliance and silence became important to them, to save themselves. They learned to be helpless, while all the adults had absolute power.

The local police started to drop in through the mid to late 1970s, acting on suspicions from locals in the small lakeside community. Homes were being broken into, food taken. Packs of cards went missing. What was it the group was into, witchcraft? They had a van they called Jupiter, full of identical kids, residents murmured to one another. All the caravans, the comings and goings. Pretty weird.

'We were led to believe that anyone outside was there to sabotage our perfect lives,' says Ben.

Workmen came one year in the late 1970s to fix electricity lines. They needed two weeks. The children were told they should talk to the workmen but act retarded, to make them think it was a special school. 'We were taught how to roll our heads, put our heads on one side, talk nonsense, garbled noises, and act uncoordinated,' said one former Uptop child.

Whenever the police came, they always left satisfied. According to Aunty Margot McLellan, a local policeman once said to her: 'I've been through every inch of this place and there is nothing wrong going on here at all.'

But the police never saw 'the Hole', a narrow, cramped crawlspace behind a pump room downstairs in the lakehouse. It had a small entrance that was concealed with a wallchart. One night at 10.30, the police came. It was unusually late for a police visit, according to one of the children who was there. The girls were woken and told to make their beds and rush downstairs towards the Hole. When they got there, the boys were already crawling in. Liz Whitaker was upstairs, talking to police, as a decoy. Margot McLellan was shoving the kids — 18 of them — into the crawlspace one by one.

Then the covering was put back over the entrance. The kids could hear noises but were scared to make any noise themselves. It was dirty, dusty, cold, and damp, and they were in their pyjamas, terrified they would be found and taken away, as they were told the police would do, to be killed or raped.

About 20 minutes later, the children heard noises at the entrance. It was Liz Whitaker letting them out; she said the police had come looking for two male fugitives, not the children.

Syd Savage remembers it differently. He told us he went into the Hole several times to fix hot-water pipes. 'The cobwebs tell me it wasn't being used every day.'

This was life at Uptop through the 1970s. The cult was trying to keep it contained and secret — unseen and unknown — but something had to give.

Then, in 1980, a ten-year-old girl went missing. Her name was Kim Halm. Her father, Hans Halm, told police she was born into The Family.

Patricia Halm, the girl's mother, had found the cult early on through yoga. She was a librarian but had become a nurse, apparently on Anne's orders. Hans was initially in the cult with her, but he was unenthusiastic, and they split up. Patricia fled with Kim, despite Hans having partial legal custody. So he called it in, telling the Australian Federal Police — because he suspected the girl had been taken out of the country — all about Uptop.

The Feds, known then as the Commonwealth Police, went and searched Uptop but couldn't find Kim. It seems extraordinary now to think they went to a cramped lakehouse and found many of the children had the same 'Hamilton-Byrne' surname yet did not launch an investigation. Police documents reveal that in fact they had started to gather intelligence on The Family a year before, telling Melbourne's state police that 'no further action' on The Family was required.

Documents we have seen also show that a former cult member, Hazel Dalton, contacted her nephew, who worked for Ben Bodna, a very senior Victorian state bureaucrat — the Director-General of Community Services — to tell him about Uptop and the life the children had there. She even drew him a map of how to get to the house. Bodna passed it all to Victoria Police, but no action was taken by them either.

Frustrated, Hans Halm hired a private investigator, Barbara Palmer, who brought with her a journalist from *The Bulletin* magazine, Dick Wordley, to find his daughter. Wordley had written the book *Cathy's Child*, about a search for an abducted child. The pair staked out Uptop, taking photographs and watching. They hired a boat for a better view from the lake, and on one mission Palmer told the media that she took her top off, exposing her breasts, to entice the children to look at her so she could get clearer pictures.

Wordley doorknocked the surrounds and also recorded some interviews with adults in the cult in the hills. In Melbourne, *The Age* newspaper was also onto the story. One of the paper's most dogged journalists, David Elias, lived in the hills, in one of the Ferny Creek streets that had become a strong cult enclave. It was an unfortunate coincidence for a cult that thrived on secrecy. His daughter had begun playing with one of the girls living over the road and had told him about her new friend: 'She doesn't have a mummy and daddy. She has lots of mummies and daddies.'

Hans last saw Kim when he dropped her off at her mother's house after a father–daughter day out and saw a white Datsun parked in the driveway. It didn't belong to anyone he knew. He also saw a silhouette of a woman he didn't recognise in a window. Kim didn't turn up for school the next day. Hans went back and found the house abandoned.

But a neighbour had seen his ex-wife and Kim loading up the car, and had written down the licence-plate number. Hans gave it to Elias, who traced it to a female cult member who admitted to Elias that she had helped Kim and Patricia Halm pack up and leave the house that day.

Elias reported his findings in *The Age* — and then a man called George Ellis, a former cult member, contacted him. He handed over 20 pages of information on who was who in the cult. The documents named a solicitor, Peter Kibby, a tall, slender man with a thatch of wavy hair who suffered from obsessive-compulsive disorder. Kibby had phobias around dirt and germs: he washed his hands constantly and would only be driven in Michael's car because he knew Michael kept it clean. He even washed his money — at a time when he was also laundering the cult's money.

When Elias contacted him, Kibby stayed on message and painted a rosy picture of Uptop and Anne's methods, denying any cult involvement with Kim Halm's disappearance. The curious lawyer was staying loyal to Anne, who had nicknamed him Pontius Pilate, after the judge in Jesus's trial. Kibby was protecting her. But soon enough he would betray her.

The Truth tabloid was reporting on the Halm case too. According to the paper's sources, Jewish 'heavies' who knew Mr Halm had threatened to kidnap a child from the cult if Kim was not returned to her father. Hans told the newspaper they weren't heavies and they weren't Jewish — one was Catholic, he said, and the other just a Methodist.

Hans decided to go to court. He wanted to get full custody of his daughter, but he didn't even know where she was. This was very bad for the cult: it was the first time they had become embroiled in a court case. The judge bucked convention by allowing proceedings to be reported in the media even though the case involved a child.

Kibby and a cult Aunty called Christabel Wallace, who was a GP, were ordered to give evidence in court about Kim Halm.

Wallace — who was from New Zealand — was physically similar to Liz Whitaker: large and matronly, and very keen on gaudy lipstick and heavy eye make-up. She had already told the private investigator Barbara Palmer that she knew where the girl was. She had also spoken to Dick Wordley. But in court the denials, under oath, continued. Wallace backtracked and said she didn't know where the child was and had not said anything to Palmer. She denied telling Wordley that a 'chain of very important people all around Australia were concerned about the welfare of Mrs Halm and her daughter'.

The judge ruled that the cult members were not telling the truth, and had given evidence 'bordering on the provocative'. He ordered for Patricia Halm, who was still on the run, to bring Kim back. She didn't. A warrant for her arrest was issued. A week later, in September 1983, mother and daughter were found in Auckland, New Zealand; they were using the names Jeannette Berger and Jeannette De Haven and were using a motel as a contact address.

All of this was likely the worst-case scenario for Anne. Her group's dirty laundry was being aired very publicly. Names and addresses presented in court, accusations, counter-claims, custody battles, a missing kid, private detectives. A solicitor and a GP within the cult identified. Journalists with reliable sources. Betrayals within the closed community.

As the children got older and began to challenge aspects of the life into which they were forced, Anne told her adult disciples that the children were projecting 'conflicts' at Uptop because of pre-conditioning. They had apparently made certain things up because it was not their 'real selves' objecting to their treatment (that is, being hit, starved, dunked, demeaned, according to the former children). She told her followers that the children she had collected and left to the Aunties to raise had two separate lives and had become confused about which was real: 'We must realise that although many have a tremendous conflict, we may have a serenity and calmness as well when we are together.'

But Anne was also loosening the reins, suggesting perhaps that she was more interested in small children than older ones. In 1985, she let six of her teenage female children, including Sarah, Leeanne, and Anouree, out of her clutches to join a dancing school in the hills. They took ballroom-dancing classes, and Leeanne also did ballet. Exactly why she let them mingle with a group of outsiders and whisperers is unclear, but she was by now a distant leader, more overseas than at home. The girls were 15. Perhaps Anne thought they were by then wedded to her for life, and that none of her manipulations could be undone.

If so, she was wrong. The innocence and utter normality of teenage girls at a suburban dancing school proved, for Anne, a disaster. The girls were taken from Uptop every Friday night to Anne's rambling mansion, Crowther House, which was behind high fences in the hills. Then they were taken to nearby Kenlaurel, the dancing school owned by ballroom-dancing champions Ken and Laurel Sims, stayed the night at Crowther, and were ferried back to Lake Eildon the next morning. Leon Dawes, a schoolteacher involved with The Family, did the driving, in Jupiter.

Dance-school staff noticed that the girls' clothes were old-fashioned but otherwise thought they were nice, and very polite. They showed no signs or abuse and never said anything to anyone.

It wasn't the act of dancing, as such, that awakened the girls, although the freedom of expression must have counted for something. It was this sudden and unfiltered exposure to the outside world, and the realisation upon experiencing it that the insular cult was dangerous — not the wider society, as they had been taught.

Sarah and Leeanne struck out on their own at Kenlaurel. They found their feet, and they met two new friends, who were local girls of the same age. Cathy and Helen were normal, everyday teenagers from a normal, everyday family. Sarah and Leeanne persuaded Anne to let them stay at the girls' house for a few nights during school holidays that year. This was unthinkable to the other kids. They couldn't believe it. 'Absolutely unheard of,' says Ben. He thinks Anne probably thought she could attract more cult members by sending her model children out into the world as ambassadors.

The girls stayed with Cathy and Helen for four days. '[It was] completely different to anything I had done before in my life,' says Leeanne. They went to McDonald's; they had home-cooked meals. Erica, the mum, was nice to them. They watched television and caught a bus to a shopping centre without adults. 'We were allowed to get dirty when we were playing,' says Leeanne, 'without getting into trouble.'

After they left that school holidays and went back to Uptop, the girls were allowed to write to their new friends. The idea that the cult was strange and the outside world was normal was reinforced in the back-and-forth of the letters. 'Our pen-friends made it clear that they thought our lives were weird,' says Sarah.

The Aunties censored the letters at first, but after a while they just let them through. This was complacency but also, most likely, exhaustion. Uptop had been running for more than ten years by this stage.

Soon enough, Sarah and Leeanne began to think about breaking free. The teenagers were by now calling themselves POAs: Prisoners of Anne. They were big and strong enough, and also smart enough, to pull off an escape if they dared. The physical boundaries were not great — jump a fence, climb out a window. But the psychological barriers were immense. They had only known another life for a matter of days.

Leeanne began to fight hard against Anne's repressive household. She had already briefly escaped to a neighbours' house in Eildon. She had jumped out her bedroom window, climbed down over a water tank, and run around the lake until she saw a house with a light on. The couple there phoned the local policeman, who picked her up, but the Aunties told them she was mentally disturbed. The police took her straight back to Uptop, choosing to believe the adults rather than Leeanne. She was underage, and so still legally a child.

The fact that the Uptop kids were all children when these things happened to them is crucial to the way this story played out. They were ignored, their allegations discounted. Maybe it was just that outsiders — such as Syd Savage — could not entertain the idea that a sophisticated regime of abuse could actually be happening. Especially when everything sounded so rosy, at least as the Aunties described it. Children's rights were not enshrined in legislation in Australia and its states and territories until, at the earliest, the mid-1990s.

Then Leeanne had a big argument with Anne over where she would do her senior year in high school and what she would study. There was an established school at Uptop, with adults involved in The Family serving as teachers. Leeanne refused to be dictated to this time. She and Anne were nose to nose, eye to eye. 'Anne went berserk, like a madwoman,' says Leeanne, 'and began hitting me around the face.' Then Leeanne was on a bed with Anne on top of her, she tells us. Anne was 65; Leeanne, 16. Anne was sitting with her legs either side of Leeanne, slapping her face. Leeanne grabbed Anne's bony wrists and slapped Anne across the face. Anne winced. Leeanne wrestled her off. Anne called out for Bill to help her — Leeanne was still Daddy's girl and listened to him — and Leeanne bolted outside and hid down near the lake. Anne was due to leave on an overseas flight that day, and when Leeanne got back to Uptop she was gone. It was among Leeanne's last memories of Uptop, and the last time Anne ever touched her.

Soon after, around the end of 1986, Leeanne had a stand-up row with Trish MacFarlane, where she threw cushions at her. Trish baited Leeanne to leave: 'Go on then. See how you would go without us!' Leeanne went up to the girls' bedroom and barricaded herself in, with her cassette player on loud. Trish turned the electricity off, so Leeanne switched her cassette player to batteries. Then she packed a bag and jumped out the window and ended up by accident, rather than design, at the same neighbours' house that she had fled to before. The elderly man in the house said to her, 'You're the same girl that ran away [before].'

Leeanne asked again if she could call the local police station. She was terrified. As far as the local police officer knew, Leeanne was mentally ill and unstable, reliant on medication. So when he arrived at the house, he came in with his baton drawn. But Leeanne spoke to him calmly about the abuse and the unspeakable life she had been made to live in the cult. He phoned the nearest community policing squad, who dealt with welfare issues, and also a kind married couple he knew in the nearby town of Alexandra, whom he was sure would look after her. She was now legally an adult and couldn't be forced to return to Uptop.

'He introduced me to these beautiful people,' Leeanne says. 'They took me in that night.' The couple, Brian and Josie Slater, already had three daughters. 'They took me into their home and looked after me.' She stayed six weeks.

By this point, Anne was in crisis mode, and Leeanne's departure only intensified things. The Family as a whole was also falling into crisis. Anne had not only seen adult members of The Family leave of their own accord, but some had even betrayed her in the worst possible way by airing secrets, acting as whistleblowers to the media. She had seen evidence of illegal actions in her group go before the courts; now her children were running away. Her message was that Leeanne had betrayed the sacred cult mantra and was 'a whore on the streets and stole and sold drugs to make money'.

Leeanne, finally out of Uptop and boarding with the Slaters, felt guilty. She was free, but still imprisoned by the idea she had betrayed the rest of the children at Uptop: her brothers and sisters. 'I did actually have a life outside of The Family. [But] I felt a lot of grief and a lot of heartache and a lot of guilt that the children were [still] there.'

A youth welfare group moved her into a sharehouse in inner-city Melbourne, and she managed to enrol at a university for her final school year. The house was dysfunctional and full of drugs: heroin and marijuana. She would sometimes leave the chaos — having come from chaos — to sleep on a park bench. The other girls in the house were 'vicious, nasty girls', says Leeanne. They didn't let her eat any of the food, so she went to charity places to feed herself and the animals in the house.

A school counsellor heard her stories about the cult over a period of months and challenged her to go to the police about Uptop.

Meanwhile, Sarah was living in the hills at one of Anne's houses but spent weekends at Uptop. She was doing her final year of school by correspondence and had a part-time job at an osteopathy clinic in the hills whose owner was associated with The Family. One day, out the blue, Cathy, Helen, and their mother, Erica, walked in. They arranged to have dinner together after

Sarah's shift finished. Sarah missed the last bus back to the hills, and Erica gave her a ride. Then Sarah did a remarkable thing. She invited Erica into the house where she lived. It was provoking a reaction — and she got one. Sarah recounts that Anne was told what happened and, by phone from overseas, threw her out of the house and the cult, saying: 'You are no longer our daughter. Go out there — go and die in the gutter.'

Erica came to her rescue again, and Sarah was taken into their home from the beginning of winter 1987. This was where it got really sticky for The Family. Erica persuaded Sarah that she should do something, or at least talk to someone, about what was going on in the hills and beside the lake. She introduced her to a private investigator, Helen Dubont, who also, as it turned out, had been talking to Bill Hamilton-Byrne's first wife. When Leeanne and Sarah and the other children were at Kenlaurel, Dubont had been there too, watching from afar.

When she met Dubont, Sarah found out almost immediately that she was not a Hamilton-Byrne, and neither were the others. Anne was not her mother. She was making it all up.

Sarah set about trying to get birth and adoption records to find out who she was. She went to the state office and asked for her birth certificate, as Sarah Hamilton-Byrne. 'I got back this piece of paper saying there is no such person. I thought, okay, well who am I?'

With Dubont, she went back to Uptop one night, secretly, and snuck in to the girls' bedroom to check on her 'family'. She left postage stamps for them.

Leeanne went to see Bill's first wife, May, who had been treated very badly by the cult and held a grudge against them. 'Do you know who I am?' Leeanne asked her.

May replied: 'I know someone who can help you.' She introduced her to Dubont. Through her, she found out that Anne was not her mother, and that Bill — her 'knight in shining armour', despite it all — was not her father. Trish had fraudulently adopted her and gifted her to Anne. 'I was absolutely devastated that I wasn't who I thought I was and that somebody I hated as a child [Trish] had adopted me, and that someone who was so cruel had [been given] me. Why didn't she [Trish] want me? Why was she part of what we had been put through? It was a very confronting situation for a 17-year-old.'

Leeanne was angry with Bill. He had betrayed what she thought was a great love between them in the most heinous way: it was all a lie; he had been lying to her all along. But she was angrier with Anne, who, as Leeanne saw it, had duped Bill and made him do it — to Leeanne and to all of them. 'She was the one that controlled everybody. I was devastated by the betrayal.'

Sarah and Leeanne were urged to go the police — specifically the community policing squad, the welfare police. They were hesitant, and in the end Dubont invited the girls to lunch with two 'friends', who happened to be female community policing officers. Over a period of a few weeks, they made official statements. They recounted their lives: the cult, the people, the beliefs, the punishments. A senior police medical officer, Dr Edward Ogden, was assigned to their case.

In August of 1987, just before Kylie Minogue's first hit, 'I Should Be So Lucky', entered the charts, Uptop was raided by armed state and federal police. Not long after 7.00 am, the police entered — they did not knock on the door. Anne was in the Catskill Mountains in upstate New York, but Bill was there. He told ABC Radio much later: 'It was a terrible shock. I served during the war, I was a pilot, and I've gone through a few shocks and things, but this was grossly rude. If I may say so. The police didn't just wait for me to open the door, they just crashed in. Poured all over the place, turning things upside down and searching the place. In all this melee or whatever we can call it, the children were being picked up by various guards and carried off ...

'(A child) ran over to me screaming and hung onto me, almost pulling my head off. A smallish policeman in plainclothes with a drape type of overcoat and revolver in his hand shot across and poked the revolver into my stomach and said, "Let her go." He said, "You're a very dangerous person." I said, "Oh, really? What about you?" Of course, [the child] wouldn't let go, I wouldn't let go, and the gun was pushed rather hard in my stomach. And then someone stepped in and took it away from him. It was absolutely ridiculous.'

Police also raided houses in the hills and a safety deposit box at a bank in the Dandenongs. Drugs — prescription and LSD, found in one of Anne's bedrooms — were also seized. The full extent of how LSD, the most powerful hallucinogenic drug ever made, was used on cult members, including children, was a story that was yet to unravel. But here was the first clue.

Anouree huddled with several other teenage children in the corner of a bedroom in the Uptop house. The police stomped through. Anouree could see that she and the others were being removed, and didn't know how she would manage herself in such dramatic circumstances. She tried, in these moments, to prepare herself. She trusted Leeanne and Sarah. She rushed into her bedroom with Sarah to grab her torch and her winter gloves, but panicked when she couldn't find them. 'We were ushered out quite quickly, out of the house, and up to the [police] bus at the end of our driveway. And we just had to keep moving. I would describe it as ... a multitude of voices, just going at the same time.'

Trish MacFarlane was on one of her two-week stints away from Uptop. She was at home in the hills. Liz Whitaker phoned her, and Trish burst into tears. From upstate New York, Anne sent a five-page letter and an eight-page document for circulation among her disciples to defend herself and justify her actions. A portion of the letter read, of the children: 'Quite a number had heart damage, others were brain-damaged at birth.'

A phone call was recorded between Bill and Anne. He was still in the hills, and police were staking him out. 'I can see them,' he told her, 'but they can't see me. I am going to get a baseball bat and keep it inside the door too. I am not taking any shit from anybody, Anne.'

Anne was also under pressure, and must have been wondering how to keep her group together, wondering how to plug the leaks and to persuade those followers she had to persevere and 'walk on'. She cried often. We can hear her cry on one of the tapes, in perhaps her most remarkable recorded discourse to her followers. She uses the word 'cult' in the context of all the sets of beliefs she perceived were competing for her attention. She is at pains to reinforce that it is not a cult member's job to remove others from practising religion but merely to help them towards the feted end point she had always referred to as 'the light'. This, she said, was a 'great adventure', the great vocation of their lives — to help others live well. Stay strong, sure, and silent, she said. Silent. When others in the circle had not.

'My dear friends,' she announced, on tape, 'there is no church large enough to hold the splendour of the light and the glory of the holy spirit. There is no creed possible for the sublime, wondrous understanding when you touch God. Only love can understand love, and only the God-like can attain to this god-consciousness filling all the spaces, whereas there is no space. Children, we are all children. Many dear old Christians have fallen flat on it, you know. We are here to give, remember that. To love. It is as simple as that. Living that others may feel your love.'

A great teacher does not look like they are teaching, she said, her usually powerful voice quavering. It is difficult to know if the emotion is genuine; it may have been an act, a performance. In any case, this is when she began to cry. 'They put you in the paper. They say you are false. You dare to be true, you dare to walk and not faint, in a strength that will never fail you. To some, mention of the Christ is so long forgotten, but the voice rises from the depths of your being with the gracious words, my friend. Lovest thou me. Lord, we have loved thee with everlasting love, and he said in the Bible "feed my sheep, help others".'

She stopped herself to apologise, her voice rising and falling with emotion. But she gathered herself. 'I'm sorry. It has been a big day today, watching, serving. It is a day of extraordinary cults. Let's face it; let's turn with great peace to the all-sustaining life of God and his Christ, in you. It's a sweet, pure, all-pervading, wondrous sprit. You know as well as I do what we have is a great treasure. It is the end of the quest when you get there to meet the Christ. No one can hinder you but yourself. Every rebuff is a challenge. So I am saying to you — go forward.'

Yet the betrayals against The Family were mounting. What would Anne do — concede defeat or walk on? A New York–based Australian journalist for Melbourne's *The Herald*, Michael Gordon, went to Hurleyville and knocked on her door. 'She appeared at times on the verge of tears,' he wrote, blaming 'religious persecution' for the raid and the accusations. But she admitted to him that she had organised forged adoption papers for children. And that she wanted to start another family of 'unwanted' children, this time in America.

4

FIRES

Detective Lex de Man's pager burred. He was at home but on call for the Victoria police arson squad. A Catholic primary school in the hills had been set on fire, and one of the school's buildings was burnt out. It was December 1987, the summer bushfire season in the south-east of Australia. It was just another fire, just another job.

Lex had joined the police in 1968 as a teenager. Before that he was working for a supermarket chain and volunteering as a country firefighter. Interested by the emergency workers he met on fire grounds, one day he walked into a Melbourne suburban police station on a whim after seeing a recruiting sign.

Lex's parents came to Melbourne from Holland in the 1950s, and at first his father didn't want him to be a cop because of the European post–World War II mentality that uniforms — whether military or police — were corrupt. When Lex sat down to dinner with his parents and three brothers, and announced that earlier that day he had applied to be a police cadet, his father got up and walked out of the room. 'We had a pretty frosty relationship there for about 18 months. I went through the police academy, and six months later I couldn't shut him up about how proud he was because he'd realised that Victoria Police wasn't like the Netherlands police. It wasn't an offshoot of the military; it tried to be an organisation that does its best for the community.'

Lex found he liked being a leader. Since he left the police, he has been a local government mayor and councillor, and also held a senior position at the same fire service he still volunteers for, the Country Fire Authority. 'I've always had this desire to lead not because I'm not a good follower but because I think I have a clear understanding when I've got a task to do of how to do it. I think it came from a couple of teachers — if you want to get something done, if you show the way and you guide people, you get people to do what you want to have done, but you get them to enjoy doing it. That to me is the art of leadership.'

Lex knew the hills — a mystery to many in Melbourne, down on the 'flat' — because of his volunteer firefighting. He got to the fire site with another detective and started asking questions, and he found out pretty quickly about a young man by the name of Roland Whitaker who had been fingered a few times for lighting fires, shoplifting, and cutting car brakes. He was a bit of a wild one, apparently. Smoked a bit of dope. He'd been through the children's court for trying to drive a stolen car through a caryard's chain fence in the middle of the night.

The boy had been to the school but was now 17. Lex asked a bit more about him. A local senior constable said to him: 'I think before you go any further, you should actually know that Roland's parents are tied up with this religious sect called The Family.'

'He told me some very fanciful story,' says Lex. 'Or what I thought at the time was fanciful.'

Roland's real name — or at least the name he goes by now — is Adam. He estimates he has had as many as five names in his life, and two different dates of birth. He landed in The Family in 1970 as soon as he was born, when he was given, in hospital, to Liz Whitaker. Then, when he was three, he went to Uptop as a 'foster', without the Hamilton-Byrne surname. He would become a persistent thorn in the cult's side. But at the beginning he was, in his own words, 'a commodity'.

Adam was born Darren Gillon. He thinks his mother and father met in the psychiatric ward of a major Melbourne hospital. His mother, who was Dutch, could not keep him because of her mental-health concerns.

The cult's adoption scam was devastatingly simple, yet it required a lot of people to be complicit in the fraud. Melbourne hospital social worker Maie Davie was a member of The Family. Maie heard about all the babies up for adoption around Melbourne. They were usually from single mothers or mentally ill mothers. She then told Anne about the child and where it was. Anne delegated a couple from the cult to adopt the child using false names, addresses, financial details, and statements given on affidavits.

And so it was with Adam. His nominal parents — the people he considered his parents — were Don Webb and Liz.

Anne became Adam's beloved 'Aunty Anne'. As he grew up, he wanted to emulate her because he was in awe of the control she exerted over others. He thought she was quite magnificent. 'The power that she had was very enticing,' he says. He and his young friends at Uptop — his new family — thought that Anne was some kind of queen, and the Aunties and the Uncles were her servants. 'She was top dog. As children, we thought she was beyond the Queen of England. We revered her.'

Anne taught them about the promise of everlasting life. 'That's all it was,' Adam says. 'We were trying to fast-track inner change so we could get to another dimension more quickly.'

The comparison he gives for Anne is odd but strangely accurate — Captain Kathryn Janeway from *Star Trek: Voyager*, a television show with which, when he watched it years later, he identified deeply: 'Captain Janeway was in command of the Starship *Voyager* and they were lost in the Delta Quadrant, and it was about their journey home. It was all about a crew that didn't know each other, and over the seven years it took them to get home they'd become a family. That's what it was like with Aunty Anne. She was in charge of her own starship ... and we were her crew.'

Lex lingered at the fire scene, talking to local police. The senior constable said he needed to meet a police doctor called Ed Ogden if he wanted to know more about the cult because Ed had met the Uptop children after the raid. Ed lived in the hills and, that day, was at a flower show. So Lex went to the show. 'I introduced myself to Edward, and his first words were "Don't get involved. If you get involved, it will be with you for a lifetime."'

Lex met Sarah, who was there because Ogden had taken her in after the raid. 'The look on her face was a look I'd never seen before,' says Lex. 'It was a look between terror and bewilderment, as if she was looking straight through us, and she didn't say a word.' He said to his partner, 'Something's going on here.'

The detectives didn't really believe what they were hearing, but it was easy enough to verify: there had been a raid at a gated compound at Lake Eildon some months before and six kids were taken into state care. The kids were not in good shape physically or psychologically. Two others had escaped leading up to the raid, including the one standing before them, Sarah. They all thought that they had the surname Hamilton-Byrne and that this woman, Anne, in her sixties, was some sort of leader or teacher or guru.

Still, it was the fire he was being paid to probe. The arson squad kept investigating it, but Lex followed his nose towards the cult and soon met the community policing people and their head, Sergeant Denise Whyte, who had been at Uptop for the raid.

Then he started looking at Adam's maze-like family history. Don Webb wasn't his biological father. Elizabeth Whitaker wasn't his biological mother — and she used to be married to some big-name psychiatrist involved with LSD trials in Melbourne. In the middle of them was this Trish MacFarlane, and all of them knew the wealthy woman in the hills who was supposed to be the cult leader. And then there were the stories that Ed and the community policing squad were starting to hear about life at Uptop: the punishments and beatings and dunkings. The sheer psychological trauma of it. The despair and lack of hope the children had felt. And this mantra that members of The Family recited, where any whiff of betrayal, or even speaking to outsiders, was forbidden: *'To thy last supper let me be allowed to stay, oh Son of God, for neither have I betrayed any secrets to thine enemies, nor have I given thee the kiss of Judas, but like a thief I pray unto thee, remember me, oh Lord, as I enter into thy glorious Kingdom.'*

'It became pretty clear that the story I'd been told about this charismatic leader of the sect started to ring a bit true,' Lex says. He hauled in Adam and interviewed him about the school fire. His 'father', Don Webb, was also there — 'I thought, *He doesn't look like a heinous criminal to me*, but we went through the motions.' Adam wasn't the arsonist; he had an alibi. But Lex had got him up close and seen the way he thought, the way he spoke, the way he deferred. His values and perceptions seemed all wrong.

Adam nicknamed the detective 'Lex Luthor', after the villainous comic-book enemy of *Superman*. He hated him. Already the cult had said that Lex was trying to destroy everything they had because in a previous life he had hated Anne, and the hate had repeated. 'We were told he was an evil man,' says Adam.

The school-fire investigation went nowhere fast. Lex started talking with a feisty television journalist from Melbourne's Channel Nine, Marie Mohr, who had already begun investigating The Family after she had followed up one of the early court cases. She had good sources in a group of ex-cult members.

'They were terrified,' Marie says. 'They really thought the sect could come and kill them. They told me stories of how Anne Hamilton-Byrne had total control of their lives, their money, their careers, and their children. Horrifying stories of people being forced to leave their husbands that they loved and take up with another person.' She learned that cult adults were repeatedly paired and split up in Anne's quest for them to become subservient, and she learned that Anne and Bill professed to love the children. 'Mind-control manipulation of a level that I hadn't come across, except for other sects.'

She had met Sarah. And she had been to Uptop, in 1985, looking for Anne but had been confronted outside by an Aunty. Several of the former Uptop children we spoke to remember the day because Marie wore a red coat and it frightened them. Marie asked the Aunty, who remained out of camera shot, whether children were kept in the house. No, said the Aunty. No.

The detective and the journalist formed a sort of de-facto team, feeding off each other for information. Mohr showed Lex footage of Anne and also of the kids with white-blonde hair singing in a Family choir. 'She wasn't the normal reporter,' says Lex. 'And as I started to get the stories about things like alleged beatings and so forth, it became clear to me that there were possibly some heinous crimes committed, and I started to dig around.'

The first place the children were taken after the Uptop raid was Syd Savage's petrol station for a toilet stop. Then they went by police bus to be fed at a kids' welfare place. From there, it was to their new home — Allambie, a community services hostel for criminal or abused children down in the flat suburbs of Melbourne. Allambie was run by the state government. They were all able to stay in a unit together. Sarah and Leeanne, the escapees, had gone with the police to the raid and helped escort the kids away, along with Ed Ogden and Denise Whyte. Sarah moved into Allambie to be with her 'siblings', and then moved out to the Ogdens', while Leeanne was living in a flat, where she had been put by welfare services.

Ben says he was bewildered and excited and scared by the outside world, and very aware that it was looking like a new beginning. 'I think it began to dawn on me: this was actually the end of it. Or ... it was different. Something new was going on.'

In bed at the welfare hostel that first night, he went over in his head all the things he had either said or not said that day. He was second-guessing his own story, as he had always had to. Then he realised he no longer had to do that — to cover things up or lie to protect himself. 'I no longer have to check what I say. I'm not going to get into trouble if I say something wrong. And I think, to me, it's probably when I realised the prison doors had opened for good. And not physical ones. I no longer had to live within the world that I had known. So that was a stake in the ground for me. And from that point forward ... I was going to do everything I could to never go back.'

For Anouree, the raid had been a blur of confusion. 'It was as if many tapes of film were playing in my head at the same time, and bit by bit every single strip of film became entangled with another.' She was hysterical, she couldn't focus, and even afterwards she couldn't remember chunks of it.

The children were told individually that Anne and Bill were not their biological parents. For Anouree, this meant finding out that not only was Bill not her father, but he was actually her grandfather. His son Michael was her real father. This horrendous betrayal manifested in her as a profound sense of loss. 'We had missed out on our parents' experiences. I'd missed out on their culture, their familial culture, what they could have given to me. What they could have provided for me.'

Anouree soon figured out her real father was betrayed by the cult that prohibited betrayal. He had been convinced to give her to members of The Family's inner sanctum. Then he was crossed again when she was taken to Uptop. 'He had some loyalty for his dad. But I think that eroded very quickly, when he discovered about us children up at Eildon.'

She knows now that Michael suffered by having to hand her to Bill. On his own birthday. 'He certainly didn't have much control of his situation, let alone anyone else's. He could see that he was not going to be allowed to look after me. So I feel so, so sorry for my Dad, 'cause he really had hardly any choice in the matter.'

Crucially, the children could be told about their parentage because the state's laws around adoption had been changed three years before the raid, in 1984. The new laws gave people access to information about their birth families that had previously been kept secret. A 60-year-old clause that stipulated birth documents be kept sealed was overturned.

Victoria was the first state in Australia to modernise its laws around adoption. The changes were mainly for the benefit of the adopted person, but the relinquishing parents could also now apply for contact with their child. The changes had wide implications: from 1966 until 1976 — the cult's formative years — more than 15,000 children from the state were put up for adoption, and it was a poorly regulated sector.

Bryan Cussen was the adoption worker charged with helping disentangle the mess. The machinations of what was happening to the children was for the most part out of the public eye. 'It was challenging to do it in a gentle way, but they [the children] almost knew. I was just confirming it in a way. They knew what was coming along.'

Bryan's job was to untie the cult's systematic string of fake adoptions, now that the law allowed for it. Aside from the cult issue, a backlog of adoption information requests had developed within the government's community services department, and very few people were getting the information they were legally entitled to. There was a wait of up to eleven years for adoptees to receive information.

'I can still remember all of us sitting down at a table in my office,' says Bryan. 'Nothing is happening, so do we use this opportunity of the state election to make a stand and put some pressure on? So a few of us did the rounds on television and on radio.

'There were the two issues running side by side. This waiting list plus The Family. That's what caught the media's attention. Were there other children? And there were women who were worried. It was an extraordinary time — it galvanised media interest beyond what we expected.'

In fact, there were thousands, tens of thousands, of women all over Australia who had given their children up for adoption during the years when it was not monitored well. How many had relinquished their babies then not be able to find out where they went, if they chose to? The Family's story helped people understand what it must have been like, and how badly a mother might need to see the daughter or the son she had never seen.

A telethon was held, with the help of Marie Mohr, and women rang in from all over Victoria, talking about their stories and the impact of the long waiting list. The issue was aired on major commercial television networks. In response, Premier John Cain appointed a new minister for the portfolio and ordered a review of the whole adoption issue — and the waiting list.

Just before the election, there was a vigil for reforms to adoption policy outside a government office in Melbourne's CBD. The children were not in the vigil but became part of the story because they garnered good publicity for the cause and helped get adoption rights prioritised in government.

When Marie had first met Sarah, after Sarah had escaped, she was rocking back and forth and only stealing glances at the reporter who had come to meet her. Marie had screened some reports about the adults who had left the cult on television. 'That made her interested in wanting to meet me. You could see the fear. She was obviously a very bright girl, there's no doubt about that. Very quickly we shared some laughs, but she was so wary of the world. Quite rightly so.'

The story Marie was involved in changed her life. She became very close to the children: 'The children and I have experienced a lot of ups and downs together.' At work, one of her bosses asked her if she was a social worker or a journalist. She said that on this job she was a bit of both. The police were also aware that she knew a lot, so they drew her in to their investigation. They also noticed that she was building a rapport with the children, whereas the police were having trouble figuring out how to relate to them — how to be with them; how to talk, how to act. Marie was more instinctive.

'I can remember one policeman saying he wanted to see me. He's a big, tough cop. I thought, *What have I done now?* I was thinking I was going to be told off for doing something naughty. We went to a private room. He just looked me in the eye and said, "What happened to those kids is giving me nightmares, I can't sleep." I understood exactly what he meant because it was giving everybody nightmares. My advice to him was the same advice as I gave myself: "They don't need our sympathy, they don't need our pity. They need our help. They need us to investigate. They need justice." He understood that.'

But the police had big problems. Key files to do with the cult adoptions had gone missing. The government, anticipating the election, ordered a new inquiry into the cult, specifically the adoptions. And while the inquiry did begin, it was never completed.

The story, Bryan Cussen decided as he took testimonies and tried to figure out who these children were, was about slavery. 'They were enslaved to the false dream of this woman, and they suffered the same fate that many slaves do in that they were imprisoned, they were made to work contrary to their own wills, they were physically assaulted, they were drugged, they were not allowed to live lives of their own choice. And that's as near to modern-day slavery as I can imagine. They were taken against their will and the will of their birth parents and captured into a lifestyle that was oppressive and for the purpose of pursuing someone else's agenda. They were made to live someone else's pathological dream.'

He was still impressed with the kids he had met. He says they were intellectually sharp but had trouble with their emotions. These kids could think a lot, but they couldn't feel. They were immune. Yet they slowly thawed, and began responding to the care they were given. No one was lying to them anymore, no one was hitting or threatening them. They did not need to hide. They were fed properly. 'Everyone was just incredibly touched and moved, and these kids, they were extremely articulate. They could engage you beyond their years.'

Cussen first located deed poll changes and birth certificates. He got court records and paperwork from hospitals and found that the same names kept cropping up — Peter Kibby the lawyer, Howard Whitaker the psychiatrist, John Mackay the psychiatrist/GP, and Maie Davie the social worker. He gave his findings to the police and told the kids as much as they wanted to know.

For Ben, who had grown into a kind and gentle young man, the news of his parentage was a bombshell. He wanted answers, but he wasn't prepared for this answer. He found out that his real mother was one of Anne's foot soldiers: Joy Travellyn, a woman Anne had supposedly cured, in a miracle, of her spinal problem.

Suddenly he couldn't see a future, just when he had begun to get glimpses. This was the hardest, most emotionally wrenching, thing for Ben: the apparent jigsaw puzzle of who he was and what he should believe in. 'That was not a good moment. And it was black and white. It wasn't fake. There was no lies involved; it was reality.'

Anne managed to contact some of the children at the welfare hostel by phone but she was found out, and social workers started listening in to the conversations. She told Ben that he may have discovered who his real mother was, but he would never know his father. Then Joy contacted him and said, 'You're an embarrassment to me. Don't bother turning up on the doorstep, I'll close the door in your face.'

He knew then that Anne had told Joy to say these things. It was cruelty upon cruelty, and Ben was devastated. 'It drove into my mind that Anne had complete control, as much as she could, over what was going to go on.'

Ben attached himself to the husband of one of the staff at Allambie, hoping to be adopted. He was trying to force his way into a real family he saw as good and kind. He was invited away on weekends with them. 'I was looking very quickly for, I guess, parent roles. Trying to find caregivers that I could depend on and connect with, that weren't transient.'

The kids stuck together at Allambie, but all were damaged and entering into periods of post-traumatic stress. At least one was suicidal. They were thrilled to be out and to be able to live healthily and constructively. They all put on weight. But it was hard to adapt from a group mentality, especially a group who had shared so much pain. Ben cites *Lord of the Flies*. 'In any environment where you put a group of people, there is a leader, there are followers, and people have to know their place,' he says. The only structure they knew was Anne's structure. 'That was never going to work for us to continue on through life. Because it was toxic.'

The children, the cult, and its secrets were playing heavily on Lex de Man's mind. He didn't have a mandate to investigate anything other than a suspicious fire, but he wanted to pursue this strange new case he had stumbled upon. His boss in the arson squad indulged him and let him follow leads, within reason.

After three months, Lex and his detective partner briefed their boss on what they knew of The Family, and were allowed to continue investigating, while also working on the school fire. After six months, the school-fire case was closed. Lex kept picking away at the cult. Names, addresses, photographs. Facts.

Media attention was now fierce. Allambie and Uptop, and the better-known cult properties in the hills, were being staked out every day. John Mackay spoke to a current affairs television show, telling an interviewer: 'Anne and Bill wanted to construct a family of these children to rear them as a family, I think for very good psychological reasons.' This was the spin: Anne and Bill as heroes, the cult as a safety net for these children.

The Herald's Ben Hills managed to speak to Anne by phone from her residence. In some of his articles, he painted a picture of good Samaritans and reported Anne as saying that she and

Bill were victims of a 'witch-hunt'. Hills wrote that after the raid came a 'hysterical media campaign', a 'crusade' accusing the couple 'of every social sin'. Hills didn't respond to a request for an interview.

He reported Bill as saying people brought orphans to Anne knowing she would help them. She was, Bill said, 'the last staging post'. To Hills, Bill denied mounting accusations of drug use — especially LSD — and any allegations of child abuse.

Trish MacFarlane fled to the United Kingdom after the raid. Her new job was as a housekeeper at Broom Farm, the homestead in Kent, for two children and two adults involved with The Family, and Anne was issuing orders to her by phone from the Catskills. On duty for the cult and far from home, she spent a lot of time in her room. She was becoming distant and withdrawn, introverted. Those who were in the house with her say she lay in bed a lot, smoking and doing crosswords. 'There was crying going on, and getting drunk and "what have I done?" and sorrow over the ruins of what she'd had in her life and what had happened to her family,' says a former child of the cult who was in the house. 'Just the repercussions, I think, hit her — of what she'd done.'

Trish later said she had hit the wall. 'I thought to myself, *What am I doing here? I just can't go on*. I felt absolutely mentally and physically exhausted, and I thought to myself, *I've worked for Anne nonstop for almost 20 years and I've never received a penny for it. Surely that's enough?*'

Trish quit the cult, six weeks after arriving in the United Kingdom, by simply walking out of the house she was administering for Anne. No one contacted her. She went to London. 'Here I was in my early sixties. I'd served Anne for a third of my life because I'd truly believed she was the Teacher or the Master, and she wasn't.'

How must this have felt? What Trish got from Anne was hope, but it was false hope. She also got what she thought was love: Anne would offer great love and friendship to the women she reeled in toward the centre of the cult. She would purport to be rescuing them from the traumas and tragedies they were going through, or she would claim to offer them a life of greater meaning and purpose than the one they were in. But then when these women, like Trish, got close, Anne would withdraw the mirage of love, and keep them hanging on.

Trish paid a terrible price. 'I couldn't believe that I had been such a fool for so many years.' The path she followed was from the tragedy of her son's death into a cult and then into a role within that cult where she enacted violence on other people's children. What is it in human nature that makes people turn like this? Cult narratives are full of it: the charismatic leader offering salvation made me do it, made me kill, made me kill myself, made me steal, made me abuse. Made me ignore right in favour of wrong. The way Trish's life played out put her in the wrong place at the wrong time, and she fell hard.

In February 1988, on a Saturday, six months after the raid that freed the children, police descended on Uptop a second time, as well as cult houses in the hills. They were acting on information gleaned from the adoption services and the children who had been freed. By now a small taskforce, which included members of the community policing squad, had been formed. Lex de Man was floating between them and his main job at the arson squad.

From both raids, eight Aunties were charged with making false social security claims — getting government benefits to which they weren't entitled. Anne had told them to claim sickness benefits, invalid benefits, and aged pensions while working as nurses, they said, but the cheques went straight to Anne. Margot McLellan was charged. Joy Travellyn, Ben's real mother, was charged. So was Liz Whitaker, who faced an extra charge over falsely claiming she had witnessed Anne giving birth to twins in the 1960s. The frauds between them amounted to nearly $AU200,000.

Lawyers for the cult cited media sensationalism and said that the women all had 'impeccable character'. Outside the court — with the women wearing headscarves and dark glasses — they were jeered at by some of the former children who had come to watch.

The women appealed but failed, and all but one were jailed for short sentences. 'Anne told us to claim some money when we weren't entitled to it,' Margot told us, just before she died. 'To apply for it we lied, which I didn't like doing, really. But I did, because I was told to, and we got some money from that. Then it was made public and we had to haul through the courts, which was … ghastly.'

She makes light of what must have been a humiliating experience. 'We had our own rooms, we had our own televisions. I remember there was a three-time murderer and all these other women prisoners, and they stood around and said "What are you in here for?" Because they'd heard of us. It taught us to stand up for ourselves. I said, "I'm not telling you what I'm in here for, and I'm not interested in what you're in here for. Here, we're all the same.'

Margot served six weeks. 'The officers were very good to me personally and they helped me with my physical work — shovelling soil and a few things like that.'

Don Webb and Adam were also raided, and interviewed about some irregularities with passports. By now, Lex was beginning to understand that some of the adults involved with The Family, including the Aunties and the powerbrokers, were victims too — of Anne. This was even though he despised them and knew that they were complicit in serious crimes against the government and children. 'I was under no illusion at the time that when you had to deal with these type of people you had to adopt an attitude of compassion. And yet they allowed it to happen and were part of it. They would have known that what was going on with these children was morally if not criminally wrong.'

Lex had been the one to tell Adam that Don wasn't his biological father. 'In those days there was never any critical incident stress–type training, or progressive training in human dynamics and so forth, so it actually came from your gut instinct.'

Adam was aggressive. Lex was trying to keep in mind that this young guy — a handsome teenager who was rude and obnoxious to him and other police and was constantly on edge, distrustful, and angry — was a victim, but also a potential rich vein of information. He had the petty criminal history, he knew people; in fact, he knew everyone and everything. 'He was very, very rude for a young person. But it's not black and white. It was never black and white with these people.'

Deep down, Adam thought Lex was all right. There was a sense of respect there. His refusal to be polite and cooperative angered the policeman, but he liked Lex. 'He was a lovely man when he arrested me. I cannot fault him in the way he treated me. He didn't abuse me. He was a gentleman. He tried very hard to give me all the facts.'

But Adam was, in his words, 'caught between two worlds'. Who did he belong to, where did he come from? 'It was just all this information coming to me. Not knowing whether that was true or not. I remember thinking that Lex was the bad person and they're telling lies. Is it Aunty Anne telling the truth or is it Lex de Man telling me the truth?'

Lex had shattered his world and his illusions. Adam was devastated, and he rolled over not long after. He agreed to talk, but he did a deal: he would tell the police what he knew in return for not being charged or questioned further over his shoplifting. Lex offered to get him out of Don Webb's house and into Allambie with the other cult teenagers, but Adam refused. 'I said to the rest of The Family, "Oh, I just told him everything that he knew anyway," he says. 'Which is the truth. I didn't tell him anything. I only just knew what I knew, and I knew that he knew what I knew. So to me it was a win-win situation, at that time. I still think I made the right decision.'

In fact, Adam couldn't see a life outside the cult. This was his survival instinct kicking in. He wasn't sure of himself outside the confines of The Family, but within them, he knew he was 'safe'.

Perhaps he considered that loyalty had limits. The loyalty of the cult members — as manifested in their vows to Anne — only gave her further permission. He wasn't being loyal to himself, after all, but to her. So where was the betrayal, where did it fit?

By mid-1989, Lex had left the arson squad and been promoted to sergeant at the city's Russell Street police headquarters. He was asked to write a report on everything he knew about The Family. There was a perception in the force that the case surrounding the Uptop children was a welfare problem, not a criminal matter. That it was about children who had possibly been mistreated, and that was all. Lex's recommendation to police hierarchy was that the cult be investigated for a multitude of criminal offences: fraud, false imprisonment, assault.

And drugs. In the course of his investigations, he had learned a fair amount about The Family's relationship to drugs. Allegations were swirling about their use of LSD. Because of this, and because police didn't know where else to take it, his report into the cult ended up with the drug squad. The head, Detective

Chief Inspector Alan Morphett, said to Lex: 'We're going to set up a taskforce. I want you to be on it, we've got a room in here for you at the drug squad and we're going to give you a Detective Senior Sergeant and we'll give you four detectives. You've got three months to clean it up.'

PART TWO

5

THE SOUND OF MUSIC

Lex and his team settled into the tiny disused office they were given in Melbourne's Russell Street police complex. Six detectives and one car. They had access to telephone books, but not computers. Also, they had no name.

'We said, "What are we going to call ourselves?"' says Lex. 'We thought of Mount Dandenong and said, "We can't see the wood for the trees, why don't we call it Operation Forest? Sounds like a pretty good name."'

Lex de Man was made second in charge. The boss was Detective Senior Sergeant Peter Spence, a storied member of the state's homicide and major-crime squads who had tracked and arrested serial killers and armed robbers. Both men were solid, unfussy old-school detectives — shirtsleeves and ties, moustaches, neatly combed hair, square jaws. Firm men, but also compassionate and thorough. Of the four other detectives, two were men and two were women.

The team was perplexed to find both state and federal police had been here before. Archives from old investigations showed they had something, but not followed up. There was that map to Uptop from 1979, the one drawn by an Aunty that Ben Bodna and his team had handed to police: '... *approx 2 miles of winding road from fork to house turn off ...*', the instructions read.

Why hadn't anyone followed the map?

By now Lex had come to know the Uptop children. He had heard them begin to tell their stories and witnessed their body language. The fact that police and government seemed to know about, or at least had strong indications of, abuse and cult behaviour but had not acted on it floored him.

The detectives rounded up all the old police files and press clippings. Within them were allegations and suspicions that the cult had been operating a child slave ring between Australia and the United Kingdom throughout the 1970s. They also found that when Kim Halm went missing, the federal police had initially refused to give state police information relating to the cult. Police sources say the Feds slowly acquiesced and began drip-feeding the state police what they knew — and it was enough to know that some prominent people were involved in the cult.

A few days after Forest was formed and shunted into that bare office in central Melbourne, Peter Spence wrote to his police bosses, outlining what he wanted to do: Operation Forest would investigate the sect and its adoption of children. It would also look at the role of drugs and probe allegations of serious assaults within the group. All the children freed from Uptop would be interviewed again. Spence noted that some of the rescued children had already become disillusioned since the raid because none of the adults — Anne included — had been charged or imprisoned.

Santiniketan Lodge had been built in Ferny Creek, and from 1969 children had been 'adopted and re-adopted and other children had been acquired', and 'the same doctor, nurse and solicitor's names kept reoccurring in the legal documents and other papers searched and held by the federal police', according to Spence. The team had also learned that newspapers — including *The Age,* which was really only just beginning to report on The Family by 1983 — had been threatened with legal action by the cult if they continued.

Police sources tell us that 12 key questions about The Family had been drawn up in 1983, but when Operation Forest was formed six years later, none had been pursued. The questions, sources told us, were basic: Why use the Hamilton-Byrne surname for the kids? Why did the birth parents give them up? Why did this couple want so many children? Where do they get the funds to fly around the world so often? What does 'Santiniketan' mean? What do these people believe in?

Spence began meeting the children. He was amazed by the control Anne appeared to hold over her followers, and he was repulsed by the cruelty it seemed to entail. But he was also struck by what he calls the 'restraint' — the way members of The Family were held inside a prison of hope and suggestion. 'I found that eye-opening, to say the very least. Something totally different to the type of work that I'd been involved in, yet just as evil, if you like.'

This was different from the murderers and the armed robbers he was used to chasing. The Family was a lot more subtle and strange, and the behaviour of its members was also much more difficult to fathom. A lot of the time the black and the white turned to grey. What was the motive, what was the endgame? Who stood to gain? As Lex had already found, the victims could appear to be perpetrators, and the perpetrators could indeed be victims. The lines between good and evil that, to Spence, were usually straight were in this case muddled and crooked.

Spence made a promise to the children at Uptop. 'When you've got your own and you see them growing up and they're healthy, and they're allowed to live normal lives, and suddenly to come across these kids submitted to all this torturous type of behaviour ... I remember sitting down with them all in the early days, and I said, "I promise you, I can promise you one thing, that I'll do my best to get to the bottom of all this, and to do something about it." I said, "I can't promise you that we will arrest someone or charge someone, but we will do our absolute best."'

Lex, meanwhile, feared the operation would turn into another token police effort based not on solving the case but on wanting to be able to say they had investigated it. And also to be able to say they found nothing. Lex detected a lack of empathy for the victims from police command, a sense of indifference. 'There was complete lack of understanding of what this cult had been involved in, and were involved in,' he says.

One day in December 1989, walking up the outside stairs of the city's police headquarters, Marie Mohr and Lex were chatting about the case. Both were shaken by the condition of the children. She challenged him. 'She said to me, "You will fail, you'll never find her, and if you find her you'll never charge her, because you'll never get her back to the country, and if you get her back to the country, you'll never get a conviction." They were the four driving challenges for us.'

The long and delicate process of re-interviewing the Uptop kids began. By now the last remnants of their dyed hair had grown out, a perfect symbol of them beginning to leave behind the past they had suffered.

The dyeing of the children's hair had been Anne's most sinister gesture towards a sort of commonality. Even now, the images of white-haired children by the lake is probably the most recognisable thing about Uptop.

The Aunties did most of the dyeing, although sometimes Anne did it herself. Most of the children were rendered a pudding-bowl blonde so white it was almost incandescent. 'She liked to model us on the von Trapp family,' says Leeanne. A few of the dark-haired kids at Uptop were allowed to maintain their natural hair colour because Bill's hair was dark, and Sarah was allowed to stay a redhead because Anne's natural hair colour was copper (although she wore blonde wigs). The rest were all turned white-blonde.

In a moment of candour, Anne confided to Leeanne — whose natural hair colour was deep black — that she ordered the dyeing because she wanted people to believe the children were hers. Leeanne's hair was bleached every week with a product called Napro. By the time she met police, her hair had become very dry and frizzy, and easily tangled or knotted. When Leeanne was 16, Anne had her let her get it cut and dyed back to its original colour.

Many years later, conspiracy theories emerged that Julian Assange, the man identified with WikiLeaks, was at Uptop. With his blond hair, he looks like one of the former children, or so it could be surmised. In fact, it was his mother's boyfriend in the 1970s, a musician, who was a Family member, Assange has said. This was his only connection to the cult.

Sarah's one and only bleaching was presented to her as a protein treatment. 'The stuff stung like mad. We thought our hair was being specially cleaned.'

And then there was the clothing. After shower time in the morning (the shower could sometimes just be an outdoor hosing by the Aunties — 'they'd wash us all using cakes of soap and we were hosed down,' Sarah said), the children would be supervised as they got dressed. The girls wore gingham smocks; the boys wore frilly shirts or skivvies and tartan pants. All wore matching blue velour tracksuits for yoga. (Velvet was another popular choice of fabric.) There were sailor suits for a time. The clothes were handed down from older children to the younger, who all had the same red shoes.

The look had an unnerving faux-innocence about it, creepy and sinister to an outsider. The children appeared, in a sense, like haunted dolls. As with the blonde hair, it was about erasing their real selves and replacing them, one by one, with a façade. They looked loved and cared for, but they were not.

Much like the von Trapps, the children also sang. They had a choir, which was filmed, and also appeared at a community festival in the hills. 'I think as we got older we were allowed to be more individual,' says Adam, 'but certainly as pre-teens we were made to wear the same stuff and that was really to implant in us that we were all brothers and sisters.'

Operation Forest established that when the first batch of kids moved to Uptop in 1971, they were reasonably well looked after. Sarah told Lex in one of her interviews that she moved from Anne's home in the hills to Uptop on Christmas Day 1971; she was three. Anne's mother, Florence, had died in an asylum in a country town near Melbourne earlier that same year. Her death certificate described her as a paranoid schizophrenic.

A new permissiveness was emerging in Australia in the early 1970s. Censorship laws were being challenged, and issues such as divorce, birth control, and feminism were in the public eye. Anti-Vietnam street demonstrations made headlines. The first television ad to feature a tampon was shown. Germaine Greer's *The Female Eunuch* was published. It was a time — at least in the big cities such as Melbourne — when previously closeted post-war white-collar suburbanites were searching for new meaning and new ideologies.

But the children knew nothing of this. All they knew was Uptop and its fences. The first arrivals in 1971 and early 1972 spent a lot of time outside, walking and exploring, and playing invented games such as 'fairies and palaces' and 'Goldilocks and the three bears'. Those we spoke to recount these times as idyllic but with sinister undertones. They were taught to clean and make the beds. The Aunties instructed them about housework and dusting. They were made to clean their own clothes in the bath. There was no running water at Uptop yet; water came from the lake, in buckets. The children would stand on chairs to help wash the dishes and assist with the cooking.

Leeanne was one of those who went to school outside Uptop: Camberwell Girls Grammar until Grade One (age six) and then to a boarding school for a short time. While she was at the grammar school, Anne and Bill would sometimes take her and Sarah to Traralgon, a regional city near Melbourne, close to where Anne was born. Bill had an office there for his earthmoving business. These trips were supposed to be a treat. They would go out to restaurants and stay in a motel room. Once, they went to a drive-in movie. The cult was so fledgling that the children were treated almost as if they were Anne and Bill's real children. 'We'd stay Friday and Saturday nights at the motel. We all slept in the same motel room, with Bill and Anne sleeping in one double bed and Leeanne and I sleeping in the other double bed,' said Sarah.

Uptop's school was set up in 1974, and the cult stopped sending the children to outside schools after that. The law had just changed to allow home schooling, and The Family wanted to educate their own. School was held seven days a week, every day of the year. Classes were conducted in the boys' bedroom, originally the lakehouse's boatshed, which was tacked on to the back of the house. The children were taught by two Family members who were schoolteachers: Helen and Leon Dawes. Their son Geoffrey, who is still an active figure in the cult today and has legal power over Anne's affairs, spent time at Uptop with his sister Megan during this time.

Leon taught only at weekends, when he had time off work. The children, we were told, used textbooks he borrowed from his day job at Croydon High School.

Whenever the school was inspected — every six months — it passed. Leon Dawes would meet the inspector, James Kelly, in the town of Eildon and drive him to Uptop. Kelly began visiting in 1982 and reported that the 14 children in the school learned English, French, mathematics, science, social studies, health, biology, music, physical education, art, and needlework. All except three were blonde. He noted that they looked like they were from Sweden or Northern Europe, but had English accents.

In his reports back to the education department, Kelly did not raise any concerns, despite observing that the group at Uptop had adopted children 'of various family relationships of a private nature'. He noted that the collective 'shuns publicity and takes great care to ensure privacy'. The family's father, he wrote, was an international engineer, and both parents, it seemed to Kelly, 'presented a balanced, liberal but controlled educational philosophy. There was no evidence of dogma, rigid programming or indoctrination.' Anne had asked Kelly to keep his reports confidential, except for briefings to his government superiors, which he agreed to.

Sarah was able to praise the teaching, despite the grim circumstances in which it was conducted. 'When we were young, they drummed reading and writing and multiplication tables into us, and the grounding has stood me in good stead. Despite everything else that happened, they gave us one of the greatest gifts adults can bestow upon children — literacy and language skills.'

However, from the mid-1970s, punishments increased for minor mistakes in school, as the detectives from Operation Forest heard from the children. Spelling errors meant being hit on the hand with a ruler or being made to bend over an oil heater and be hit with the ruler on a bared bottom.

Kelly, say former cult members, was impressed with Leon, particularly his teaching credentials. The reports he wrote for the kids were glowing. He identified Sarah as the school's star student. But it seems clear to us his inspections could have gone further with a few questions asked beyond how the children were doing in maths and English.

In the 1990s, when Operation Forest first started talking to Dawes, he was uncommunicative. Now 87, he has also remained elusive with us. We asked him and his son Geoffrey, who both live in the hills, to talk to us about the cult and the school. Geoffrey replied to an initial email and phone call but no further attempts to contact him. Both father and son have repeatedly declined to talk. However, Leon did write us a two-page typed statement, delivered by Michael (the man who had introduced us to Anne). In it, he claims to not know where the Uptop children came from. 'Anne stated that her children (now a sizeable group, whose origins were to me unknown) would in quite a number of cases be unable to survive in a rough and tumble school environment,' he wrote, 'even in an expensive religious school. Anne wanted a very high level of achievement.

'The school [at Uptop] in the first years was settling students for the process of learning,' he noted. 'The going was demanding, and high standards were starting to be accepted.' Physical punishment was used in response to 'rudeness or wilful incompetence' because it was 'widely accepted practice'.

He wrote that his wife, Helen, had graduated as a teacher and then worked at a teacher's college. He had a science degree in pure mathematics and physics from the University of Melbourne; had headed up maths departments in Victorian government schools; had studied maths curriculum in the United Kingdom, America, Russia; and had taught young teachers. He said he had written or edited four high-school maths textbooks.

We met Kay Scott, a potter who lives quietly in outer Melbourne. She married Helen Dawes' brother in the 1980s and got to know the Dawes family, but never joined the cult: 'I had never heard of the sect and it was years into knowing Helen that I got to know what it involved. I thought it was just cranky followers of Raynor Johnson; she kept giving us Raynor Johnson books and asking us did we want to go to the Santiniketan Lodge, and I just thought "God, I'd rather clean the oven."'

One day in the early 1980s, she was visiting Helen's parents with her then husband. 'Helen rushed in with this little blonde child and said, "I'll be a few hours. Can you look after this girl?" And she said she has to write a letter to her mummy. And this kid was tiny, light as a feather; she sat on my lap and wrote a letter to mummy, being Anne Hamilton-Byrne in England. We had this little girl for a couple of hours and helped her write the letter, a dear little thing, and I look at the pictures of the kids all blonde and I wonder which one she was. Dear little face, and the hair — white-blonde hair. They all looked angelic, with the blonde hair, their features were obliterated.

'She wrote her little letter and we had it all tied up in an envelope by the time Helen came rushing back in and grabbed the child and rushed her out. I thought, *That was strange; what a strange little person.*'

Kay got to know Helen and Leon Dawes' children. Geoff was tall and blond. Megan, who was at Uptop, was 'strange and different', says Kay. 'She struck me as if she wouldn't kill a fly and if you did kill a fly she would be overcome with sadness. I took her to the beach and she'd never leave your hand alone. Megan always called me A.K.: Aunty Kay. We were running along this beach one day, nothing on it, and she said to me, "I want to scream, can I scream?" I said, "Yeah, you can scream. Scream!" She said "Really?" and I said "Yes!" and she came out with this little scream, so sad. I said, "That's not a scream." I thought *Strewth, this poor kid.*'

As well as conventional lessons, the Uptop children also did at least an hour a day of 'spiritual reading' or listening to taped talks by Anne's favoured spiritualists. These were Hindu, Buddhist, or Christian tracts selected to fit in with Anne's jigsaw of beliefs. She also made the children read *Life in the World Unseen* by Anthony Borgia, a New Age text written in the 1940s. Borgia was a medium who claimed to be communicating with a dead British priest about life after death. The children read the Bhagavad Gita, the Upanishads, and the Puranas — all ancient Hindu stories and philosophies.

Most importantly, they also read *Satsang with Baba* by Swami Muktananda, which was a small book featuring a series of questions and answers by the now-disgraced Siddha Yoga guru from southern India, whom Anne revered and envied. He was one of the foremost Indian yoga evangelists in the 1960s and 1970s, and by the time he died in 1982 he was rich — his yoga foundation had 11 ashrams and hundreds of meditation centres worldwide.

Anne's property in Hurleyville, in the beaucolic Catskill Mountains near New York, was very close to a Muktananda ashram, where she took children from Melbourne to bow at his feet. She bought the house specifically to be close to him. Muktananda visited Melbourne three times in the 1970s — 1970, 1974, and 1978 — and set up an ashram in the suburb of Fitzroy. He also visted Uptop. He gave Anne the name 'Ma Yogi Shakti'.

The Uptop children meditated and did yoga every day. 'It was very much a Buddhist and Hindu way of life,' says Ben, 'with this very strong theme of Swami Muktananda's philosophy of the shaktipat (spiritual energy transferred by touching), the spiritual awakening, the kundalini (energy released to help a spiritual journey), the power within you that comes out through the third eye. I grew up with that.'

Ben recounted to us the daily routine from the 1970s. There was a lot of cruelty at Uptop, but there was also a lot of mundanity: sameness, a relentless sameness. Anne viewed Uptop as a monastery, and life within was monastic. Exercise and yoga was strictly enforced; it was in this context that food, or the denial of it, became a weapon. The children were bored, restless, and confused. They knew what Christmas, Easter, or birthdays were, but these were only celebrated when Anne was there. At all times they were expected to look and act the same — any individualities in their personalities were flattened.

'We would wake at six am — at five am in summer,' Ben says. Then he laid out for us the following schedule.

6.00 am:	wash, clean teeth, make beds
6.10–6.30 am:	dress into tracksuits
6.30–7.15:	hatha yoga
7.15–7.20:	relaxation
7.20–7.30:	get changed
7.30–7.45:	Swami Muktananda tapes as well as a tape of Anne's (sometimes alternated or sometimes both)
7.45–7.55:	chanting
7.55–8.10:	meditation
8.10–8.30:	sprints to the front gate and back
8.30–8.55:	breakfast and set up the school room downstairs
8.55:	first bell

9.00:	school begins
10.45–11:	recess
11 am –12.15 pm:	schoolwork
12.15–12.30:	spaceball
12.30–1.30:	lunch
1.30–2.35:	schoolwork
2.35–2.45:	recess
2.45–4.00:	schoolwork
4.00–5.00:	pack up the classroom, tidy bedrooms, vacuum, clean showers
5.00–5.15:	meditation
5.15–5.45:	dinner
5.45–6.00:	a spiritual reading
6.00–8.00:	homework, clean teeth, perhaps watch television

The 'spaceball' Ben refers to in the timetable was a game, but even it was about conformity. Anne had invented it. The children stood in a circle outside and threw a ball to one another; she presented it to them as a tool towards connectivity but it was really just throw-and-catch.

At Operation Forest, Peter Spence broke his golden rule of policing, which was to never take work home with him. He was realising how challenging and different this investigation was. His phone or his pager would ring after hours and it would be one of the kids wanting to chat, as trust developed between him and the children. Peter drew his wife into the case, as a way of sharing the burden, and she also began to get to know the children and pitch in with support. 'I think it just goes back to the fact that you're dealing with children,' he says. 'You can see the pain and the suffering that they've gone through over many years, and they recount all these things. And as they do that, you become more attached to them. You're not supposed to as a detective, but when you're dealing with vulnerable children it can just have that effect on you where you become personally emotionally involved.'

On one search of Uptop for evidence, police found tiny graves in the garden with little white crosses on the mounds, marked with dogs' names. They dug them up, searching for human bones, but it was just dog bones. Lex describes the grim task as eliminating all possibilities from their enquiries.

He saw his role as gaining trust from Sarah, the boldest, and the others. The children were starting from a position of not trusting him at all. 'Sarah and the other children were told from the beginning of their memories that police were there to shoot kids. If you saw a police officer, hide, run.'

An investigation such as this needed him to demonstrate patience and empathy. There were no quick fixes. 'To get to know Sarah, it was a process of time: talking, and letting her to come to understand that there was a genuine concern for her and her brothers and sisters,' says Lex. 'The way you approach the investigation can't be the norm. You've actually gotta think outside that square about how you approach them, how you take statements from them, and you need to have a lot of compassion when you're actually talking with them. And try to understand. I still don't think today that I can understand what each of these children went through in their early years.'

The most horrific of the stories began surfacing only when the taskforce detectives had built up enough trust with the children. Sarah told us: 'I think there were things that happened to me under LSD, but it's a bit difficult to disentangle what was being said and put in my head, and the hallucinations that you get, from actual assaults. But I do have a scar on my lower left abdomen, which is where I was cut and blood was smeared over me, and things were said about that. I was to be implanted with something that would destroy my sexual organs from the inside, and in a way I think that's sexual assault.'

In his written statement to us, Leon Dawes said: 'There were absolutely no sexual crimes committed!!! 'None!!!' (The exclamation marks are his.) 'The manifest untruths spoken in so many other of the other public statements made about life at Eildon must surely call this most shocking statement into question as well.'

Several of the former children, in interviews with us, say that when Leon and the partially blind boy were alone in a bathroom, after the boy had been disobedient, they heard loud noises, like the sound of a body crashing to the floor. Leon denies anything happened. Michael, Anne's most devoted follower, does too. 'They would have said these things in the process of asking for money from Anne,' said Michael, referring to compensation cases some of the children began, much later, as adults. 'The lawyers will create a victim. Lawyers are very good at that. Create a victim and ask for money. Leon got cancer; his career was destroyed. Who is the victim? Actually what happened was the children heard some bumping around through the wall. But that was [the boy] self-hurting himself. But it came out [as if] Leon did it. He's not aggressive at all. The children thought they heard it but they didn't see it.'

That is true. They didn't see it. We weren't there when it happened, and neither was Michael — but several of the former children we have interviewed independently have given identical accounts of what they heard coming from the locked bathroom. The Uptop children told us the boy's way of coping was to dig his heels in and say the same thing over and over again — something like 'you're going to come and take me away' — and refuse to eat. He was taken to the bathroom, and the door was locked.

'Several days later he had an epileptic fit,' said one of the former Uptop children. 'We did not know what was happening at the time — he just keeled over, frothing at the mouth, tongue lolled out, in seizure.' The witnesses allege the boy was taken to see specialists.

The written statement Leon sent us does not mention this. Instead, he lists the things the children did outside of their Uptop schooling that he saw as positive: playing cricket, getting books from the Eildon library, playing tennis, going on bushwalks. 'On practically all of our excursions malted milks/ice creams were bought,' Leon wrote. 'There was the occasional (and exciting) speedboat trip on the lake.' Under 'night time activities', he wrote: 'On TV, *The A-Team* — an action thriller which was put into action by the kids! Also games' nights where chequers or card games were played (including possibly chess?). When Bill was there, some amusing silent movies were very popular, as well as seeing a film of themselves which they found very enjoyable!'

When James Kelly came for his inspections, the children would give music recitals. On one visit, it was Liz Whitaker's birthday, and, unusually, a spread of cupcakes and sandwiches was made for Kelly's benefit. One of the kids took a cupcake but dropped it in front of Kelly, who, as any adult would normally do, simply picked it up and handed it back to the child. Several of the Uptop children remember this as an extraordinary event because they were never allowed to help themselves to food — and if they did, they would be punished rather than rewarded.

Outside in the Uptop garden one day, Leeanne and another boy were playing in the dirt and disturbed a bullant nest: large black and red ants with venom and big eyes. These ants were all through the trees at Uptop. Leeanne was 13, she recalls, and the pair were making pathways on the dirt for the insects. They were caught by Anne and Liz Whitaker, who collected two jars full of the ants and told the children that these would be tipped down their shirts as punishment. Leeanne and the boy ran inside and hid behind the couch. 'I was so scared and petrified of these hundreds of bullants on my body biting me. I remember the fear and terror.'

The two were taunted and threatened with the jars. 'They got as close as being right in front of me and I just remember screaming, and my "brother" — my brother and I always fought, like we were a typical brother and sister; we fought all the time — I remember grabbing hold of him and holding so tight because I just thought, *Well, maybe he might protect me.* He was part of it as well.'

Anne and the Aunty never did it. They stopped short, in a horrible, loaded episode full of implied violence and torture. 'It was probably one of the most frightening things I've been through,' says Leeanne. 'The memory of it is horrific to me.'

One of the youngest of the rescued Uptop children spoke to one of two female detectives in the Forest team. She has asked, through her Uptop 'brothers and sisters', not to be identified. For the police, she became a symbol of how acute the physical and emotional deprivation at Uptop could become.

Twelve years old when she was rescued, the girl weighed only 20 kilograms, and was under 120 centimetres tall; that's 12 centimetres shorter than the shortest girls usually are at her age, according to growth percentile charts. 'She looked like a four- or five-year-old,' says Sarah. Anne said when she was pregnant with the girl — which she never was — a UFO flew overhead. That's why the girl was special, and also why she always developed a patch of redness on her forehead when she got upset.

The girl was diagnosed upon release with psychosocial short stature, a condition where kids under extreme stress stop growing because they can't produce enough growth hormone. She didn't speak until she was five. Cult Aunties Trish MacFarlane and Liz Whitaker were told to inject her every second day, in the bottom, with what Sarah believed to be a growth drug imported from Germany. She slept for days at a time and was bruised from the injections.

After being freed, she grew 11 centimetres in a year. But she has no memory of anything much at all that happened to her at Uptop. 'It's a complete blank slate,' says Ben, who was very close to her. 'There is no memory.'

This story affected Lex and his police colleagues deeply. A child whose growth was stunted by cruelty and an emotional vacuum seemed to them a powerful symbol of all that was wrong at Uptop. They quietly vowed to one another to press on and on, in a bid to try and right, as best they could, the wrongs of the cult.

6

SACRED MANNA

'The Aunties would sometimes say, "Have a moggy, you're feeling upset,"' says Sarah.

At Uptop, the children were all on an extravagant daily dose of vitamins and supplements — vitamin A, vitamin B, vitamin E, yeast tablets, kelp tablets, vitamin C, and liver tablets. Yet because they were also hungry, the vitamin C tablets, which were like orange-flavoured lollies, became a form of currency as if they were smokes in a prison. One biscuit was worth ten vitamin Cs, two big apples, or three small apples. They were saved and stashed and swapped.

Many of the former children also remember being given psychoactive drugs — Anatensol, Serepax, Mogadon, Valium, Largactil, Stelazine, and Tofranil — to make them docile. These would often be crushed up in food.

Yet it was LSD and psilocybin (magic mushrooms) — the 'sacred manna' in Raynor Johnson's initiation — that were used most insidiously, on adults as well as the teenage children. Many claim that the two drugs were Anne's primary weapons in her armoury of persuasion, and for this she had one man to thank.

Howard Whitaker was an eminent Australian psychiatrist. Liz Whitaker was his first wife, until he left her for another woman. In her despair, Liz moved deeper into the heart of The Family to become an Aunty. Howard was deeply involved himself until he retreated abruptly and was declared bankrupt late in 1969. He told Operation Forest: 'Call me Dr Gullible.'

Whitaker rose to prominence through senior appointments at major Melbourne institutions through the 1950s and 1960s. He was a balding, rounded, Catholic man with large spectacles, Rumpole-esque, and he spoke with a stutter. He loved to fish and be in the mountains, and had helped establish a ski-patrol rescue service. But he was an evangelist for LSD, one of the most powerful hallucinogens on the planet. Whitaker was among the first psychiatrists in Australia to experiment with it in therapy on the mentally ill.

To the Citizens Commission on Human Rights (CCHR) — an arm of Australia's Church of Scientology — Whitaker was public enemy number one; Scientologists had always, and still do, considered psychiatry an enemy. Melbourne's Scientologists kept a dossier on Whitaker throughout the 1980s and called him 'Australia's Timothy Leary'. But in fact Whitaker began using LSD in therapy on returned Korean War soldiers in Melbourne in 1954. Leary, the American counterculture figurehead of the 1960s, didn't try hallucinogens until 1960, in Mexico.

LSD was legal for therapeutic purposes when Whitaker began experimenting with it in Melbourne. In the 1960s, he was getting it straight from the Swiss manufacturer Sandoz in liquid form, in ampoules.

The Family's inner circle of power and influence can therefore be seen as Raynor Johnson, the academic and spiritualist, on the left; Howard Whitaker, the well-known psychiatrist, on the right; and Anne, the yoga teacher and guru, bethroned in the middle as God.

Whitaker originally met Anne through Johnson in 1963. The two men were friends from the University of Melbourne. This was just as Johnson was falling head over heels with the idea of Anne being his spiritual Master. Whitaker confessed to police that at the time he was mixed up in his religious beliefs. Johnson told him he knew a spiritual teacher and medium who could help him.

Two nights later, Whitaker sat with Anne at Johnson's home at the university. They talked about religion. She told him she could see auras and the future, spiritually heal those in need, and commune with the paranormal. He returned and saw her around ten times, and then she told him he should try and enter her spiritual realm. 'I was reading up about the things she was on about ... Christianity, Hindu religions, Muslim religions, and I checked up on different things she said and I was quite impressed,' Whitaker has said.

Anne contradicted earlier accounts to others by telling Whitaker her own guru was Indian and lived in Queensland. She wore a blue medallion, which she said she got from the guru. The medallion was inscribed *Via Crucis Via Lucia*: 'the way of the cross and the way of the light'.

Whitaker liked her. He considered her friendly and warm. He told Lex if he had his time again he would be more knowing and be able to recognise her as simply 'remarkably intuitive, like the gypsy fortune tellers'.

Anne initiated Whitaker into the group in May 1964, at Johnson's house, in a ceremony that lasted two hours.

'The initiate promised obedience to the Teacher,' Whitaker recounted to Lex. 'Anne said because of her status as a guru she was able to take over responsibility for resolving our karma … and that's how we took steps on the path towards ultimate liberation.'

She stressed the importance of loyalty and the severity of the ultimate crime of betrayal by citing the cult's mantra, which Whitaker was told was so secret it couldn't even be written down. 'The oath and obedience and secrecy is repeated over and over,' he said. 'That's the hold Anne has on people. After May 1964, quite quickly Anne started to tell me what to do with my life.'

Whitaker told Lex that in these early days Johnson was the conduit towards what Johnson and Anne were calling 'the Group'. Michael describes it in terms of a sports club, with Anne as president and Johnson, at the time, as the 'number one ticket holder'.

After he was initiated, the meetings were all about meditation and prayer, and she switched between Hindu, Buddhist, and Christian teachings. She used a Christian cross but it was turned upside-down to swing the teachings away from death and into, Whitaker said, 'life salvation … the cycle of birth and death'.

Anne told early followers that at the beginning of every astrological age a saviour, in the Christian sense, or an avatar, in the Eastern religious sense, arrives on Earth to rescue humans from the wheel of birth, death, and suffering. She said it was the dawning of a new age and she was the avatar. She said that after Christ there was always meant to be a female, citing the Maitreya from Tibetan mystical literature: a female Buddha.

She wanted people to think that with her help they could exist forever in a spiritual sense, having vanquished the past. LSD and psilocybin gave an illusionary glimpse into these things: it gave grand visions, nightmare visions, wonderful visions, and distorted visions of self and time and place. We have heard from many individuals that she often personally guided people through their 'trips' with suggestion and innuendo; they were putty in her hands. In Whitaker, she found someone who could get it for her beneath a veneer of respectability.

Whitaker himself described psychedelics in therapy like this: 'It opens up a person's unconscious memories so they re-cover, re-live, re-experience traumatic things that have happened in early childhood or early adult life. It facilitates release of a whole lot of emotion and helps the person come to terms with what's happened and undo the hangups.'

Before he met Anne, he had been mentored and influenced towards LSD by a community of Melbourne medical scientists who started using experimental therapies during World War II. One was Dr Alex Sinclair, who studied the notorious 'deep sleep therapy' (DST) in the United Kingdom and then used it on World War II troops in the Middle East. The therapy rendered patients unconscious, via barbiturates, for days or even weeks to try and cure them of conditions such as schizophrenia.

Deep sleep — with LSD and ECT — was supposed to be the new frontier in the emerging science of Australian psychiatry. But it was quickly disgraced, and led to a Royal Commission in Australia over 26 deaths in the 1960s and 1970s at Sydney's Chelmsford Private Hospital, where it was used with unusual zeal.

Whitaker also followed the work of a British psychiatrist, Dr Ronald Sandison. Sandison went to a conference (that was later revealed to be linked with the CIA) on LSD and mind control in 1959, where he spoke about reliving birth. Whitaker spent time with him in the early 1960s. Sandison came up with the term 'clearing' for a therapeutic LSD trip, a term The Family adopted as their own. The CIA used LSD in their notorious MKUltra program of mind control experiments from the early 1950s until 1973 to counter interrogation and torture tactics used by Soviets on captured Americans in the Korean War. They administered

LSD in some instances without the patient's consent. The CIA bought the LSD for MKUltra from Sandoz.

In the mid-1960s, Whitaker visited Sandoz in Basel, in north-western Switzerland, and met Albert Hofmann, the famous chemist who had discovered LSD during World War II by synthesising psychedelic fungi.

In Melbourne, as the 1960s moved towards the 1970s, there were soon 19 Melbourne psychiatrists using it legally in therapy. Three of those 19 were members of The Family, with Whitaker at the head. All three practised from a private hospital called Newhaven, in the conservative Melbourne suburb of Kew. Over time, ampoules of the drugs found their way into group members' homes in the Dandenong Ranges.

Newhaven still stands, though it's long been converted into a private home. The building is a glorious Gothic mansion built in 1892 by wealthy tea tycoons. They named it 'Goldthorns'. In the 1950s, it was a clinic run by Robert Kiel, a psychiatrist who was also interested in LSD as a therapeutic tool. His head matron was Joan Vilimek. Anne was a frequent presence there (as well as running yoga classes elsewhere), even though she wasn't a qualified nurse. Vilimek became a member of The Family and later bought the hospital. When she died in 1979, a year after buying it, she left her estate to Anne.

Whitaker's LSD experiments at Newhaven began under Kiel. LSD was given to an estimated 4,000 patients across Melbourne between 1962 and 1970. Whitaker gave it to 100 people in 328 treatments in 1960 and 1961 alone and then, in 1964, published a paper in *The Medical Journal of Australia* outlining its benefits, credited as a consultant at the Royal Women's Hospital and a lecturer at the University of Melbourne.

Whitaker's paper shows the people he gave LSD to suffered from depression, personality disorders, or sexual disorders, specifically 'male homosexuality, voyeurism, exhibitionism, premature ejaculation, impotence, frigidity and vaginismus'. They consented to be injected and were then tranquilised five hours later with chlorpromazine and amylobarbitone. While on LSD they were blindfolded and often wore earplugs.

Whitaker wrote that patients were encouraged to let themselves go into 'phantasy' and that the psychiatrist could become a hallucination of something frightening or something loving. He listed seven varying reactions, from 'pleasant phantasy and ecstasy' to 'explosive' re-enactments of the past, and concluded that psychotherapy with LSD had better and quicker results than without.

Yet LSD and psilocybin were just beginning to be understood. It was only 1964, and there was a climate of acceptance that the drug, if trialled, could be useful. That's why it was flooding into Melbourne — and Newhaven — so liberally and legally. But in 1967, Sandoz got the jitters. By then the drug had got out into the community, embraced by hippies and the counterculture movement, and was being used and manufactured illicitly. Sandoz decided they only wanted to supply it to clinics such as Newhaven with government approval. Albert Hofmann himself wrote a passionate letter to the board of Sandoz, stating the case for continued use of LSD in therapy, citing a 'magic circle' of study into hallucinogens that found tiny traces could 'radically affect the psychic processes and mental functions'.

Whitaker began lobbying the Victorian state government's chief medical officer, Dr Ralph Farnbach, and won. He was asked to sit on a committee to help draft some new laws allowing LSD and psilocybin to continue to be used.

Notes from a meeting held between Whitaker and Farnbach show that 700 ampoules of LSD and psilocybin would cover a month's use at four Melbourne clinics, including Newhaven.

Receipts from Sandoz show the drugs were shipped from Basel in Switzerland to a Sandoz warehouse in Sydney and then transported to a government office in central Melbourne for distribution to psychiatrists.

One of the Newhaven psychiatrists was John Mackay. Today his wife, Olivier, who is in her eighties, visits Anne at the nursing home and does her washing. The other psychiatrist was New Zealand–born Dr Harry Bethune, who had been a medical officer in Korea and was described by a former member of The Family as 'weird — he had a Frankenstein complex. He was mad keen on zapping people with ECT (electro-convulsive therapy)'.

Things at Newhaven got out of hand pretty quickly. In 1969, the Australian psychiatry governing body moved to tighten restrictions around the drugs when health department inspectors found LSD and psilocybin stored in an unlocked cupboard. Unbelievably, they appointed three Newhaven doctors, including Whitaker, to draw up a new code of ethics, even though at least one of them was in breach of the original code.

For many adult members of The Family, Newhaven became a home away from home. They would come into the hospital with a bag and stay the night among the regular patients who had been referred there by a GP or a counsellor. Most would sign in under fake names to avoid being traced. These 'patients' would be taken to small, single consulting rooms with a bed and injected and left for long periods. One of the doctors might interview them while they were under the influence.

Anne was often there. Others from The Family worked there as nurses. A former cult member remembers one time she was inside: 'I heard the man in the next room moaning and weeping. I said, "What is it, what is it?" And he said, "I'm covered in blood." He was sitting on the bed with his legs crossed, and he said, "I'm so evil, I'm back 4,000 years ago, all the blood, all the blood!" I said, "What is the blood?" He said, "It's all the people that I've mutilated while I was still alive. I'm such an evil person. How can God love me, how can I be saved?"'

'He ended up one of her most devoted disciples,' she said. 'So that's the sort of thing that was going on. It was pretty heavy stuff. And it was all secret.'

The same former cult member also helped a man who was hallucinating spiders. 'He was suddenly aware of something coming in the door, and it grew, and the whole atmosphere around him was terrifying, it became this huge spider. Huge, filled the room, and he became aware that it was drawing him into its mouth, and the psychiatrist saying, "Just go with it, just go with it. You're being tested, just go with it. Trust Teacher. Trust Teacher." So he did, and he told me that it was the most repellent experience being eaten, chewed up, digested by the spider, but then he came out into the light, and he fell out of bed, and he fell on his knees, and he said, "Jesus, Jesus, save me."'

A real-estate agent in The Family, John Balfour, had left his wife and children and gone to live in the hills. Balfour had been involved in a group called Subud, a yoga movement spawned in Java, and met Raynor Johnson, Harry Bethune, and Harvey Barnett, a spy with the Australian Secret Intelligence Service (ASIS) who later — in the 1980s — became the head of ASIO, the Australian Security Intelligence Organisation.

One Saturday night in 1969, he took his 19-year-old daughter, Alana, to a party held by members of The Family. Alana estimates that there were maybe 30 people there, drinking alcohol and talking. Most were male. 'They hovered around Anne; she was the centre of attention. [They were] mostly professional-looking men — one identified himself as a lawyer, one was an architect. Anne looked stunning, beautiful. And she was so much the centre of attention. She would lean over to touch you on the shoulder to say hello and try and make a connection, but I didn't talk to her. I didn't feel drawn to her. I was determined not to be. The people all looked like they had dead eyes. It was very strange.'

Her father had been urging her to go to Newhaven for therapy. She didn't want to. But eventually she acquiesced and went, at 9.00 am one morning. She was told that she would be given a mild dose of psilocybin. Dr John Mackay came in and introduced himself soon after she arrived, saying that he had seen her at the party.

Alana was blindfolded and injected. The intensity of the trip she had has led her to believe it was a strong dose of LSD, not a mild dose of psilocybin. 'It was far too extreme.' Alana — who used the name Insiah at the time and says she was 'spiritual' — did not see God on the drug. In fact, she only saw a void where God was supposed to be.

This vision of nothingness has stayed with her ever since.

'I went to a place where there should have been a God and there was nothing there. [After that] I was not able to function. I had severe depression. I was convinced that I would commit suicide. It was an incredibly strong experience, and whether or not someone was guiding me then I don't know. My whole belief in God was stripped away.'

Michael Byrne, who was Bill's son and Anouree's father, was given the job of being a 'guide' at Newhaven for patients on LSD, sitting with them during their trips and encouraging them to think about certain things. The clinic became a recruiting ground for The Family and a halfway house for existing members who were deemed to need treatment — a 'top-up', according to a former member. Byrne told Lex de Man during the investigation: 'You can use the drug to instil an idea in somebody's head. Disorientating them to put in a concept. Brainwashing.'

Lex de Man was staggered by this revelation. Not just that such an activity could actually happen under the authorities' plain gaze but also the — for want of a better word — amateurish way it was pulled off. The way he sees it, Anne arranged for intelligent adults to be dosed up on the drug, wore a 'billowing white dress, shone a few lights around', had a bit of a whisper, and bingo! She was Jesus. The reality was a little more subtle, but only just.

'These professional people,' Lex says, 'who in their daily life were at the peak of their profession, who had gone through a traumatic experience in their life, who needed some psychiatric care, went to this private hospital to receive treatment. So it was discreet. Then, coming out of the LSD experience, they actually believed that she was Jesus Christ. But in the female form. You've gotta ask yourself, how does that happen to professional people? They were actually convinced that they were seeing the Almighty.'

Whitaker was so keen on psychedelics that he dosed his own son David, who was inducted into The Family when his mother and father joined. David was injected with his father's liquid LSD or psilocybin as many as 20 times, beginning in 1968.

David is now a straight-talking, well-adjusted farmer living a long way from Melbourne. He escaped the cult long ago. He remembers that he first met Anne when he was seven, and he didn't respond to her as those around him seemed to. 'She was obviously very powerful, she was obviously directing things … I didn't like her at all.' He found her bossy and overbearing. He and his brother nicknamed her 'Big Ball' — 'a big blonde, brash woman, very charismatic sort of person, very powerful person, she had a huge presence about her. She used to tell us what to do. She'd come around to the house and we'd hear her telling our parents what to do and they'd immediately react. Do whatever they were told. It just didn't seem right.'

David's first dosing happened at Anne's grand house, Winbirra, in the grove in Ferny Creek. Children were initiated into the cult with either LSD or psilocybin — usually LSD —

when they reached 14. Some were injected and then tranquilised with sodium amatyl (referred to as 'stoppers'), then dosed again. David was dosed for two days.

'The second day,' he says, 'Anne managed to convince me she was Jesus.' David's father had injected him and he was told to lie on a couch. The curtains were drawn against the sunlight, and Anne began whispering, 'Who is Jesus?' She repeated it four times, and after the fourth the boy replied, 'You are.' She said, 'You always knew.'

His father came back in, and then his mother. 'He reinforced the fact she was Jesus and the one true Lord and so did my mother, and I guess my excuse for believing that was I was only 14 and they drugged me. And I was stuck in that for the next decade.'

The sessions were called either 'clearings' or 'going through'. David was mentally stronger than some around him, so even at 14 he was able to survive the gruelling trips by fixing his mind on the corner of a room and 'gritting my teeth and waiting'. But still, it had an intense effect: 'Imagine a 14-year-old kid into his second day on LSD.'

From that first 'clearing', the effect lasted three months. David saw the colours on the wall bend and morph into one another while he was under the influence of the drug, and those colours persisted. He couldn't shake them. 'For a long time afterwards, I'd have a sensation that I was lying in bed and I've shrunk down to the size of a pea and the whole universe is sort of rushing past.' He didn't hate the sensations, but he didn't like them either. Mostly he knew that if these things were happening in his head, something wasn't right.

The sorts of questions Anne asked him while he was drugged were, he says, 'Can you look at why you're so wicked?' or 'Why don't you do as you are told?'

There was a sexual element as well: 'She'd ask questions about your sexual thoughts, your sexual desires, your sexual fantasies, what you liked, what you didn't like, why you didn't like it. She'd plant all kinds of weird things in your head about whether you were breastfed and whether you were homosexual or whether you weren't.'

This sort of regular drug use was happening all around him, so it didn't seem unusual at the time. Anne used LSD; her inner circle used it. 'It was what everybody was doing in our family group,' says David. 'It was reinforced by everybody around me. I was told in no uncertain terms that I would go crazy if I told anyone about it, so what could I do? I couldn't really go to school and tell my teachers that Daddy's giving me LSD and the woman across the road thinks she's Jesus. Who's going to believe that?'

In cult circles, Anne called the drug 'the herb' or 'the dream machine'.

She used it with Whitaker at his home, according to Whitaker's own accounts to police. There's no evidence she had used it before this, but she was certainly aware of its power. She used it with her second husband, Michael Riley; when he proposed, he once said, they were both on LSD.

She would sometimes take one of these two drugs, sit in a chair, and gather children at her feet to make predictions about their futures. 'She used to do an extraordinary thing,' a former cult member says. 'She used to go into samadhi — the ancient idea was that masters on Earth can go into this samadahi situation and be in touch with masters elsewhere, like a trance state.'

The cult treated LSD like a kind of sacrament. In reality, Anne had seized on the powerful, mind-bending effect it had on people when suggestion was used on them again and again. She knew the grail it could hold if given to others she wanted to control. And under Whitaker's prescription, it was legal.

Adam, the boy Lex had interviewed about the suspicious fire in the late 1980s, today claims he had LSD as an eight-year-old. He says he can't remember exactly what happened — he may have found some, he may have been administered it — but he remembers the effects vividly. 'I was scared, I was alone. I just remember being in this world of colour, ever-revolving colour. It was just constantly purples to pinks to reds to greens to blues — you name it. And I'd walk into it, and it was as if I'd walked into jelly. That's what it felt like. It scared the hell out of me. I've had LSD as an adult and that's when I realised that the experience I had when I was a child was exactly the same.'

At Trish MacFarlane's house in Ferny Creek, wedged into it as she was with John Mackay, a stream of adults from The Family would come to the house to stay the night. They would bring overnight bags and usually be picked up by another cult member in the morning. When John came into the bedroom where they were installed, Trish had to leave.

Bill came onto the scene through Newhaven, to seek treatment for Michael and also for his then wife. Bill already knew Don Webb from the Rotary Club out in the country. Cult folklore has he and Anne meeting beside the road in Gippsland dairy country as he supervised excavation work for his business, but it's far more likely he met her at Newhaven. Bill was handsome and wealthy, but his wife, May, was said to be mentally ill. Michael also had symptoms of mental-health issues and drug addiction, and both he and his mother were kept at Newhaven. Bill and May — together and separately — also lived with Trish for some time.

'It soon became common knowledge amongst sect members that Anne and Bill were having an affair,' says Trish. Anne froze May out, keeping her in Newhaven for long periods, often absolutely alone. Michael met and fell in love with a young woman named Treena, who Mackay had treated for mental illnesses at a large psychiatric hospital in Melbourne, Larundel. The two had Anouree, who was gifted — or, she says, sold — to the cult. Treena died in June 1974. She was 26.

Administering drugs to consenting adults was one thing. But the testimonies that Operation Forest detectives were taking from the Uptop children about drug use was harrowing. Once they hit 14, the children went headlong into a regime of 'going through' on huge, relentless doses of LSD — much like David Whitaker had already done.

When she was 14, Sarah was sent to Broom Farm, in the United Kingdom, for her initiation. The scenario she remembers was typical of the way it played out for others we interviewed: one morning, a morning not of her choosing, she was given a piece of toast, had a bath run for her, and then was put back to bed in a nightie. She was given a tiny piece of paper with a coloured mandala printed on it: acid. Her experience was 'utterly beautiful and yet completely terrifying'. By this time, the legal supply of the drug had stopped, so the cult was believed to be sourcing it illegally.

Mostly, among the hallucinations and auditory distortions and unstoppable vision streams, Sarah was scared. She saw her skin falling off, she saw bones and maggots and a corpse, and she felt 'alone in the universe'. She remembers Anne laughing at her and calling her names.

As the trip wore on, she could not tell whether it was day or night. She heard some noises in the kitchen and figured it was evening. Then she hallucinated all night, and as the drug began to wear off, she was given more. And then a few hours later, given more again. She thinks that several days and nights passed. Even for a seasoned adult drug user, this was overkill.

For Sarah, this was the moment her life changed. It was her

initiation into the cult, but it was also dangerous and horrifying. She says it left her unresponsive, disengaged, and 'catatonic'.

Sarah 'went through' three more times that year. The psilocybin mushrooms grew wild in the paddocks of Broom Farm and were ready to pick each November. One of Sarah's jobs was to find them and spread them out on sheets of paper in a back room to dry — and because she had been traumatised by LSD, she started eating the Broom Farm mushrooms on her own, to escape. Her attitude was 'if I can't die, I may as well get high'.

She came back to Melbourne, to the hills, and the regime of drug-taking continued. This was around the time when she and the other two girls were first allowed out to the dancing school. Each time she had the drug it was not as bad as the first, but each gave her flashbacks of the horrors that had come before.

During one interview, Lex heard that outlandish suggestions were made to the teenagers while they were on the drugs. One of the girls was told that she was Elvis Presley's daughter. Anouree was informed that she was a reincarnated Martian. The children were told that Leon Dawes was a war pilot with the Red Baron, and Leeanne was a Tongan queen. One the boys, according to Ben, was convinced a snake was coming out of his eye.

Leeanne says: 'I remember feeling very weird and seeing lights and shapes, and weird things like circles, or just colours. It was strange; it was just awful. I just remember being right out of my body.'

Anne, we were told, had a jar full of LSD blotters at her house in the hills — 'small squares with a flower on them', recalls a former child of the cult. Anne shook baby powder around this child after she had been told curl up in a foetal position while on the drug. 'Handel's Largo' was playing, and Anne loomed over her saying a prayer.

The adults had more control over where, when, and how much of the drug they took. Even as an ageing Aunty, Margot McLellan used it. It was part of the cult's fabric. 'It's like looking into a big black hole and diving in and having a look at what you really are,' she says. '"Man know thyself and thou shalt know the Universe." That's true. I had a good look at myself.'

Michael tells us about a time when he took psilocybin in the hills ('a look-in'), and Anne, a soprano, started singing to him. 'It was the most beautiful thing, the most beautiful thing. The sweetness of the voice was just so nurturing and so wonderful.' She would come and go with the adults too, intoning messages, making suggestions.

She would say to him, 'Have a look at this, Michael.'

'And when you see it, it comes out with such a feeling of light, and lightness, the "aha" moment is like an epiphany. It's really like that. And you actually get to see what you needed to see.'

He says it was while on hallucinogens in his early days in the group that he realised his biggest wish was to be loved. 'I went back to being a little child, and I was in the middle of a ring, and I was quite a beautiful child. I had a huge head of black hair. And people just adored me and I loved them ... and I wanted to get back to it, I needed to get back it, or I'd be warped or unbalanced. And so that's what it was about. It was very therapeutic for me.'

The image of being in the centre of a ring has stuck with him. 'Have you ever had somebody or an organisation come up to you,' he says, 'and you realised they believed in your potential and what you were capable of? It's a most wonderful thing. That's what The Brotherhood [as the cult was also known to its members] provided for me.'

Whitaker introduced the man who would become the cult's lawyer — and a central player in the rise and fall of The Family —

to Anne in 1964. Peter Kibby had been treated by Whitaker at Newhaven for his crippling obsessive-compulsive disorder. He already knew Joan Vilimek. Whitaker gave him LSD. On Kibby's first trip he imagined himself being reborn and panting very heavily. But Whitaker's therapies didn't work, and by the time he met Anne he was suicidal.

Kibby thought Anne was beautiful, and she reportedly told Whitaker that Kibby had a blue aura around him. She read to him from *Yoga and the Bible* by Joseph Leeming — which concentrates in part on Surat Shabd yoga, or yoga of the sound current. Then she gave him copies of two more of her primary texts. The first was *The Secret Path* by Paul Brunton, who was a British neo-Hindu spiritualist who had met the Indian gurus Anne also looked to, Meher Baba and Ramana Maharshi. The second was *Autobiography of a Yogi* by Paramahansa Yogananda, an Indian yoga monk who had travelled to California in the 1920s. All members of The Family were expected to have works by Brunton, Ramana Maharshi, and Yogananda in their shelves.

Anne told Kibby she would save him from his mental torture. His OCD was based on a phobia of germs. He washed everything he touched, and he washed his body and hands constantly to the point where he developed a severe skin condition.

Kibby started going to the cult's meetings, hosted by Anne and Johnson, on Monday nights in a church in central Melbourne. The meetings moved to a suburban Methodist church and then to the National Herbarium at Melbourne's Royal Botanic Gardens. Soon he met a woman — Barbara, who would become Barbara Kibby — at the meetings. She was a patient of Whitaker's too, being treated for depression. Barbara had been in the group awhile by then. Anne had already encouraged her to marry two other Newhaven patients: a young criminal who had been referred there by the courts, and a psychologist who was a cult member. Then she suggested Peter. 'I was very taken with this man,' Barbara says. 'An older man, well spoken, a lawyer.'

She knew that he had a chronic psychiatric condition. 'I had absolutely no idea how difficult it would be to live with a man who had a very bad case of OCD.' Barbara needed to wash her hands all the time as well, in order to touch him.

In 1965, Anne told Peter Kibby to go to India. He quit his job and went with three other members of The Family, including Johnson's daughter, Maureen, and Anne's biological daughter, Natasha. He stayed for two years doing voluntary work in a medical centre in Tamil Nadu. When he came home, he moved into a granny flat out behind another member's house in the hills.

Then he went on another trip — to Tunbridge Wells, near London, with ten members of The Family including Natasha, Johnson, Don Webb, and Liz Whitaker. On trips to London, the group would go the British Psychical Society in Belgrave Square to see mediums. On the way back to Australia, they all went to Israel to meet Dr Thomas Maughan, the head of the British chapter of The Druids.

Back in Melbourne, Anne ordered Kibby into Newhaven for three months of 'treatment', where the doctors dosed him on LSD and psilocybin. Whitaker also gave him ECT. During one LSD session, Liz Whitaker read him sections about betrayal and Pontius Pilate from the Bible. 'I said, "Who in the hell does Pontius Pilate think he is; doesn't he know I'm the Roman governor?"' Kibby also saw Christ: Liz says 'his face appeared to show love, compassion and forgiveness and his eyes were blue'. From then on, 'Pontius Pilate' was his pseudonym within the group.

Anne was still trying to cure Kibby of his mental illness. She had promised him she could, but of course she could not. In 1969, according to Kibby, she ordered he have two leucotomies — a form of radical brain surgery. Both were supposed to cure him but neither did. Peter Kibby married Barbara, moved to another house in the hills, and had a son, Matthew, whose middle name, at Anne's prompting, was 'Howard'.

But by 1969, Lex found, Howard Whitaker was over it. His tenure had been brief but crucially important for the group, but that was it — he was done. He excommunicated himself late that year, just as the group was consolidating and growing in strength and just before the first batch of children began to arrive at Uptop.

'He just disappeared,' says Barbara Kibby. 'He didn't talk to anybody about doubts. He just went.'

Whitaker's end was inglorious, but it opened his eyes. He was running low on funds after opening a new medical clinic in expensive East Melbourne on Anne's persuasive recommendation. The clinic was lavish, with marble fittings. He had also bought a big property in the hills because she had asked him to, even though he never lived in it. Meanwhile, he was also paying maintenance to Elizabeth; Anne had set a high amount after lobbying hard during the divorce to make sure Liz came out on top. He told Lex it was all a 'swindle' and that Anne had decided that his ex-wife Liz was more useful to her as an Aunty than he was as a storied psychiatrist.

Whitaker couldn't pay his taxes, and sold a Mercedes and a property he owned, but Anne told him to persist with the new clinic even though it was in strife. Eventually the courts, through the Australian Tax Office, declared him bankrupt. 'It hit the fan as far as I was concerned,' he told Lex. He said he started to see through Anne and had begun to consider many of her teachings 'crap' and many of her methods devious.

When Whitaker left, The Family had around 200 members. By this stage, most adult members were paying ten per cent of their income to Anne, ostensibly as support for 'unmarried mothers' and other charitable causes. He said Anne had changed through the 1960s from a benevolent mystic to a cruel, greedy controller.

The cruelty: this was what Operation Forest was trying to understand. And they were getting somewhere, despite scant resources. They had all the children's testimonies by now, recording the details of the brutality and the abuse and the hunger. The heads thrust into buckets of water at the lakehouse, held by the hair. Hiding in the Hole when police came. The drugs and where they came from. What they needed now was solid evidence. Whitaker's admissions weren't enough to build the case.

Meanwhile, Adam had turned 18 and was on the outer, estranged from the other Uptop children and deeply conflicted between loyalty to Anne or betrayal. He had joined the Navy. And he was in trouble, facing four charges of threatening to kill after making a series of phone calls to Operation Forest with threats towards Sarah (who was speaking out), detectives, and Marie Mohr, the television journalist. He had been told that one of the police who raided Uptop had hit the woman he knew as his mother, Liz Whitaker. He felt protective towards both her and Anne, so he made the calls from a restaurant he was working at up in the hills.

In one of the calls to a Forest detective, he said he knew where the detective lived. 'You haven't got the balls to do anything to me or The Family.'

Adam can now see how angry he was as he started to have doubts about The Family, and The Family began to fall apart. 'A frustrated, angry young man,' he says of himself then. He was enraged that no one was standing up for The Family when one of the twisted truths of life for him was that it was the only real family he had. He felt The Family had protected him, and now they were being attacked. 'I don't fear authority. I used to thrive on destroying authority. That's how my nature has been. I don't do that anymore. I've grown up. I'm beyond all that now.'

It started as he hit his teens, with The Family active and at its most abusive and conceited. He was living in the hills as a foster of the cult and would sneak out, go to one of the forest carparks in the hills, and cut car-brake cables with a serrated knife.

He set fire to the house of Don Webb, the man he knew as his father, and tried to set the bushfire-prone forest alight. 'I was crying out for help,' he says, 'and I didn't know how to ask.'

While for him the cult meant family and security, it came with a sense of injustice. Right and wrong were skewed. Anne was his mother, Liz was his mother, but no one was his mother. When he was nine, he opened one of Anne's letters. He was then living over the road from her in the grove in the hills. He was sprung by an Aunty but soon walked back home over the road, thinking he had got away without any consequences. Yet an adult in the cult was already on the phone to Anne when he walked in. 'I got belted black and blue to the inch of my life,' he says. 'She had no right to do that; she hurt me very badly. But she was made to. Aunty Anne put the orders out and they obeyed, whether they wanted to or not.'

He went to school bruised. 'Nothing was said. No action [was taken]. I do not have any memory of the teacher saying, "Where did you get that from?" If you get belted just before school, surely a teacher should know. Back in those days, that didn't happen. Everything was hush-hush, not only in The Family but also in the real world.'

When he started his campaign of mischief with the fires and the brake cables, he was sent away to the United Kingdom. But he was travelling on a fake passport and there was a problem at customs at Heathrow, and he was detained. Then a British member of The Family named Max Deacon, a prominent London homeopath, turned up and told customs that Adam was in need of treatment, and they let him in. He was sent to boarding school.

Adam was bumped around from home to home, country to country, rootless and restless and kicking against the pricks. He felt part of The Family, but as he entered adulthood, he didn't know what to do. When he felt threatened or aggrieved, he lashed out, such as with those phone calls. He decided he needed to stand by Anne once and for all. His anger mounted when ASIO — the Australian government's spy agency — forced him out of the Navy. 'Aunty Anne wanted me to join the Navy. I was going to be a cook in the submarines. I'd always wanted to be a submariner. To me, it's like being in a starship, just travelling and exploring space that you've never been before. So that's where I wanted to head in my life.' The ASIO officers declared him a security threat to Australia because of his associations with The Family.

Marie Mohr told the Forest detectives that even before he had threatened her, she was living under siege, with nuisance phone calls in the middle of the night because she was seen as so vehemently anti-cult and was exposing their crimes. She already knew Adam and had interviewed him about the cult, in which he was friendly and open, but then, she said, he changed. Because he didn't yet know who he was.

For Forest, however, the investigation was escalating fast. The LSD culture of the group and the integral role of Newhaven were now on record, through the children's and Whitaker's testimonies.

But where was Anne? No one yet knew, but it was clear she wasn't in Melbourne. She'd been gone since about a year before the raid. The problem was that Forest was struggling for resources. The police's crime department command, according to Lex, were still not taking the case seriously. As head of the taskforce, Peter Spence was growing increasingly frustrated at his bosses' unwillingness to commit money and resources to the investigation — they still perceived it as a welfare issue, as 'a few heads dunked in a few buckets', he says.

Victoria's police force was at the time in deep crisis over an escalating tit-for-tat shooting war between suspected armed robbers and police. The police code of being a 'brotherhood' was being tested just as Adam's sense of loyalty was being tested. Two young cops were gunned down in late 1988 as a grim payback, and the shootings went on for months. These shootings became a big political issue, draining resources and preoccupying the force's commanders, during the formative days of investigating The Family.

Marie Mohr went to the United Kingdom looking for Anne. Her crew flew over Broom Farm. Then she heard that Anne was in Hawaii, staying at a supporter's house, so she went there too. She and her large television network had more resources than the police. She tracked Anne down and confronted her, with a camera rolling. It was April 1990. Anne and Bill had just got out of their car. Anne was wearing a crisp white shirt, her hair impeccable, heavy earrings hanging down towards her collar. The camera focused on Anne as Bill lurked to one side. Anne smiled through gritted teeth.

MOHR: Have you got any comment now about why
          you kept the children locked away for so long?
BILL: No comment.
MOHR: Why not?
ANNE: They were not locked away.
MOHR: You don't call keeping them at Lake Eildon
          for all those years —

Anne puts a hand to her chest in a gesture of fright, smiles, and begins to walk away.

MOHR: Can you explain to me why you treated the
         children like you did?

ANNE: Can you explain to me why you are so rude to me?

MOHR: All I want is answers as to why the children were
         treated like they were, why they were beaten.

ANNE: You are only believing the children. You have
         not listened to us at all.

Marie wanted to know if Anne loved the children so much, as she always said she did, why hadn't she seen them since they were taken from her? 'There was a disconnect on so many levels,' Marie says. 'It's all theatre to her, presentation. "Look at my children! Aren't they beautiful?" Not the touch-feely being-a-mum side of it. They were an experiment to her, I'm sure they were.'

That same year, another Auntie was charged by Operation Forest: the GP Christabel Wallace. At 75 years old, she was fined $AU5,000 in Melbourne's County Court — amid much media attention — on three charges of making false statements for passport applications and two charges of making false statements in statutory declarations. She pleaded guilty and admitted lying about being present at the births of two girls in the 1980s. Wallace had declared they were twins born to Anne in Sydney. They were not. The judge told her: 'The way you have ridden roughshod over the fabric of society involves considerable deceit.'

Then, in an extraordinary twist, a senior Melbourne politician was briefed in secret by police. Rob Maclellan was the Liberal shadow minister for police and emergency services. Police went to him with their mounting frustrations about the lack of resources, even for interstate travel to interview former children of the cult or potential witnesses.

Both Lex and Peter Spence deny they were the ones directly leaking to the politician. 'The matter came to me through anxious and unhappy police,' says Maclellan, 'and I responded to that by going and speaking to senior police on a confidential basis. I would never, even to this day, say who it was because I gave my word to that person.'

The abuse, drug experiments, and mind control he heard about had happened under the watch of Liberal state governments during the 1970s and 1980s, but Maclellan stood up in the Victorian parliament in May 1990 and likened the story to Germany under Hitler. He cited 'medical experiments on children' with the aim of producing a master race:

> We're not talking about Transylvania, East Germany, Brazil, or the madness from the Nazi Germany. We're talking about Victoria. This occurred around Eildon, in the hills just outside Melbourne. Most of the children involved were children of unmarried mothers who had consented to their adoption, under circumstances where they were persuaded that their children had been born malformed, or spastic, or something like that, and that they were better off without the children. It is baby snatching in anybody's language. The police are saying, 'for gods sake Parliament, State of Victoria, give us the resources to do the job'.

Maclellan regrets the Hitler reference now, but says he needed to make a point strongly. This was child abuse he was talking about, endemic child abuse that was in a sense sanctioned by the state because it had been systematically ignored despite several police recommendations in the late 1980s. He suggests that those associated with The Family might have been able to block efforts to find answers because they held jobs of influence. 'I'm not into conspiracy theories. But I do believe that the sect that we're talking about, that is the group of "believers", had people who were not necessarily signed-up members, but supporters, sympathisers, and that they deliberately cultivated people in influential positions that might protect them and might make what they were doing more successful and more easily accomplished.'

Maclellan repeated much of what he had said in parliament on commercial radio. The next day, Melbourne's *Sun News-Pictorial* tabloid, which had the biggest circulation of any newspaper in Australia, published a story based on a leak from police — a red herring, as it turned out — that the taskforce looking at the cult was now investigating three suspicious deaths of women who had transferred property in the hills to Anne.

Nine days later, homicide squad detectives joined Operation Forest. The taskforce moved from dilapidated Russell Street to the St Kilda Road police headquarters, and they were given a computer and a data analyst so they could better cross-reference everything they had found out.

Then came the breakthrough.

Through their intelligence, police got word that Peter Kibby had left The Family. He wasn't the only one who had deserted Anne, fed up with her apparent manipulations over money and marriages. He said it was due to cumulative mistrust over many years and the fact that Anne had asked him repeatedly to perjure himself.

Kibby also knew that his only chance of survival was to roll over if ever the police knocked on his door because, given his illness — which had stayed with him, affecting his marriage and losing him several jobs — he would have a difficult time in jail.

It was the ultimate betrayal in the eyes of the cult that he essentially administered. To them, he was destroying the sanctity of the mantra he had recited all those many times. But if a person renounces a set of beliefs they come to see as morally wrong, is it still betrayal?

Lex soon established that Kibby had OCD and had trouble holding jobs because he was showering for up to three hours a day, using multiple cakes of soap, and the routine was making him constantly late for work. The Forest team also found he had been through Newhaven, and that he had handled almost all the forged Family documents. 'If you're looking for a suspect of a crime, and the solicitor's turned against the client, there may be an opportunity for the solicitor — without breaching the old professional relationship — to talk to you,' he said. 'We got to know of Pontius Pilate. We ascertained that Peter Kibby was his right name and he was the person who had done a lot of the transactions on the official documents, and one thing you learn as a detective is that official documents lodged with a government agency — the golden rule is that a document doesn't lie. A document can be falsely signed or forged, but the document actually tells you the story.'

He and Peter Spence started looking for something small and non-cult-related that Kibby had done wrong in order to reel him in. They found a statutory declaration that Kibby had falsified. Then Lex found that Kibby was living in the hills but working more than 200 kilometres away for a law firm in a small farming town called Camperdown, west of Melbourne. He and Spence drove there in September 1990. 'I felt that the key to the activities of the cult probably lay in the brain of Peter Kibby because he had done all the documentation on transactions for all the houses the cult had bought for Anne, and on some of the births. So imagine if we could get the solicitor for the sect leader to turn

Queen's evidence. We could — for want of a better term — bust the case wide open.'

The detectives made a big show of it. They walked into the law firm where Kibby worked and asked to see him, but were told he was in a meeting. So they strode into his office anyway, handcuffed him, and waltzed him down the country town's main street to the local police station, where they questioned him about the dodgy stat dec and charged him with fraud but let him out on bail until a court hearing. They knew that, having been charged with an offence, he could no longer practise as a lawyer.

And then a deal was laid out. 'As we were leaving, we said, "Peter, this is what we're doing. If you wish to talk to us about the cult and about Anne and so forth, it may well assist in the court proceedings in the future."'

A week later, Lex's phone in the Operation Forest office rang. 'This really animated and, I have to say, delightful voice was on the end of the phone saying, "Lex, Peter Kibby. I'd like to have a cup of coffee with you."'

Lex would get to know this unusual man very well. Peter Kibby was about to sing like a bird.

7

SANTINIKETAN

He sat at the desk in the cramped, grey interview room at Melbourne's St Kilda Road police headquarters with his elbows on the table and his hands in the air. He was careful never to put his hands on the desk and he was careful never to accidentally touch Lex.

Peter Kibby's epic Operation Forest interview lasted three months, conducted four days a week. He was picked up on each of those four days from his house in the hills by police and driven into central Melbourne. He liked a proper lunchbreak every day. When he had a toilet break, it would be a long wait for him to re-appear in the room because of the obsessive handwashing.

Lex describes Kibby as a Geoffrey Robertson figure: intelligent, courteous, polite, well dressed, and very, very cultured. 'You could imagine Peter standing up before the Bar in the Supreme Court.' He had first met Anne in 1964 and by now it was 1990; that's two decades or more of intimate knowledge of her books. He knew almost everything there was to know about Anne's methods, her contacts, and the way her mind worked. He knew about her idiosyncrasies and the ways by which she persuaded people to part with money and property and sign documents they were not supposed to be signing.

At first, he was a little tense. But then he relaxed into the process. 'After the first couple of weeks, I think he started to enjoy the experience — the notoriety of it,' says Lex. 'It was a relief to Peter that he was able to tell everything about Anne because he was so angry at what his life had become and what Anne had done to him and what he'd seen Anne do to others that he didn't hold back.'

For police, it was a coup. There were theories and abstractions about how The Family had operated and thrived — and there were the testimonies of vulnerable young people making allegations that, in many cases, could not be verified — but there was scant evidence about the backbone of it: the financials, administration, and adoption processes.

'No one had ever had the ability to get so close to the inner sanctum of the sect, and we had the key here — Peter was the key to the door,' says Lex. 'Establishing the trust, gaining his confidence — having a banter at times and having a bit of a joke. That was the way that we were going to find out what the hell went on.'

One of the first things Kibby told Lex about was the partially blind boy that Leon Dawes had been present with in the bathroom at Uptop. Kibby had heard about the child before he met him. The boy had been adopted by John Mackay and his then wife, Jeanette, when he was a baby, but he was handed straight to Anne. So first Anne had needed to be appointed the child's legal guardian, and she had turned to Kibby. Kibby told Lex he went to a Family event at a house in Ferny Creek: 'They had with them the baby ... Anne and Bill were playing the mother and father figures.'

Anne told Kibby to change the boy's name by deed poll. The adoption papers were signed by senior members of The Family. The deed poll document, Kibby told Lex, had a forged signature on it, of a Family member and mainstream church minister named Jim Armstrong, who was not in Australia at the time of the signing. Another member of The Family had forged it in Kibby's presence, he said. Anne signed the document too. Kibby went to the Registrar General's office in central Melbourne with it in September 1974. 'This was the first of the deed-poll changes Anne had wanted me to do in an effort to change the children's names to Hamilton-Byrne,' he told Lex.

The next child's paperwork was faked in exactly the same way six months later. He was adopted by one of Johnson's two daughters and named Raynor, after her father, but given to a cult member called Miriam, who had changed her surname to Hamilton. She then gave him to Anne, whereupon his name was officially changed.

Names were a very important cipher in The Family. They were bestowed on people not only to give them a new identity and create the impression that they belonged to Anne, but also to lend status and meaning within the cult. Many of the girls at Uptop were given names beginning with A. Like the hair and the clothing, the names rendered them facsimiles of one another and of their leader. It is strange that Johnson's own daughter named the child of a faked adoption after her father, and strange too that Miriam changed her surname to Hamilton, as if merely saying she was in Anne's 'family' was not enough, but in the context of the cult's obsession with names it made sense.

Next, Kibby revealed another effective method the group used to hide identities. In this fraud, an adult member of the cult — in the situation Kibby recounted, Beryl Hubble (Raynor Johnson's daughter, who was later known as Christine Fleming) — changed her name by deed poll to Anne Hamilton-Byrne. Kibby signed as a witness. He would come to do this often, but the Hubble case, in the winter of 1975, was one of the first. The aim was for Hubble to be able to then sign as Anne in deed-poll changes for the children. Lex showed Kibby copies of documents where cult members had signed as Bill also. Kibby admitted to Lex that he himself had forged multiple signatures.

In January 1976, Kibby told police, he went to England for six weeks. Anne was already there, and he visited her at Broom Farm. She looked pregnant, and she was wearing maternity clothes. She was faking a pregnancy, and she did it often. One of the cult women had the job of making smocks for her — 'Hundreds,' she said, 'in one style. She seemed to be pregnant all the time.'

When both were back in Melbourne two months later, the story went around that she had given birth to a girl. As far as Kibby knew — at least at the time — Anne was 44, but he said he never really knew her age because she lied about it and had had a lot of cosmetic surgery. But he found out later that she was 56 at the time of this apparent pregnancy, and was just pretending to be pregnant. The child she claimed to have given birth to — the tiny girl who would rarely speak and would later suffer psychosocial short stature — was in fact another woman's child, who was given to Anne. Yet followers were told that Anne had given birth to the baby and that the other woman's baby was sick and had gone to live in another Australian state for treatment.

Then Kibby began on the property scams. Broom Farm, he revealed, a 17th-century homestead set on three hectares, had been paid for by donations Anne received — so-called 'loans' that he believed she never intended to pay back. The two-storey house had five bedrooms, plus there were separate sheds, garages, and stables. There were pretty borders of hedgerow, and fertile emerald-green paddocks. Don Webb flew from Melbourne to the

United Kingdom twice to do architectural work on the property.

While the property was being purchased, said Kibby, Liz Whitaker flew out with $AU10,000 in cash stuffed under her skirt to put in the Broom Farm fund.

He detailed an eight-year saga that had occurred in the 1980s, and had led to him being investigated by both the state's fraud squad and the Law Institute of Victoria, which watches over lawyers. Anne wanted her homeopath in London, Max Deacon, to buy a house in the Dandenongs, in the area that had become a stronghold for the cult. She allegedly told Kibby to organise it and persuade Deacon to give Kibby and Anne control of his money. Anne told Kibby that she and another cult member had loaned Deacon $AU50,000 at high interest. Kibby was soon paying money from Deacon's bank account into Anne's to cover the interest she said she was entitled to from the loan.

After the house was purchased, Anne — with Deacon's consent — gave Liz Whitaker power of attorney over Deacon's affairs as well. Liz took out a $AU37,000 loan against Deacon's house in the hills, which was being used by members of The Family. (He was still in London.) But the loan repayments were not met. The money had gone straight to Anne — and Deacon, Anne, and Liz all turned on Kibby and stripped his co-power of attorney while he was under investigation. Liz Whitaker informed him a psychic had told her that two men stole the money. 'I would say this story, without doubt, would have been Anne's idea,' he said.

Anne's mansion in the hills was purchased in 1976, Kibby explained to Lex. It was owned by a woman involved with The Family who had it under her company, Audette & Co. Anne bought it from the woman for $AU60,000 and renamed it from Bray Lodge to Crowther House. (The law firm Kibby was working for at the time was Weigall and Crowther.) He said that there was no contract of sale, and that Anne merely told the woman that she would repay her in 'two or three years ... I doubt whether Anne ever paid [her]'. Anne bought it under one of her aliases: Fiona MacDonald.

Kibby told police the grand old house was Anne's main home when in Australia and that she had held spiritual classes there, for a short time, under the name 'Melbourne School for Esoteric and Exoteric Studies'. He also told police a surprising fact: that in the 1970s the house was a small café, or tearooms, on weekends. 'Members of the sect would make scones, tea, coffee, et cetera, for the general public. The staff who worked in the tearooms were all members of the sect and working at Anne's direction.' It was a nice little earner, and a sideline that stayed essentially hidden from the police.

Crowther was used for weddings among members of the cult too. Leon Dawes was married there; Michael's second marriage was conducted there. Dinner parties would be held with the cult's inner sanctum, and all the Uptop kids would be driven to Crowther in Jupiter to spend time with the guests. Anne sometimes wore a distinctive bright red dress to the Crowther parties. Several former cult members remember the red dress.

She got her hands on another lavish hills property, called the White Lodge, in 1979. Howard Whitaker had owned it after it too was bought a company with links to the cult. After Whitaker went bankrupt and left The Family, Anne decided to turn it into a child-minding centre for children of the cult who were not at Uptop. It was renovated to suit, with the bathrooms featuring small hand basins. But the child-care centre never eventuated, and the house lay empty until Anne, according to Kibby, told him to transfer ownership of it to her, under her pseudonym Fiona MacDonald. She then charged cult members $10 a head to meditate inside, he said.

To Peter Spence, these were extraordinary revelations. It was, it seemed to him, a systemic institutional failure. The hospitals had not detected the fake adoptions. The police had failed in previous investigations to get anything done. The government was never interested in probing too far.

He recommended a Royal Commission, the highest government-led inquiry possible for institutional crimes such as corruption and systemic abuse in Australia. The Royal Commission into deep-sleep therapy, which investigated the deaths of 26 patients and 19 suicides at Sydney's Chelmsford Private Hospital in the 1960s, had just finished. Spence could see that the parallels with The Family were strong: psychiatry, drug experiments, frightened patients. He also knew that many would not speak unless compelled: he had tracked down a psychiatrist with links to The Family based in another state, New South Wales. The man was not implicated in any crimes but had worked at Newhaven and seen a lot of things. He refused to give a statement to Forest but told Spence he would give evidence before a properly constituted inquiry.

Spence wrote a long and detailed report on what Forest knew: 'The sect, the treatment of the children, the way in which they got hold of the children, the use of the drugs on numerous people including the children ... I suggested that the only real way forward was a Royal Commission, where many, many of these people could and would come forward and give evidence of what actually took place over those years.'

Royal Commissions in Australia are put in place by governments, either state or federal. In this case the decision would have fallen to the state government because most of The Family's activity took place in the state of Victoria. But Spence says that his recommendation never got as far as the government. Even if it had, he now thinks the chances of a high-profile commission being established were always slim: inaction by government agencies would have been embarrassing for any government of any persuasion, and a Royal Commission would have brought it into the open. There was a nagging sense that the cult and the allegations around them were in the too-hard basket for the authorities. 'I have a theory that [the cult] had enough influence to prevent further investigations being taken forward in the early days, and then it would have been politically embarrassing if we had we had a Royal Commission conducted in 1990 or thereabouts,' Spence told us.

According to Marie Mohr, the government would have asked itself, 'What are we going to get out of it?' 'Look how long it's taken for any commission into the Catholic Church. It's the same reasons. It's hard. It's difficult. I think the reason we needed an open investigation was how [the practice of forged adoption] was allowed in the '60s and '70s, where children were literally stolen. Senior social workers, doctors, nurses were manipulating the system to take whatever child they wanted. They got passports under phony names. They were sect members doing Anne's bidding. They had no qualms in making fraudulent statements to the system because the system is nothing compared to their divine one.'

Spence agrees: 'I think it would have all ultimately been very embarrassing for quite a number of people. There's no doubt that there were tentacles reaching right to the top.'

Nevertheless, at the time, Spence was floored by the news. To him, the idea of a public commission was 'totally off-handedly rejected'. What would it take? Royal Commissions had been called for less, but the old adage is that governments don't want them unless they know what the answers will be.

He called a meeting with police command—the state's assistant commissioner for crime and a detective chief superintendent.

They were told that Forest detectives were struggling with the emotional toll of the case because of the fragile children they were meeting and the allegations they were hearing. The death threats from Adam had also affected the team; police hierarchy feared that some of the taskforce were too close to the case and were losing their sense of objectivity.

Spence also conceded it was unlikely that criminal charges against Anne or adult cult leaders for crimes of abuse or assault committed against the children would stick because there was not much evidence except testimonies, and the evidence, in police speak, was 'stale'. As witnesses, the children weren't great: damaged, shy, prone to memory lapses. They had also all been housed together after the raid, which could lead to accusations of 'contamination'; that is, they could be accused of making sure their stories matched. Also, Spence and his bosses were asking themselves whether the children should be subjected to cross-examination in court — should they be caused any more pain? An internal police report from mid-1990 recommended no, they should not be: 'Any attempt to bring them into court as witnesses will only further exacerbate their already fragile psychological wellbeing. There are lessons to be learned by those agencies entrusted with the welfare of children being adopted in this state. The main thrust of this investigation should be to ensure that this situation cannot happen again.'

However, the consensus was that the fraud charges — the forgeries and faked documents — would stick and would not require any of the children to give evidence. Plough on, came the order from police command. See what turns up.

Armed with warrants, Operation Forest searched a house in the hills and found two kilograms of marijuana and nearly $AU3,500 in cash; they charged a fringe cult member with drug offences. A shrine to Anne was also found in the house. Police carried out surveillance on other houses in the hills, trying to track the names and finances of those they suspected were involved.

Meanwhile, Anne had issued a writ for defamation against Channel Nine over a television news report and was expected back in the country anytime.

Operation Forest had by now drafted the FBI and Interpol into the investigation. Interpol found out that a person called James Hamilton-Byrne, who had been one of the children Anne claimed as her own, went to an embassy in Honolulu to get a new passport. He agreed to talk to police but refused to return to Australia. Lex found out all about Raynor Johnson's pivotal role in setting up the cult and secured himself a copy of Johnson's diary.

Then Liz Whitaker tried to fly the coop. She had been under surveillance, and was arrested while about to fly to London and charged with perjury over forged signatures, based on Kibby's evidence and the documents to which he had led police. She was let out on bail but ordered to stay in Australia. This led Anne to try harder to stay hidden. Her lieutenants were falling; Anne must have known they were getting closer to her, step by step.

Howard Whitaker was long off the scene, having since taken up various psychiatric roles in Melbourne and in country towns. He had refused to see anyone linked to the cult except patients he considered in dire need. Yet, despite his past, he was a member of the state's Mental Health Review Board from 1987 until 1998.

Whitaker's son David had begun to edge himself out too.

Anne had always wanted her group to be self-sufficient. She wanted her own teachers, lawyers, doctors, and nurses, with the kids all educated and tended to medically within the confines of the group. She also believed that they needed to be able to feed themselves because of a looming apocalypse. So — in a repeat of her mistake in sending Sarah, Leeanne, and Anouree to a local dancing school — she sent three men, including David, to an agricultural college two hours north of Melbourne to learn how to be farmers.

David had been living with the cult in the United Kingdom. He first arrived in Britain in the mid-1970s. Already he had learned the best way to get on with his life while still living within The Family networks was avoidance. If Anne didn't see him, she couldn't tell him what to do. 'If she saw you, she'd say, "Oh, bloody hell, we've got to do another clearing." Or she'd say, "You need to do this"; "You need to move to England"; "You need to move back to Australia." If you didn't actually see her, she didn't mess you about so much.'

Sending David to farming college was a 'fundamental mistake', he says. It was outside the group's circle of influence; Anne thought the young men she sent to the town of Dookie were rusted-on followers who would never falter in their beliefs and never, ever betray her. But at Dookie David would mix with ordinary folk in a student dormitory and see life outside the cult — 'Normal people doing normal things,' he says.

It didn't take long for him to see the light: straightaway he met a fellow student called Cathy, whom he would eventually marry, and who would help extricate him from The Family. Cathy saw right through it all from the beginning, David says: she would call Anne's teachings 'bullshit, a load of rubbish'. However, Cathy didn't realise the extent of it — 'initially when Cathy met Anne, she didn't realise how significant a person she was in my life. She just thought she was the weird aunty.'

David decided in the very late 1970s, halfway through his three-year course, that he wanted to leave The Family. Anne's plan to school him in farming for her benefit had apparently backfired. But not for long.

David finished his course, and went to work on a farm in country New South Wales. He wanted to keep away from the hills, as far away as possible, but something was still in his brain — a little of the cult's magnetism, an inextricable pull towards the people he knew and who knew him. He wanted to betray them by walking away, like his father, but he couldn't yet. After a year on the farm, Anne rang him up. The power she had over him was still strong. She convinced him to go back to England.

Anne wanted to control David, he believed. She knew Cathy had led him away from the cult and she wanted to draw him back. She never thought that Cathy would go with David to England. David was not yet strong enough to refuse Anne's orders, but he was strong enough to take someone with him who could potentially stand between him and 'Big Ball'.

The couple set up in Tunbridge Wells, near Broom Farm, under Anne's instruction, and David was made to study osteopathy and get a job. They stayed for four years, from 1980. Adam was sent to live with them for a time because he was causing trouble back in Melbourne. David thinks this was also to drive a wedge between him and Cathy because Adam was a handful, and Anne thought it would be too much for Cathy. 'She tried very, very, very hard to break us up. Did all kinds of wicked things.'

One night after a dinner party at Broom Farm, David tells us, Anne tried one more strategy on Cathy to spoil her relationship with David, and things came to head. She started picking on someone Cathy knew — who wasn't there — and told Cathy not to trust her under any circumstances. Cathy knew it was a game, a tactic. They left the party, and Anne followed them out to their car, still heckling. 'Cathy wound up the car window and said, "We're never coming back to talk to that mad bitch again." And I thought, *That's probably about the end of it*. And I'm pretty sure that's the last time I saw Anne.'

David and Cathy got married and came back to Australia. David wrote to his mother, Liz Whitaker, who was ensconced at Uptop, and told her he was finished with the cult. Then he bought a farm some way out of Melbourne to begin his new life: 'To put a bit of space between us and these lunatics.' He started getting letters from members of The Family criticising his decision and sticking up for Anne, and the letters kept coming, and then, just as Operation Forest was being pulled together, he decided to make a stand. 'I felt that just walking away wasn't quite enough. I wanted to attack her power base, which is of course her people, and also I had decided that the only way I would survive the whole thing was to break all contacts, and that required burning all the bridges and slamming all the doors.'

With his brother, who had also distanced himself from the cult, he typed up a two-page A4 document — 'our thoughts about the cult and what a load of crap it was' — and took it to the Santiniketan Lodge one Sunday night in 1988 when he knew it would be busy. The cult was in a period of high paranoia and secrecy after the raid and the formation of a special police squad to break them up. David says all he wanted to do was help others get out.

The brothers put the open letter under a windscreen wiper on each vehicle, and then stood at the door handing them out. The letter cited a cult-spotting checklist David Whitaker had seen in *The Australian Women's Weekly* and adapted it to ask a series of questions about Anne and The Family. 'If you believe that Anne Hamilton-Byrne will lead you to enlightenment and that The Family is something other than just another cult, you are either very afraid or incredibly gullible,' Whitaker wrote.

The questions he and his brother posed were:

1. Does Anne wield total power and absolute authority?

2. Does Anne make absolute claims to absolute personal infallibity [sic] or divinity?

3. Does the doctrine of the Family foster the view that its way is the only way to liberation or God?

4. Does Anne rule autocratically?

5. Does dissention and disobedience to the Family bring with it the consequence of punishment, either physical, mental or emotional?

6. Do the doctrines of the Family foster personal fear and guilt?

7. Does the Family require moral indiscretions to be performed in the name of the 'cause?'

8. Is it a requirement of membership that all your ties with former friends and family are broken?

9. Is it a requirement of membership that all your worldly goods be surrendered to the Family upon entry?

10. Does the Family foster intense daily ritual and routine, leaving its members little room to make decisions for themselves?

11. Does the Family require its members to seek new recruits from the wider community?

12. Are recruiting, proselytizing and fundraising activities the only acceptable form of social contact outside the Family?

The answers to these questions were not as straightforward as perhaps David hoped, but he had still made his point in brutal fashion. He and his brother wrote that if followers of Anne answered yes to more than two of the questions, 'It is time to stand back and seriously evaluate what you are letting yourself in for. THINK ABOUT IT!!'

Why has Anne not returned to Australia after the Uptop raid, the letter asked. Will her 'so-called blue light or any other bullshit' protect her? She lives in the lap of luxury, with expensive cars, while her members' mortgages keep turning. Does the money go to deserted mothers or lost cats and dogs or the homeless or development projects in the Third World, as Anne sometimes claimed it did? 'Don't kid yourself! You are financing Anne's personal wealth and for what?'

Everything she does is about power, David and his brother wrote. Power and control. She made many cult members change their name not for their benefit but for hers. She made some become nurses and go to England and funnel invalid pensions into her bank account. She made others leave their husbands or wives or, indeed, their own children. 'What is pathetic is that you are still stuck in the rut.'

The letter asks cult members to do two things: ask questions of each other about their lives and their regrets, and 'get out now. There is life after Anne and the Family!'

David and his brother copped abuse at the Lodge that night. But David also knows of one cult member who left: 'probably not as a result of it, but it certainly helped them along the way'. Then a few weeks later he got a letter, which he says was obviously dictated by Anne. It was about betrayal and the grim consequences thereof. David had betrayed Anne spectacularly, but by now he didn't care because he had allowed himself to believe in the idea that it was not betrayal if it was right. 'The letter was full of stuff about how if you allow somebody to put out the light in your heart — that is, drag you out of the cult — you'll be in darkness for ever. All the normal sort of bullshit they went on with.'

He wrote his own letter back, but with an extra ingredient. 'I went out in the paddock and I got a little piece of cow manure, wrapped it up in a plastic bag, put it in an envelope, and posted it back with a note saying: *Next time you want to send someone bullshit, send them the real thing.*'

He has never been approached by anyone in The Family since.

After David's letter, Anne sent her followers a recorded discourse. She knew, of course, that the Uptop children were talking to police. She knew that the police had a taskforce set up to find her, and she knew that a fellow named Lex de Man was leading the investigation. She said that unenlightened people, even members of The Family, had a strong tendency to doubt. She invoked doubting Thomas, the disciple who could betray his God, noting, 'We become preconditioned before we begin to use the divine power … often half a lifetime has to pass before we can recover and be able to eliminate what personality we assume we understand from our early time in life.'

She said it was natural for people to wonder, but not natural for them to betray. Young people — the children who had spoken to police — had assumed fronts that caused a barrier between the physical self and the enlightened self. Later in the discourse, she refers to one former child who had confronted her after the raid and asked her why the cult was so cruel to children. 'She is a very troubled girl. She was up there too and she was telling me she saw someone bashing someone and someone else having their face put in a washing pan and she mentioned one of the nurses — I can only say it wasn't Liz — and another one belting a little boy with a bat, and it didn't come with the aura, it didn't come right, so I am telling you she needs prayers.'

Sarah, she said, had betrayed her and had cancer as a result. (Sarah never had cancer.) Anne told followers the disease was karma for betrayal for breaching the cult's mantra. '[Sarah] doesn't have much time left, and it will happen to Anouree and the rest because, the poor little beggars, they can't live holding onto this, they are being forced. So naturally, all of us, we have to do what we can in prayer and meditation.'

In the tiny police interview room, two months in, Kibby was not only telling police all about the nuts and bolts of The Family but he was also endearing himself to Lex. 'Peter liked to have a bit of a laugh and a joke. He'd often tell jokes and talk in very posh tones about a particular individual, but at the same time he knew some great colourful language. You know you shouldn't, but as a detective I got very close with Peter.'

Kibby tried to explain to Lex the exact nature of Anne's charisma and why he had been convinced to work for her. Even Lex admits that Anne had a certain magnetism about her: 'When you look at the early photos of Anne, Anne was what you'd call a stunner in her days. In her early life, she wasn't too bad on the eye.' He believes she used her charms on men in the group and men who might join the group. No one ever admitted that to him, but he has a hunch. 'All Peter used to say was, "God, she's a good looker," in his very articulated Geoffrey Robinson voice.'

But Kibby was primarily a deep well of information. 'You want to do an investigation to find out if any crimes have been committed, so with Peter it was going through each of the various documents for him to affirm his involvement and his knowledge of how the document was created and who was involved.

'You want to make sure you cover every piece of knowledge he had because he was a solicitor for Anne. It's not a thing to rush. We were actually able to take our time to get it right, even though we had a lot of pressure on us. I knew we'd get information that people had surmised for years but never had evidence for.'

He talked about Anne's biological daughter, Natasha, and a property she had bought in the hills enclave right back in 1967: Little Woodford. The house was occupied through the years by many members of The Family, and when Natasha split up with

ABOVE: A group of children in front of the main building at the Old Melbourne Orphanage in Brighton, Victoria. Anne Hamilton-Byrne and two of her six siblings spent time here as Anne's parents struggled with finances and the mental health of Anne's mother, Florence. *(Pictures Collection, State Library of Victoria)*

LEFT: Anne (far right, second row from top), nine years old, at Sunshine Primary, a state school in Melbourne's industrial western suburbs. At that time, Anne was known by her birth name of Evelyn Edwards.

ABOVE LEFT: Anne in the 1930s, before she began a series of cosmetic procedures and facelifts to maintain the illusion of youth.

ABOVE RIGHT: Dr Raynor Johnson, co-founder of The Family. A renowned British physicist, Johnson emigrated to Melbourne in 1934. He met Anne in 1962 and became convinced she was Jesus Christ reincarnated.

ABOVE: Dr L. Howard Whitaker and Elizabeth Whitaker (nee Black) on their wedding day. Dr Whitaker, who became a follower of Anne's in 1965, was one of the first psychiatrists licensed to use LSD in the state of Victoria. Liz Whitaker, a registered nurse, also became a devoted follower.

ABOVE: Anne in the 1960s with her harp. A soprano, she claimed to have sung at charity evenings for the British Empire Society in Melbourne.

BELOW: The first group of children were gathered at Winbirra, Anne's house in the Dandenong Ranges, before they were taken to a Lake Eildon property called Kai Lama, or Uptop, in 1971. From left, Sarah is second; Anouree, third; Leeanne, fifth.

ABOVE: The 'Hamilton-Byrne' children lined up in their best clothes to be baptised at St Mary's Catholic Church in 1978. In the left row (from front), Anouree (second), Sarah (fourth), and Leeanne (back). In the right row, Ben is third from the front.

ABOVE: Adam (formerly known as Roland) at Uptop. Adam was taken to Uptop as a three-year-old but was sent back to the hills after about four years because he was considered too difficult to control.

ABOVE: Five of the boys with bleached-blond hair who believed they were Anne and Bill Hamilton-Byrne's children, including Ben (front right).

ABOVE: A studio portrait of Anne and Leeanne. Many members of The Family were given this photo to place on the altars in their blue rooms, where they worshipped Anne.

ABOVE: Anne Hamilton-Byrne in a David Hamilton–inspired portrait in the bush around Lake Eildon, in the late 1970s.

Anne loved animals, and had many dogs and cats at her properties. Some in The Family claim that she treated animals better than children.

BELOW: Bill and Anne Hamilton-Byrne with Adam. Adam remained loyal to Anne and Bill well into his adult life.

ABOVE: Former Victoria Police detective Lex de Man, who spent nearly five years on the Operation Forest taskforce, which finally succeeded in extraditing Anne and Bill Hamilton-Byrne from the United States in 1993.

ABOVE: Anne and Bill Hamilton-Byrne arrive at Melbourne's County Court to face charges on 15 November 1993. Adam is by their side. (The Age, *John Woudstra*)

her husband, David Cook, the house was transferred to trustees to hold it for their son, Richard. But Anne, through Kibby, got hold of the property in the 1980s when she gave him a cheque to discharge the mortgage. Then Anne, again through Kibby, took out caveats on the property to keep it away from her daughter: 'So Anne could annoy Natasha, as they'd had a falling out,' he told police. He said bags of documents were buried in the garden of Little Woodford, but he didn't know exactly where.

Kibby's trump card to Lex was the information he revealed about an alleged set of triplets. This disclosure marked the point where Lex knew he might be close to being able to lay a charge on Anne and bring her to court, quickly. She always claimed she had had triplets in Auckland, New Zealand, in 1970: James, Lyndon, and Sarah Hamilton-Byrne. Sarah remembers that when her birth certificate was changed and she suddenly became a Kiwi, she swapped allegiances when following the cricket and started cheering for New Zealand. 'We never really knew our age or date of birth,' she says. 'It was all about subjugating ego. We weren't allowed to start letters with "I" or really use the world "I".'

In fact, Lyndon was born as Mark, in a suburban Melbourne hospital near the hills. Kibby admitted to forging a passport for him — along with other cult 'witnesses' and forgers who had changed their names. Mark's biological mother said that one of Raynor Johnson's daughters, Beryl Hubble, had accused her of trying to have an abortion because the baby had been born with a wounded head, and then she arranged for the baby to be taken away and adopted out.

Operation Forest found that Lyndon, who had a birthmark on his head, had his name changed to Lyndon Hamilton-Byrne by forgery and was baptised in that name in a Catholic church near Uptop. They also found that Anne made a legal declaration to authorities in New Zealand some time later that he and the other two were triplets, that their births were never registered properly because she took them overseas after giving birth, and that Bill was their father. 'All three children are living with me and their father in Melbourne and are alive and well,' she wrote. Liz Whitaker and Pat MacFarlane filed supporting documents. Lex knew they must all be false. Kibby had said as much.

As the triplet scam was being enacted by Anne and her enablers, the grand hall in the hills, Santiniketan Lodge, was being built. Raynor Johnson had bought a house up there, which was once owned by former deputy prime minister of Australia Sir John Latham: Anne told him she had seen it while astral travelling. (Although she told her followers later that she saw a rather more mundane sale advertisement for it in the newspaper.) Johnson was 62. He always thought he and Mary would go back to England to retire, but now he was a student of Anne's they planned to stay.

Sir John had built a small outbuilding on the property to use as his library. The cult converted it into a place of worship called 'The Little Chapel', or 'The Healing Chapel', but they soon outgrew it. They could fit only 25 on each floor of the chapel's split levels, with Anne holding court from a special chair upstairs, her talks amplified down to those below through a sound system. She accumulated the money to buy a block of land over the road, adjoining the beautiful Dandenong Ranges National Park: 'That's the ideal spot I'm looking for to put a hall,' she said.

Santiniketan Lodge still stands. Acolytes of Anne's insist they use it several times a week even today, but when we visit the site it has few signs of life. Outside are underground water tanks with chains leading down off the corners of the roof to help direct the rainwater in. Someone — presumably an intruder — has plastered graffiti on an outside wall, only partially erased: *What Are The Chains For?*

Michael, who has taken us to the Lodge, lets us inside its doors. The power is off. He doesn't want us to linger too long but agrees to allow us to take a look around. We see blue lights lining the long hallway towards the main room, where plastic chairs are stacked up on top of one another. The heavy orange curtains are drawn tight. Anne's purple chair, with a small table, embroidered tablecloth, and antique lamp, are in place up the front — not that she has sat in her chair for a long, long time. There's a big crucifix on the front wall.

A laminated order of service from the 1990s, sitting discarded on a table, calls for a 'silent mantra' upon entry to the dusty Lodge. Michael fills us in on how a service would be conducted: a meditation tape would play for ten minutes; then there would be five minutes of 'healing' before the 'Teacher's Tape', or Anne's discourse, followed by some meditation, and then 'Handel's Largo', an aria that Anne loved and had ordered be played as she entered the lodge, bathed in blue light, in the cult's boom period of the 1970s.

A smaller adjoining room is the cult's library, and the shelves are now full of hundreds of Raynor Johnson's old books: Swami Muktananda, Robert Browning; astrology, astronomy, theology, history, philosophy, and yoga. The library has plastic roses in vases and cheap prints of Francis of Assisi, the *Mona Lisa*, and Rembrandt's *Mother and Child* on the walls.

Despite these touches, it seemed to us that even the building — the once-grand Lodge — has been betrayed. It seems unloved and unused. 'The world works its way and people are too busy now, or too tired or too old,' says Michael. 'I suppose it happens to every institution or church as people get older. [Yet] it is our privilege to keep it as it was always meant to be.'

Today the Lodge is worth an estimated $AU2,000,000. In 2015, a local real estate agent said: 'It is an amazing piece of land, very unusual. It backs onto the Dandenong Ranges National Park. Most land around there is hilly with a lot of trees but this is flat, open, and sunny.'

Just after it was built, local men staged a protest outside with placards, apparently angry that their wives were spending long hours at the Lodge doing yoga and spiritual training instead of being home with their families. The building cemented Anne's group of adherents as a cult because it was a place of worship, a fulcrum, hosted by their charismatic, controlling leader. Members all lived nearby. Johnson was literally over the road, Anne down the street. The Lodge formed a sort of bridge between them, a place to be reassured that this was the right path, that no wrong was being done.

Inside Santiniketan, only the Teacher could speak. It was from here that Anne's discourses were either delivered or broadcast (from cassette tapes she recorded elsewhere). Johnson described these tapes as 'the most precious possession' of the lodge and The Family. To him, they would 'presumably one day become the scriptures of the new age'.

Anne's recordings are long. Sometimes in the making of them she was interrupted by cats or dogs (she always had dozens of animals around her). 'Oh, hang on!' she says in one, leaving the microphone running. 'Pussy is going for doggy.' She might also stop mid-discourse: 'By golly, I have gone to town!' On another, 'Now, folks, it's getting on, time to — it's ten to eight, oh golly, yes!' as if she was chairing a community meeting — which in a sense she was, but no one else was allowed an opinion. Anne had quite an odd accent for an Australian; she sounded aristocratic, as if she had been invited into the parlours of royal families and taught in private girls' schools — both of which she claimed to be true, but neither were.

Sarah told us she eventually figured out that Anne spoke in

circles. 'It was a kind of double-speak.' She would trail off and leave statements hanging, inviting listeners to infuse them with meaning. She would refer to her followers, silent in the lodge, by the familiar 'old thing' — as in, 'You don't want to lose your self-respect, old thing!' (This comment was during a sermon about the value of silence and how betrayal damages the soul. 'You still can not talk to anyone besides your Teacher,' she said. 'Always keep your spiritual treasure hidden within you. These are not for the vulgar people and the gaze of humanity. You don't want to lose your self-respect, old thing!')

The recordings have common themes: I have witnessed miracles and bliss and invisible worlds. I myself am a miracle. I have chosen you and you are special. Say nothing, even though it is amazing. Do not betray me.

'I started [the group],' she said. 'I had to start it. That was divine orders. That was the divine vision. You are the one being rescued. I also have to force you and push you toward meditation. It is the most secret key towards the most secret treasure. All the truly true paths say the same thing, my friends. That to be true we want to reach God and we do need to have a lot of patience and perseverance and help others into purity of their body and their mind.'

In many recordings, Anne made clear that helping others to get on the path is crucial. They were recruitment drives. She always appeared to want more people, more validation, more money, more power. 'It's quite an intense spiritual footstep that you have to take to help them. Spiritual grooming, it is called.'

Ian Weeks, Raynor Johnson's former student, believes Johnson saw Santiniketan Lodge as a benevolent project based on the Indian model of an ashram — 'a conference-centre kind of place for learning and study. That was Raynor; he did such things.'

Just after Johnson bought his house in the hills, Anne had visited him. She looked sick, and said she had cancer and might die. 'The thought that She might have to leave us (including the dozen or more souls whom She had called and initiated),' he wrote, 'while all of us who were so ill prepared to do her work, distressed Her greatly.' They meditated and prayed together.

Not long after, she was sick again, and Johnson was told she had died for several minutes overnight but was revived. She was playing with games of guilt and dependency, and fostering loyalty.

She also spoke with Johnson about the looming apocalypse. She said the evolution of the universe had been stalled because there was not enough love on earth, but she had spoken to her heavenly father ('He is more personal than you know') and begged for a little more time for the planet: 'Its degradation and lack of "Love" were holding up the evolution of other planets in the cosmic timetable. The time available for change was now short.' If 'flying saucers' came in spring, they had journeyed from another solar system and carried life much more advanced than ours, and it would be a warning that Earth was godless and that they wanted to take over. Anne told followers that she had flown in a UFO.

Johnson's biographer, Alan Moore, wrote that Johnson would remain interested in extraterrestrials all his life because he thought they were alien civilisations trying to contact Earth to help the move towards the new age.

Johnson became somewhat overcome by the divine power he thought he was gaining access to. He was humbled when he tried unsuccessfully, by magic, to heal Anne's nose — 'which would have avoided the necessity of surgery'. She also told him the Bible was wrong because records and writings from Biblical times had been lost in a 'deluge'; in fact, she said, Jesus had died on the cross as recorded but then revived himself and lived until the age of 68.

Anne also told Johnson that in a previous life he was a naval officer for Lord Nelson in the Napoleonic Wars. According to Anne, Johnson had drowned while serving Lord Nelson. His daughter Maureen was an 'attractive debutante' in love with Nelson, while his other daughter was a 'young midshipman or lieutenant'. The film star Jane Russell was also there, in Anne's imaginings, and Johnson, the Napoleonic hero, had been in love with her.

These conversations between Anne and Johnson occurred during the cult's most formative days, when recruits were flocking in. Michael joined in 1971.

Michael is the one who sits with her still in the dementia wing; his paintings are on her wall. He makes her tea, he plays music to her. He says even though she has physically withered and can no longer speak in her commanding way, she is still magnificent. He appears for all the world to love her and be in love with her. 'Still perfect-looking, most magnificent even in her walking, Anne has great inner power. When I first met her, everything went through me, and some people can't tolerate that because of their insecurities and fears and they feel they have to fight and defend themselves. They are easily threatened because they are living a lie. One of my favourite things Anne used to say was, "People put so much energy into being what they are not." And aren't they? The world is full of people being what they are not.'

Michael met Anne through Maharishi Mahesh Yogi — the Maharishi — the celebrity Indian yogi who entranced The Beatles during their psychedelic period and founded the Transcendental Meditation movement. The yogi collected Rolls Royces and had a pink private jet. He visited Australia in 1967, when Michael was 19, and this turned out to be Michael's first formative step towards Anne.

The Maharishi had just held his celebrated first lecture in London. The Beatles, Mick Jagger, and Marianne Faithful had turned up, and then followed the yogi to Wales. (Later they would all stay at his ashram in India, where much of *The White Album* was written.)

Michael was a law student at Melbourne University. 'I went to listen to a talk. He didn't talk philosophy as such but gave a method of meditation which stopped the mind.' The Maharishi was being put up in an apartment in St Kilda. Michael went and met him the next day. 'Everything changed,' he says.

Michael's family are wealthy, from the upper echelons of establishment Melbourne. His uncle on his mother's side, Sir Zelman Cowen, would become Australia's governor-general in 1977, after a distinguished career as a legal scholar. Michael, his uncle, and his father all went through the prestigious Scotch College and then studied at the University of Melbourne. After he met the Maharishi, Michael dropped out of law — which troubled his family — and enrolled in Indian studies.

Michael's father tried to rescue him from Anne's group, hiring a 'cultbuster' and taking his son on a pilgrimage to Israel to see family and be among the roots of Judaism. He tried to tempt him with a job through family connections in a hospital in Tel Aviv. None of it worked. Michael had found what he was looking for. He told his mother that Anne was his spiritual mother, which didn't go down too well. His father, meanwhile, was 'freaked out'. But Michael already saw himself as a true man of God, which in his mind meant he had permission from Judaism to become a seeker.

Another Hindu yogi came to town: Swami Nithyananda from South Africa. Michael had a bushy afro by now; he was, he says, 'Indianised'. Raynor Johnson invited Nithyananda up to the hills. Michael was invited too, but his invitation came from others not connected with the cult.

He drove up to The Little Chapel with two visiting Indians from Sri Auribindo's ashram in Pondicherry, in southern India.

Michael says he heard Anne in the forest before he met her, a voice in the trees. Anne greeted Michael at the door of The Little Chapel with the words, 'I have been waiting for you.' He said he immediately felt 'known', and a physical sensation of what he calls 'energy' passed right through him.

After that, he stopped looking for the one who would enlighten him. He had found her. The energy that he says passed through him was blue. 'The blueprint of life, the goodness of it all. I'd wish that upon everybody, even you.'

While talking with Michael, he often asked questions of us, or referred to us in terms of the cosmic plan he perceives to exist. What do we want for our lives, our children, our film, our book? Is this why he wanted to spend so much time with us: to preach and proselytise?

Before he was initiated into Anne's group, he worked for a summer in a firetower in the bush. 'I had a baby fox that I had rescued,' he says. 'It had rickets. I brought it back, and [Anne] healed it.'

Barbara Kibby also became engrossed in the cult at The Little Chapel. Howard Whitaker had given her LSD, for depression, at Newhaven, and recommended she do yoga with Anne. Two months later, Anne invited her up to The Little Chapel for 'advanced yoga'. Anne was, she says, 'ageless'. She saw her as a mother figure because her own mother was an alcoholic, and in and out of hospital. 'I didn't have a lot of mothering,' she says.

Barbara says the cult always had more women in it than men. Anne also lured in a lot of gay men because she accepted their sexuality and often sent them to London, which, in the 1970s, was more liberated — at that time, homosexuality was illegal in Victoria. The women, she enticed through yoga. Raynor Johnson made sense to Barbara when she heard him speak about Jungian archetypes: 'We all have a vision of the perfect mother.'

She joined the cult, but could not see Anne as a supreme being or as Jesus. However, she wanted to get closer to make sure. She wanted more of a sense of belonging: more attention from Mother, more care. 'As I got more involved in the group I really enjoyed the yoga. It kept me fit. I liked the sensation of doing the yoga and the way my body felt. That was a good thing. But I had this yearning to belong to Anne's group of people, and the more I tried to belong the further away it seemed.'

Anne pushed her away, Barbara says, as a tactic to bring her in. Barbara and other women in the cult found that no matter how much they did for Anne — giving her money, changing jobs and husbands, going on weird diets, working at Uptop and Newhaven — it was never enough. 'Nothing was. She would say all we had to do was just follow what she said.'

The Santiniketan Lodge was used in part, recalls Barbara, to dress down followers, usually women, who had displeased her. If they dressed in a certain way they would be called 'sluts'. This was surely hypocrisy from Anne, who was likely aware of the power her own physical appearance had on some men. Some women, Barbara included, took to taking Mogadon from before they entered the Lodge in order to zone out and dull the criticisms they faced.

But despite this, Barbara was sucked into the vortex. So was her husband, Peter. And as Lex de Man was preparing to extract from Peter the finer details of Anne's strange games and scams, Peter Spence discovered that in 1971, as the Lodge was filling, the then Liberal premier of the state, Rupert Hamer, was given a journalist's entire dossier on the cult and said he would begin an official government inquiry, but never did.

The dilemma for the cult in 1971 was that they wanted to stay hidden, but once the Lodge was built they couldn't. It became busy, with streams of traffic going in and out from a narrow, forested residential road twice a week. There were more than 200 members by now. Locals were starting to pry, and starting to wonder.

The first media report on The Family was in the Ferny Creek local paper, the *Knox & Mountain District Free Press*, in May 1971. Reporters were acting on phone calls from people around the area. Some had told the paper that they were scared after they heard rumours of breeding programs, drugs, and devil worshipping, and the paper called Anne a 'high priestess'.

At the same time, the television journalist who ended up handing his dossier to the premier, Philippe de Montignie, had taken calls from former followers of Anne, and he staked out the Lodge from the bushes for ATV-0's (now Channel Ten) *Dateline* program, showing a full carpark — VW Beetles, Holden HQs — with cult members scurrying out, wrapping themselves in blankets, and driving away. Part of the news footage shows de Montignie hiding in the trees with binoculars.

'In those days, people who lived up in the hills were all considered a little bit mad, a bit like the Melbourne version of "hillbillies". But upon investigation, it turned out to be a very interesting story indeed. We went up there, no one would talk, or very few people would talk. All the information that I got came from people who had left. We called it a "cult".'

'It was dark and grey and raining, so it added very much to the atmosphere of what we were filming. But the people who were disaffected referred to things like brainwashing, husbands and wives swapping all the time, children who didn't know who their parents were, just a whole range of really odd things. I think the thing that really struck us was that no matter which way you looked at it, it seemed wrong. I can understand people wanting to live alternative lifestyles — we probably all would like to do that — but this was way beyond "alternative".'

Dateline ran three stories. 'The fact that this sect did exist,' says de Montignie, 'that there were quite major, major names involved in the sect, that there was probably some form of cruelty to the children at that time [made it newsworthy]. They seemed to all be locked away, you just never got to the kids. In today's era, I'm quite sure, the police or state authorities would have been in there and cleared it out. The husband and wives changed names all the time too. We found one week we'd be talking to Mrs Smith, and next week she'd be Mrs Brown. It just didn't seem quite right, and it certainly was not a good thing for the kids. And that was really the focus of our stories.'

But The Family's first brush with the mainstream media went well for them because through their connections they were able to complain to Channel 0 about the coverage and demand the right of reply in a 'friendly' interview with Johnson.

'I thought Raynor was a really lovely man,' says de Montignie. 'He was just charming in the way he dealt with you. He didn't impose his view onto you. He told you his view, but he told it in a very friendly and charming manner. I can understand people being taken in by him. However, my feeling was that he was an unintended front man for The Family and that in fact the ropes were really being pulled by Anne Hamilton.'

Channel 0's owner in 1971 was Sir Reginald Ansett, the newly knighted baron who owned Ansett Airlines. He knew Johnson because he had been Ambrose Pratt's friend, and also the friend of Supreme Court judge and Melbourne University board member Clifford Menhennitt, who sources have suggested was close to the cult. De Montignie was summoned to the Dandenongs to a judge's house — he says he doesn't remember whether it was this judge — with two other men, including a solicitor. 'I suppose pressure was put on, now I think back to it. The main reason for asking me for a drink was supposedly to show me that these were decent, ordinary people, that they would never be involved in drugs or anything like that. So it was probably a bit of propaganda. It didn't sink in at the time.'

Then came the call from Ansett. 'It would've been maybe the second day after it went to air,' says de Montignie. 'Reg used to come [to the TV network office] everyday. He'd fly in, in his helicopter from Mt Eliza, and land on the front lawn there, and spend half an hour with the Board and then buzz off. Well, on this particular day I got hauled in to talk to him, and he didn't say that he'd been leaned on, but it was obvious that somebody had been in his ear about it. And I got told off … certainly told, in no uncertain terms, that I had to do a follow up, and it had to be a friendly one.'

Johnson seems to have played it somewhere between extraordinary naïvety and bold obfuscation for *Dateline*. He described the cult in terms of a suburban yoga club; already the message was, very firmly, 'nothing to see here'.

De Montignie had asked, in the interviews for his *Dateline* reports, if the cult broke up marriages. Johnson said that marriage as an institution was in trouble anyway, right through society, and the cult's 'liaisons' and splits were reflective of that. De Montignie asked him if there was free love or partner-swapping. 'By Jove!' replied Johnson, like the educated, privileged Englishman he was. 'No.'

There were plenty of children in and around the group, he conceded, but only because they were being looked after, like babysitting, by different adults. He denied any drug use and said the group was made up only of respectable citizens and he threatened to sue anyone who called it a baby-farm.

When the dust settled, de Montignie took his original research, without making copies, to Premier Hamer. He wanted state authorities to find the children and make sure they were safe. 'We felt a strong-enough case was there for an investigation to do with child abuse,' says de Montignie. 'The drugs, well, if they wanted to do that, that really didn't concern us much. If they wanted to wife-swap, that's their business, but it was the kids that really worried us, and we felt it should have been investigated.

'So we contacted him, and he invited us in, and we took all our material. Now I don't think we even had photocopiers in those days, or if we did they would have been very basic things, so we took all our original stuff. Bit sad, in a way. We should've photographed them, I guess, before we took them in. But you can be quite naïve, I guess, at times, which we were. We didn't think it would get swept under the carpet, but I'm sure that's what happened, that it was just shoved to one side. He promised that he would investigate further, and there'd be a proper formal inquiry, and nothing ever happened. It just went away.'

After *Dateline*'s series, *The Truth* tabloid paid a visit to the lodge painting a glowing account, trying to discredit *Dateline*, reporting that the group was peaceful and that Johnson, whom they suggested was the leader, was 'about as sinister as Santa Claus'.

8

BLUE ROOMS

In the Operation Forest interview room, Lex Man could see that Kibby was becoming bolder. He was enjoying the process of being interviewed, and, now that he trusted them, telling police more. Lex could even see that sometimes Kibby was excited by the prospect of doing good with all the information he had. The relief was palpable. 'I remember he said to me at one stage, "I feel like bloody Sherlock Holmes."'

Kibby detailed for Lex a nasty little trick Anne tried to pull in 1980 on a property in the hills called Werona. Kibby acted for both buyer and seller. The Supreme Court was later told that 'undue influence' may have been exerted on the owner, a cult member called Winifred Lugton, to sell it.

Lugton gave the money from the sale — $40,000 — to Anne, and Anne in turn gave it to a company called Faffete Pty Ltd. Don Webb and John Mackay were directors, according to Kibby. Lugton, who was 65, died ten days later of a brain haemorrhage. Two other women who had gifted properties to Anne also died, of the same cause, around the same time. Police found no link between their deaths and the cult, but all three had been swiftly cremated, which prevented deep investigation. The Werona money was then allegedly moved from Faffete to Anne's daughter, Natasha. The buyer never got her title deeds, so she sued the Lugton estate for them. Kibby lied in court and said the money was to repay debts in the United Kingdom. It was later found that affidavits certifying the debts were false and countersigned by a posse of cult members.

Then came an even more audacious scam. In 1985, Anne managed to get a court order excluding her old friend Joan Vilimek's three daughters from their mother's estate, worth $AU620,000.

Vilimek was the wealthy cult member who owned Newhaven, and also a small property near Uptop called Sunny Corner. She died in 1979. Her husband Jaroslev, a horse breeder, had passed away before her, in 1974. They had no biological children together, but Marion had three from her previous marriage and had adopted, with Jaroslev, two boys, Gavan and Rohan. The parents formed a trust fund for the five kids and put Anne in charge of it. They also entrusted Anne and Peter Kibby with their estate. But, according to Kibby, Anne removed him from this role — and then excluded the three daughters, two of whom were cult members, from any of the money, instead directing it to the two boys, over whom she had control.

As Kibby related such incidents, week after week, Lex began to feel desperately sorry for him. He felt that Kibby was a good man who had been exploited. Above all, Kibby was a victim. 'Peter was not a bad person, but Peter was a person like many others in the cult — he'd been deceived through his illness to do things for Anne because he had a true belief that he was actually doing this on behalf of Jesus Christ. He truly believed that she was who she said she was.'

Kibby had become vindictive and angry over Anne's treatment of him. 'Towards the end,' Lex recalls, 'he used to say, "She's just a fucking bitch. This is what the bitch has done to me. This'll fix the bitch!"'

Kibby also started to talk much more about Trish MacFarlane. Lex led him down this path because, like Kibby, she had left the cult disenfranchised and with a lot of secrets. She had co-signed a lot of the fake documents too. She had been a trusted acolyte, but she was now on the outer, of her own choosing, and Lex could not help but suspect she must be full of regrets and misgivings. Lex worked on convincing Kibby to unearth her and persuade her to talk. For the good of the children.

One morning in November 1990, Lex drove to the hills as usual, as he had been doing four days a week for nearly three months, to pick Kibby up and bring him to the city for another session. 'He was over the moon. Couldn't wait to get into the police car. "I've got news for you," he said. "I did speak with Patricia last night."' She was still in the United Kingdom. She had been there since the raid. She was living near Winchester, in the south of England.

Says Lex: 'He had convinced her that I wasn't an ogre and that I could be trusted, and that she should talk to me. So I was pretty happy with that. Except she was in the UK. So we arranged one night — nighttime in Australia and daytime in the UK — to actually call Patricia.'

Trish MacFarlane agreed to talk to Operation Forest. But not in Australia. 'It was a great moment for Peter, because Peter had helped us to establish a link with one of the two supposed Aunties that had administered some of the treatment to the children at Eildon, and had convinced her to talk to police,' says Lex. 'And I don't think that would ever have occurred without the trust that had been built up through Peter Kibby.'

————

Lex de Man went up to the tenth floor of the St Kilda Road police complex. All of the force's specialist crime squads were housed in this building, a large glass tower. Standing beside him at the urinal was the assistant commissioner for crime, one of the men right at the top of the tree.

Lex was on the verge of a breakthrough for Operation Forest, but it was bittersweet because Trish MacFarlane wasn't prepared to come back to Melbourne. The taskforce was under-resourced; it would take Lex a couple of months to get approval to go as far away as London. But she was central to the story.

Not all men talk at the urinal, but these two did. 'We're standing there, the two of us having a bit of a chat, and the boss said, "So, how are things going with Operation Forest?" I said, "Not bad, sir. I think we might have a breakthrough, but I've gotta bit of a problem." He said, "What's that?" I explained to him that MacFarlane, one of the main offenders, wanted to turn, and would speak to us, would give us full details, on a written statement. And he said, "Great — when are you going to get it?" And I said, "She's in the United Kingdom and she won't come back." And I remember him turning to me and saying, "So get on a plane and get there."'

This was in early December 1990. Within a week, Lex and a female detective senior constable from Forest were in Britain.

They interviewed Trish in a British police station in Winchester, in the forensic science building. She confessed straight up to police that she could never see herself 'dobbing' Anne in to the authorities — her word — but that she found herself with only that option after 20 years as a 'neophyte'. She said the Aunties were victims too, and that she hoped the children would eventually understand this.

At first, Trish said, The Family was good. All of the cult members we spoke to say this: that right in the beginning, when it was just yoga, it was terrific. Trish was vulnerable and at a low ebb following the sudden death of one of her sons in that car accident, when he collided with a milkman's cart. Anne had been helpful and kind — despite turning up unannounced at her house — and by sending her off to become a nurse, Trish felt that Anne was helping her further by plunging her into an environment where she was among suffering all the time. 'There were lots of people worse off than myself,' she said.

Anne was the answer, or at the very least she could provide or point to the answer, and Trish was soon convinced the answer for her was to go to Uptop. 'To me, Anne in the early days was everything. Her talks to us in the chapel were brilliant.'

But things changed. The way Trish saw it — in hindsight — it seemed as if she drifted into subservience and blind loyalty through a combination of mind control and a sort of enforced apathy. Although, with her, this sense of subservience was tempered. Liz Whitaker, she said, was always scared of Anne, but she never was. 'I obeyed her and did as I was told but was never frightened of her.' She also said she never liked Whitaker, even though the pair were handpicked as senior enforcers at Uptop. 'I never got on with her.'

Trish served and was victimised by Anne for so long, it was perhaps inevitable that the misgivings piled up. She flirted with escape once, way back in 1971, fleeing from a cult house in Ferny Creek after an LSD session.

She was injected with LSD at Winbirra and at a house in the hills belonging to Joan Vilimek. Like the children, adults such as Trish were told to get in their pyjamas or nighties and get into a bed. Classical music would be playing. After a session when she had been injected in the crook of the elbow, with Anne coming and going from the room, as was her method, Trish told Anne that she was Beethoven. John Mackay was there too and at that point, Trish said, put on a Beethoven record.

The next morning, still feeling under the influence of the drug, Trish realised there was no milk in the fridge, so she jumped in her car and began to drive. She got all the way to Eildon from the hills — over two hours' travel — in a daze. She kept going, 'way past Eildon because I wanted to get to the other side of those mountains'.

But the car started playing up. She had to pull over at a mechanics' workshop, and it was going to take a couple of days to fix, so she checked into a bed and breakfast, still under the influence of LSD. She asked the management if she could borrow a nightie, and stayed for two days. Then she drove back to the hills. Once she returned, Anne told her she had put a jinx on the car so it broke down and Trish would not be able to escape. But it wasn't a serious bid for escape. It was more a gesture — in her clouded, scattered mind — that, deep down, she felt something was wrong.

When she finally did leave the cult, after the raid, Beryl Hubble, Raynor Johnson's youngest daughter and a rusted-on supporter of Anne's, wrote a letter that Trish was certain Anne dictated. Hubble (otherwise known in the cult as Christine Fleming) had terminal cancer by this time. The letter read, in part: 'Patricia, it was you that dunked the kids in the water. You were the Aunty that was hardest on the children. I'm going to come back and haunt you and all the people who have left Anne.'

Trish threw it out.

Just before Lex arrived in the United Kingdom to talk to her, Trish had seen a lawyer in Guildford. She wanted to prepare herself for what was to come. The lawyer told her that she didn't have to say anything if she didn't want to. But she did want to. When she first met Lex, she told him that she didn't want any involvement from the Australian Consulate or High Commission

— she just wanted to talk. She wanted to go back to Australia one day and hoped to be free to do so, but more importantly, after 20 years of unpaid work at Eildon and in the United Kingdom for Anne, she had seen the light. She wanted police to know exactly what the circumstances were, as she saw them, around certain incidents, methods, activities … to clear up the 'misconceptions, rumour and innuendo'.

When Lex first met Trish, he thought she was distant and matronly. 'That cold face, that very harsh face,' he says. 'That was her exterior.' But soon he and his detective partner heard enough from her to conclude that she was the same as Kibby, the same as Johnson, the same as both Whitakers — 'brainwashed into the cult'. Picked on at a vulnerable time. 'She was a bit of a character, one of those loving Nannas, but underneath that you knew that she had actually perpetrated some terrible things on the kids that were at Eildon.'

Trish's emotions were up and down during the long series of interviews. She cried and laughed. 'She was very defensive at times about some of the claims that were made, but at times she was really regretful at some of the activities that she had been involved in,' says Lex.

She confirmed the detail of Leeanne's adoption into the cult in 1968: she was merely summoned to the Royal Women's Hospital in Melbourne by Anne and Joan Vilimek, she said, addressed by her incorrect surname of Webb, and given the baby with the crooked jaw she had 'adopted'. Then she gave the child to Anne.

She admitted to signing false documents to do with the child in front of a suburban justice of the peace in 1970, two years later. There she was to see, for the first time, documents signed by Anne and Peter Kibby changing Leeanne's surname to Hamilton-Byrne. And she was happy to tell police that her second son, when he was around 21, was part of a pathfinding group Anne sent in the early 1970s (by ship) to the United Kingdom to establish the cult's British footprint.

Trish's son left the cult soon after, and, following a stint as Anne's driver, hooked up with Anne's daughter, Natasha. They and four others set up house on a property in Crowborough, Kent, called 'The Olde Cottage'.

Another ship went to the United Kingdom, Trish told police, in late 1972. She was on it, with Anne and Bill, Johnson and his wife, and one other adult member of the cult. They rented a cottage in a village called Wadhurst, in Sussex, from Joan Vilimek's daughter. John Mackay came over and stayed with them, she said, and then he and her son were sent ('for some unknown reason') to the Himalayas to go trekking.

The cult's pathfinders found Broom Farm in Langton Green, Tunbridge Wells, 20 minutes away from The Olde Cottage but much larger and grander and more historic. It would become Anne's bolthole in the United Kingdom, and of course the site of some horrific drug-related experiences for the children as they got older.

Anne and Bill stayed at The Olde Cottage as members of The Family fixed up Broom Farm for them. It took a year of weekend work by eight male cult members, including John Mackay. The whole house was stripped and refurbished to house Anne and her new husband — all the carpets and tiles were replaced. The men were never paid for their work, but Anne gave them money to buy materials. Trish and, by now, Liz Whitaker, who had joined them in Britain, cooked the men food while they worked on the house. Anne and Bill didn't help, according to Trish.

The cult expanded its UK operations even further into Guildford, where Trish and four others lived in the same street — Pilgrim's Way — with Maie Davie, the social worker affiliated with the cult who facilitated the fake adoptions from Melbourne hospitals. Trish and several of the other women were nurses, working through an agency.

One night Anne started ringing around. A group of cult members needed to go to Italy. It was all very urgent. A wealthy, elderly American woman named Esther Beare was sick and needed nurses. Anne got the contract. She had the nurses, after all. Her contact with the Beares — Esther's husband, John Beare, was an Englishman who served 18 years with Scotland Yard, including heading an anti-corruption squad — came about through Howard Whitaker. His former secretary, a cult member, had gone to Europe after Whitaker went out of business and ended up working for the Beares.

A former member of The Family told us: 'Mr Beare thought Anne was pretty good. She said she had all these miracle cures that could help Mrs Beare. [Mrs Beare] was about 90 and Mr Beare was fighting with her relatives because she was the one with the money and her relatives were fighting to make sure that he was disinherited. They did everything possible to say the marriage wasn't a consensual one. He was 50 or 45 or something. They were absolutely outraged because he wanted the money. He had to have all these people around to prove this poor old 90-year-old was getting all the attention that she needed.'

The cult nursed her at two houses, one a mansion near Genoa, and the other huge house beside Lake Como, in northern Italy, near the Swiss border. As the old lady was bedridden with dementia, her much younger husband was spending a lot of time at home. 'He was looking after her shares and her finances,' says the former member, who asked not to be named. 'I stayed beside the lake for a year, then I was told to go somewhere else. He used to send me Christmas cards every year. We had to sign to say we wouldn't write about it or go to the papers. I just think he married this woman who was super-wealthy. Anne used to visit her, and Mr Beare thought she was a wonderful woman.' John Beare wrote to Trish — because one of the nurses had told him about her, and given him her address — to summon her there after the first wave of nurses had been through, but Anne didn't let her go. She held her women on a tight leash, Trish believed, to control them.

Anne's connections to Melbourne society were also still strong — around the same time her nurses were looking after Mrs Beare, another squadron were tending to the dying former governor-general of Australia and government minister Lord Richard Casey. He died in 1976. (Michael's uncle, Sir Zelman Cowen, became governor-general the following year.)

Trish also told Lex that a fundamental rule of being in The Family was to have a blue room. It was a place in their homes to meditate and pray to Anne. This was, Trish believed, a further way for her to infiltrate their lives, even away from the lodge and the coterie in the hills homes, and concentrate their collective focus around her. The colour was supposed to be a channel toward her, a tunnel. The chosen room could be any room in the house, but it had to be completely blue. Blue was spiritual. If there was no spare room, a corner of an existing room should be used. Outside light must be blocked out. Anne gave members photographs of herself to be used in the blue rooms.

Why blue? One of Raynor Johnson's flights of fancy was blue light, and Anne had adopted the idea from him. Johnson had met a yoga master in the 1950s and continued writing to him. The Venerable Sumangalo, an American from Alabama whose 'western' name was Robert Clifton, gave him the idea, because he told Johnson he had been treating a woman possessed by occult forces but had exorcised her with blue light, flowers, incense, and bowls of water. Ancient teachings, he told

Johnson, showed blue light to be the most spiritual.

At her house in the hills, Trish had used a spare bedroom, which she painted blue and hung with dark-blue velvet drapes. She put in a dim blue light bulb, and arranged a table with a crucifix and a photograph of Anne. Trish told Lex she was supposed to meditate for up to an hour twice a day in the blue room, in the lotus position. 'I was pretty bad at meditating full stop,' he remembers her saying. 'I always got bored and went and did something else.'

She was punished for her apparent transgressions. One of Anne's feared methods — apart from name-calling in the Lodge — was called the 'rounds of the kitchen', where the enraged Teacher shouted down those she had gathered, admonishing them and threatening their journey, their pathway.

Trish said Anne kept a blue ice-cube tray at Uptop for a kind of voodoo. She would write the names of her enemies or her traitors — those who had betrayed her — on small slips of paper and freeze them in the tray so the people named suffered or got sick or had a terrible accident. Beyond the ice trays, of course, she would freeze them out in daily life.

When she accused cult members of transgressions in the lodge, others would also take down these names and repeat this freezing process at home. At Uptop, Trish and Liz would often answer the phone and it would be Anne with a new list of names for the ice tray. Old enemies were removed, new ones added. Trish told Lex the voodoo was hard to explain but that she considered it 'magic', and Anne had more 'magic' than anyone else around her.

A regular frozen name was Hans Halm. Anne had allegedly put a false story out among cult members after Kim Halm had gone missing that Hans had been sexually abusing Kim, as well as another girl — 'the little girl next door'. In addition, the very word 'Uptop' was taboo for cult members — they knew about it, but they weren't allowed to say anything or betray the mantra of silence. But people like Hans broke out.

Lex and the detective stayed in the United Kingdom for six weeks over Christmas and New Year. They interviewed six current or former cult members, including Trish, Max Deacon the homeopath, and Trish's son. They also met with local police around Kent and Hampshire, and with Scotland Yard's extradition squad. And the information they were gathering was filling out their picture of Anne and her Family substantially.

Some rank-and-file cult members came in quickly during the passion of the 1960s and early 1970s culture of 'seeking', and exited just as quickly. Some stayed for long periods and then edged away. Some were courted fiercely and submitted, but later fought the power that was trying to engulf them.

We meet Fran Parker, who fell towards Anne through Raynor Johnson, like so many, in a middle-class search for meaning. Fran had been working at the University of Melbourne's main library through the 1960s, and found inspiration on the library's shelves — specifically, in Johnson's books. 'He wasn't just an ordinary physicist, if they can be said to be ordinary,' she says. 'He was a physicist who was spiritually searching.'

She went to a series of his lectures and, like Trish MacFarlane, was so enraptured that she approached him afterwards. She asked him if he could recommend any good yoga teachers. 'Of course he said, "I would love to do that," and he gave me Anne's phone number. I went home and I rang her straightaway, and this lovely voice answered me. It was an entrancing voice, full of depth and love and encouragement, and I said, "I'm from Dr Raynor Johnson's classes," and she said, "Is your interest in yoga for physical health, or something perhaps more religious?" And I said, "Well, it really is a spiritual dimension I'm longing for, but I realise you have to do the hatha first, and I really want to start there." And she said, "Oh darling, you're so ready."'

Fran went to the yoga with her then husband, John, and met Anne. 'There she was. Entrancing, beautiful. Loving. And everyone there seemed to be on a similar wavelength. They were just lovely people who were sincerely looking for the spiritual dimension in their lives, even if they weren't quite aware of it yet. From then on, one thing led to another.'

Fran and her husband moved up to the hills. She knew there were adoptions happening: that adults were being assigned children who would then often disappear. Then, Fran says, Anne phoned her and told her to go the Royal Women's Hospital in Melbourne. "Frances," she said — she always called me Frances — "your little baby Jamie has arrived. Now jump in a taxi and go off to the Women's Hospital, and ask for Nurse such and such, and there he will be."'

Fran didn't think twice. To her, nothing was wrong because the nice people in The Family who had jobs and a good education and spoke so well and were so kind ... they were all doing it.

When Fran arrived, the baby was in an incubator. 'I just fell in love with that baby at first sight. He was beautiful, very little, and he kept on trying to pull out his tube, and I thought, *What a determined little guy, I really love that; he's just perfect for me.*'

The baby had to stay in hospital for a while. The nurses taught Fran how to feed and bathe him. The doctor who delivered him was a member of The Family, as were the social workers organising the adoption. She was told that his parents were English migrants who had split up. Fran's husband was surprised, but went along with it. 'I took him home, and I was just so happy. He was gorgeous. He started growing up, and he was a playful little boy. He used to sit in the car seat beside me — they didn't have capsules in those days — and he'd be laughing happily, and we'd look at things out of the window, and we got closer and closer.'

Her cult friends told Fran about Newhaven and about Anne being a version of Jesus. 'These beautiful, clever, wonderful people had literally experienced ecstasy, they had seen her glorified with beautiful light around her, an exquisite spiritual angelic sort of ecstasy, and they would also have seen hideous, ugly things about themselves.' She believed them. But: 'We didn't think of ourselves as a cult,' says Fran. 'I mean — that would have been ridiculous.'

Soon her husband was put into Newhaven. Their marriage was in trouble and he was unhappy. Fran got the sense that he was being pushed away from her because he was defiant at times and stood up to Anne. He was beginning to be viewed as a liability rather than someone who could be easily moulded. Fran resisted LSD herself, so she wasn't in the inner circle. She was operating in a sort of vacuum.

She and her husband eventually split up. Anne encouraged the split and told her it was for the best and that she had a safety net in The Family. 'She said, "Don't worry too much about your future. You stay with that little boy. You'd look after him, whatever would happen, [even] if you had to live in a room." I said, "Yes, I would." And she said, "Don't worry, darling, you won't have to do that."'

For Fran, this was the moment she realised she was in too deep, but to turn back would be to deny the promise and the hope that had been offered. 'We were destined to have her for our Teacher. We could either follow the path, or else know that this wonderful thing had happened and we'd rejected it.'

Fran also saw the feeling around the cult change from 'love and light' to a new seriousness. Newhaven was increasingly being used a threat: Anne reportedly warned many that if they didn't do as they were told she would have them interred and left there. 'Anyone who hadn't gone happily along and had marvellous experiences under the drug ... I used to think, *How can I be so reluctant, look at these wonderful people who are so intelligent, they're so professional, they're so loving, and they're people without any really bad habits or cruelties about them. They're just a bunch of great people.* How could I have these doubts? You were made to feel ashamed of yourself if you had any doubts.'

Fran went to Newhaven under duress, and the psychiatrists tried to weaken her by using emotional triggers. 'They'd sit at the end of the bed, and they'd try to goad me, or they'd get me emotional about how unhappy I was. This was just so contrived, and I just said straight out — "I have never seen myself as a yogi or a saint. I want a spiritual dimension to my life, I want to live a good, loving life." I was brought up as a Christian, I said, but I don't see myself as going further than that.'

Fran had drawn a line in the sand, outwitted the psychiatrists, and resisted LSD. So Anne betrayed her by painting her, in cult circles, as a chronic liar.

Fran found out later that the same trick had been pulled on other women in the group. She saw Anne try to break their spirit on the way towards total submission. 'She wasn't giving love — she was offering it and then taking it back.'

Fran had agreed to let John take their adopted son, Jamie, to England. He was English and she consented to letting the boy meet his father's family. Fran's new daughter — born after Jamie, to her husband, before they split up — was being looked after by relatives. Fran began studying nursing under Anne's orders, including a stint working at a Melbourne hospital, a strategy on her part to remain safe and stable until she could properly escape and get what she wanted: her child, her son.

'Of course I was heartbroken about my little children, being with different people to be looked after. My life had turned out to be very, very, different from the life that I'd wanted to work for and to be a family. That had been taken, but thank God it didn't break my spirit. The real pain was the pain of not being able to protect him, to be with him, to take care of him. The pain was that he needed me and I couldn't get there. It was loving him that spurred me on to finish the nursing and get through, because I kept feeling within me that I would get him back. I would get him back. And that's why I could just keep on, keep on.'

She finished her nursing stint, passed her exams, and called Anne. "Oh darling, you've finished your nursing," she said, "and I hear you came second in the state. What do you want to do now?" I said, "I want to go and see Jamie in England." "Oh, I don't think it's time for that," she said. "No, no, no, no. You'll see him, though." So I just went home and I waited.' Fran would see Jamie again, but not for some time.

While Lex de Man and his detective were probing the UK connections of the cult — and hearing about Trish's central role in it — detectives in Melbourne were taking a fresh look at a curious and seemingly suspicious case at Newhaven from the 1970s.

Kevin Storey worked on the tools at Melbourne's shipyards, as a fitter and turner. He was 49 in 1975, when he died in Newhaven. He had been admitted twice before with depression after his father died. He was given numerous rounds of ECT and a milder version of deep-sleep therapy — called narcotherapy in the 1970s — with sodium amatyl.

Storey's nurses were Trish MacFarlane and Barbara Kibby. They considered him gentle and unassuming. He had a single room on the top floor of the grand old building, and he had brought in his own cassette player for his long stays, of up to four weeks at a time, to play classical music: Brahms and Beethoven. He was a compulsive diary-writer, and entries around this time, his wife told us, have just one word: 'nervy'.

Storey didn't like the ECT — sometimes known then as shock therapy — because it made him drowsy and vague and unsteady on his feet. He started feeling worse; he became suicidal. He was put on a heavy program of narcotherapy, where a patient is dosed to the point of almost being asleep, but not beyond.

Storey's doses were every other day. His wife visited him on his rest days and found him uncoordinated to the point where he couldn't open his tobacco tin. Trish or Barbara sat beside his bed while he slept; a psychiatrist came in and out. Late in the month on one of these two-day cycles, Barbara Kibby came into his room one morning and found him dead.

To the great surprise of the Storey family's funeral director, there was no autopsy on the body to find out how he died. His wife was told he had a heart attack.

Then, 17 years later, as Forest was hearing testimony from Peter Kibby and Trish MacFarlane, the Citizens Commission on Human Rights, the Scientologists' anti-psychiatry sleuths who built up the dossier on Howard Whitaker, started digging into Storey's death. To them, it spoke loudly of extreme psychiatric practice with sodium amatyl causing death. They told the state coroner and Operation Forest what they had found out, and the coroner re-opened the case. Forest detectives couldn't find records of Mr Storey's time in Newhaven, even in an off-site storage facility where they had found other hospital documents.

Operation Forest began re-interviewing everyone involved in the Storey case. The coroner had asked the Forest taskforce specifically because of the hospital's link to The Family. Police called in the psychiatrist who had been treating Mr Storey. He was grilled by detectives and denied injecting Storey.

But there were other curious circumstances. Mr Storey's wife said she was told that Newhaven would cover the funeral costs. Barbara and Trish went to the Storey home to deliver flowers. Mr Storey's 1975 diary went missing, never to be found.

The coroner had these snippets, but little else to go on.

The death was 17 years earlier. He didn't place much stock in Trish's evidence: she was deemed an unreliable witness because she had told a few different versions of events.

The verdict that Storey died from heart disease stood. It was a classic red herring: a case of cult-related suspicions around Newhaven leading to police following a blind path.

The Family had also been linked with the coroner's court not long before, in 1988, after the raid at Uptop but before any significant police investigation into the children's claims against members of The Family. This one was even weirder.

Michael had a sister, Cypra. Cypra died in strange circumstances that year, aged 37: she was found naked on a footpath in the suburb of Toorak, where the family home was located, after apparently falling from the third floor of a car park. Cypra was a wild bohemian, but troubled. She was never in the cult, but skirted it. Former cult members think she was schizophrenic.

A coroner ruled her death a suicide because she left a suicide note and was suffering from depression. But Michael's brother, John Helmer, an investigative journalist who has spent much of his career based in Moscow, challenged the finding. He tried to have the case re-opened, in 2010, claiming his sister was being aggressively courted by the cult and that the investigation into her death was shoddy.

John Helmer's legal action failed, and the coronial finding stayed as it was, but he established, representing himself in the Supreme Court, that the coroner's signature on the original coronial finding had likely been forged 'by person or person's unknown at the Coroners Court'.

According to Anthony Leigh — Michael's adopted son and Cypra's beloved nephew — Cypra made a lot of noise about Uptop. He told us that when he was 12 he started telling her what it was like and she started talking around town about it. He considered Cypra his 'surrogate mother'. His brother Jerome had been through Uptop and had told him stories.

He told Cypra everything he knew. 'The kids weren't theirs, they'd beat them, they abused them, they put their heads in a cold water bucket, they fuckin' didn't feed them properly, they fed them rotten fruit, and so on, and so forth.'

Cypra, he says, was his friend and protector, as much as she could be: 'We were very close, [she was a] very beautiful lady, crazy as a cut snake.' She was shocked by what she was told and started talking to Nana and Papa. Papa had already tried to extract Michael from the cult. 'The truth was that Papa had engaged a private investigator to investigate the sect,' says Anthony, 'and the goings-on in regards to his son. So Jerome was removed from the sect house in Eildon.' He went to live with Michael, and Anthony.

Michael says Cypra was pushed off the carpark roof because she wouldn't have jumped herself. 'I think there was foul play,' says Michael, 'but not like what John thought. I don't think she jumped off the building. She didn't quite have enough courage to jump. So a friend pushed her. That was the foul play. She wasn't schizophrenic or depressed but she was a bit psychotic. I think it came from having a couple of abortions. She was a beautiful person. She was very interested in what I was doing, but she didn't want to hurt Mum and Dad. I don't know if she told anyone about the abortions, but I know about them. It was all locked up inside her and she heard voices telling her how terrible she was. She used to drink and take drugs to try and stop the voices. See, I was closer to her than John. Cypra and I were very close. John was away studying. It took years for it to come out of me. Anne would say 20 years later, "You have never got over your sister dying, have you?"'

Cypra sang in a rock-and-roll band with famous Australian musician Lobby Loyde and worked during the day as a postie, delivering mail. A friend of hers from university days told us: 'She was outspoken, she was very confident, she had long hair. She would wear a fur coat and wear her hair over her fur coat; she was very glamorous. She believed in the *I Ching*. She was odd. What touched me about her was on one hand she was intimidating and angry — *fuck the government* — but when it came to me and I was confused about something, she was very nice.'

University students were drawn into the Newhaven vortex too; it had become a thing for them to go in, take LSD, and have a chat to a therapist. Cypra's friend had just finished university and was working as a teacher. Someone she knew who was depressed had gone in and got treatment, and it sounded all right to her. She didn't know it was a cult headquarters.

The first time she attended Newhaven, a doctor gave her psilocybin and then LSD by injection, but she soon realised it was a seduction attempt by the cult. 'I came close to the devil. I don't believe in hell, I don't believe in anything like that, but they were evil, and I had no idea at the time because I was totally naïve.'

Michael laughs at this. He laughs at a lot of things people say about the cult, 'The Brotherhood'. He doesn't believe in the devil either, and laughs at the suggestion that Anne was — is — the devil. 'All the great beings have entered into the Christ consciousness to a greater or lesser extent. It's a great state of being. It's not a person as such, it's a consciousness. And you'll see a lot of the great beings have touched upon that, and have entered into it. What Jesus was saying was that he's one with the Universal Consciousness. Different religions put it in other words, but it's all the same.'

Michael is an incredible contradiction. Why did he walk away from his family, one of the most prominent Jewish families in

Australia? He says he has not rejected anything, and even though he has worshipped in The Family, he is still a Jew. 'There is a wonderful power of living in Jewish people. I am very proud of that. This is why they are wonderful musicians, philosophers. That is the greatness of the eternal flame.'

Yet he thinks Anne is possessed of the same purity that Jesus had. And because of that, she joins the ranks of the 'great beings' — Jesus, Buddha, Mohammed, Ghandi — who have lived on Earth, or at least are reported to have lived on Earth. 'One of the first things Anne said to me was, "Michael, if you were meant to be Indian you would have been born Indian, dear. But you were born here as a Jew so you have to come to terms with who you are."'

He has had two weddings during his time in The Family and three children, one of whom wasn't biologically his — Anthony, who has been called Johnny. He is in touch with all of his children and, from time to time, his former wives. He has helped Anthony through addictions to prescription and illicit drugs.

Anne has helped Anthony too, in her own odd way. He first met her when he was a boy of six. She pronounced him her godson. He spent time at Broom Farm in a big cult mob in the 1970s. Now, he has the vulnerable air of an ex-addict: jittery and tattooed. 'She had that aura — even then I remember thinking, as a kid, she had an aura about her. The awe that she struck among her followers, if you like, was palpable. She was a redhead, and I mean very red, a striking, striking woman. Amazing eyes, eyes that looked through your soul.'

In 1999, Anthony was at the height of his addiction and crashed his car late one night on the fringe of Melbourne's sprawling suburbs. Anthony has written about it in his life story, which, at 120,000 words, is longer than most novels. He shared it with us.

Smash, crash, lights flashing, the thought that I am not ready to die yet; I am all of a sudden aware of how I have been on a path of suicide for months. All of a sudden the car stops. I look over and there is [my friend] John, unconscious but having some obvious problems breathing.

I jumped out of the car and for some reason threw the bonnet off the car. We were off the road a good couple of hundred meters. I went to check on John.

We were in the middle of no where [sic]; there were no street lights and I was off the road behind trees in a paddock. I had to run from the car to the road trying to flag down a passing vehicle through tall grass black berries and undergrowth. I ran back and forth checking that John was still breathing. I had no luck in getting a car to stop; finally I stood in the middle of the road until a car stopped and he luckily had a mobile phone; I had my mobile stolen only the day before.

An emergency helicopter flew John to a big hospital in central Melbourne. Anthony went to another hospital in an ambulance. He was told that John was close to death. 'I can remember the police coming in and asking a few questions; but the only comment I can recall was that one of the cops told me that I had not even braked and the car had become airborne as it left the road.' John did not survive.

Anthony's natural father — a member of The Family — took him in for a while and then made him go and stay in a motel. According to Anthony, this was when Michael rescued him. 'He took over, you know. It had been a week, by that time. And he'd found I was in the motel, and he said, "Bullshit," and he took me up to his house in the hills. And so I started staying there, and went into hiding.'

Then, the insane part. According to Anthony, Michael and Anne raised $AU3,000 for him. They wanted him to fly to Paris and join the French Foreign Legion. There was a hotel room waiting, booked. 'Get a new name, and new identity, and so on and so forth, so that was the plan, and I went off to do that,' says Anthony.

He was robbed twice in Paris as he tried to find the fort where the Foreign Legion did recruiting. But he found the place — Fort de Nogent — in eastern Paris and started to fill out forms to join. When they asked for a drug history, though, he was honest. 'Of course the French Foreign Legion wouldn't have me,' he says, 'because I had the worst drug history in the world, and at that time they weren't taking drug addicts because they didn't need any canon fodder.' He was thrown out of the fort.

'So off to Amsterdam I went. I get on the phone to Anne and she says, "That's okay, do what you like. When you're ready, go to the farm in England, and give us a call and we'll see you then." When I finally shot the Channel to England, I had 20 quid to my name.'

Anthony found himself back at Broom Farm again, in the bosom of the cult. He has always been in and out, too wise to dive in but too comfortable to break away completely. He fell between the cracks of what might have been a secure life, a surrogate family who were not his family, and the cult.

'I personally have had dealings with the leader, Mrs Hamilton-Byrne through out all my life,' he wrote in his long manuscript. 'She claims to be my God Mother as well as [the] reincarnation of Christ. The dreams that I can remember reflect the scared little boy who was trying to get along in an alien world all alone.'

After the raid, Michael became the cult's gatekeeper — literally. He shooed *Age* journalist David Elias away from the gate at Santiniketan Lodge many times, marching down the long gravel driveway in the forest with a torch. 'I realised he [the journalist] wanted to belong,' said Michael. 'If only he could come in and see. Everybody wants to belong to something meaningful.' He kept telling us as we were preparing this book that he didn't mind talking to us because we were non-confrontational and interested in detail beyond the salacious. But Michael's reputation with ex-cult members and the children from Uptop — even though he never went there — is as a difficult man who is complicit in the cult's methods.

We had seen one small illustration of this. In 2009, when *Sixty Minutes* were allowed into Crowther House with Sarah, ostensibly to see Anne, Michael was there, sitting out of the camera's frame. When the interview with the elderly Anne became aggressive, he stepped in, waving his arms around frantically and berating the television reporter.

But Michael wanted to talk to us, and talk he did, many times, for many hours, usually at tea rooms or cafes up in the hills, or at his house. He wasn't so friendly in the beginning, and until he decided he wanted to meet us he would often not answer his phone, or answer it and not say anything, or give a few brief responses and then hang up. But ultimately he was generous with his time. He opened the lodge for us; he showed us to Anne's bedside. He has a studio under the house where he used to sell paintings, and he even gave us two each — paintings of our auras. After we were given the first of our paintings, we thanked him, and asked why our gifts? He said he was into giving things away and not transferring art from person to person in a 'commercial' way. 'Life can be full of these moments: momentous surprises, in a way miraculous,' he said. 'It is living in the moment, it is intuition, the language of the heart, and images are the language of the heart, whereas words and intellect are the language of the mind.'

One day we were talking about the Lodge. We started talking

about what the land might be worth. Michael shut us down. He said there was no point talking about money. 'What's the land of the Catholics worth? Or the Anglicans? Billions! With my paintings, I realised when I got out of commercial worlds they got better. A certain way of living is money-free. We relate everything to money. But it is false. You can't take it with you, and it lets you down when you most need it. If you want to have a short-term way of working out the truth of a guru, it is whether they charge. Once you start charging, you open yourself up to a very rapid downward spiral.'

But, we said, somewhat incredulous, Anne asked for money. She appeared to love money. 'No. Anne didn't ask for money. Anne often worked out people's inheritances or things that came with money. A lot of people think she wanted all the money for herself, but Anne doesn't need money. This is the grievance. Sex and money are most of the reasons why people leave a spiritual group; mostly money. But Anne is independent with money. And I know a lot more than you think I know.'

He's also convinced Uptop was, in the main, a good idea. He doesn't believe the children's stories of what happened there, and attributes any problems to overtired Aunties. 'There were disciplinarian things that came out of the weakness of the two ladies, Elizabeth [Liz Whitaker] and Pat [Trish MacFarlane]. I wouldn't have liked to have been on the backhand of Pat, a tough bird. They loved Anne, fantastic ladies, but chronic tiredness does things to people. Kids are exuberant and demand even-handedness and that goes out the window. People don't know what's gone on. They only know what's been written in the papers.

'I had one son up there — and he hates the thought of it but he is well because of it. He is a strong, great person. Compassionate, kind, physically well, and I believe his basic structure was created in those years that he was there.'

Back in the police forensics building in Winchester, Trish MacFarlane was unloading. She had lost furniture, she said, from the house she shared with John Mackay. She told them everything she knew, and she felt better afterwards. 'I feel a different person,' she told the detectives, at the end of her interviews. 'Much freer, and at peace.'

The detectives showed her three notebooks, Lex recalls. One outlined the daily Uptop routine, from dawn til dark. The other two were 'Mummy's Rules' and 'Nanny's Laws'. These volumes included Anne's handwritten instructions about how to treat the children; they were The Family law.

The Uptop Aunties also had a cashbook and a weights-and-measures book, which were kept in a kitchen drawer, Trish told Lex. The latter was a lined school exercise book where the weights of the children — especially the girls — were recorded. Trish told Lex that Anne always wanted the girls to be slim, despite being 'tubby' on occasion herself, and was 'phobic' about their weight. Three of the kids — two girls and a boy — were very small. One was the child Lex had discovered had psychosocial short stature. Anne's rule was that height had to relate to weight, so if a girl or a boy was short, he or she must also be skinny. The rulebook stipulated quarter-serves of dinner and weights in pounds that must be lost by the time of the next measure.

The detectives were interested in the incident where the boy from the cult was in the Uptop bathroom with Leon. Lex has revealed to us they found reference to the event in 'Nanny's Laws'. The evidence is a single piece of foolscap paper, handwritten by Liz Whitaker and dated June 1983. Parts of it were covered over with blue texta — homemade redacting. The incident was described as being an outburst from the boy, who was taken upstairs to the bathroom by Leon Dawes. Lex says the phrase 'thrown to the floor in judo hold' was covered by the blue texta, but he was able to still make out the words.

Another page, according to Lex, described a phone conversation between a cult member and Anne about the incident. He said it read, in part, that the boy was to be left alone in future and that 'another turn could be fatal'. However, it said another child was free to be slapped across the face for being naughty.

Trish also fleshed out details of Anne's strange pregnancy in 1975, which Peter Kibby had begun to describe. Anne had told Trish she had a hysterectomy, but then she was suddenly, apparently, pregnant. Police now believe the pregnancy in question was fake, and that the child Anne told everyone she had given birth to was in fact born to John Mackay's new partner and future wife, Olivier: the woman who takes Anne's dirty laundry from the nursing home and returns it clean, to this day.

Trish had one more nugget, recalls Lex. Just after the Uptop raid, at 2.00 am, she was at home, over the road from the Lodge. She heard cars going in: the clanging of the gates, the tyres on the gravel. She crept over in her nightgown to have a look and she saw three men digging holes and burying black plastic bags. They spotted her and told her to go home and mind her own business. Lex says Trish told him the three were 'close-lipped types' within the cult, the type of men who would never tell secrets.

PART THREE

9

HURLEYVILLE

Where was she? Where was Anne? The Santiniketan Lodge had been bugged and photographed — detectives lying in the dirt in the hills, hidden by trees and undergrowth, snapping cars, identifying who owned them — and while this was all useful intelligence for police, the cult's central figure was nowhere to be seen. Her properties in Melbourne were under surveillance, her passport details on high alert, but there was no sign of her.

The Operation Forest detectives returned to Australia from the United Kingdom in late January 1991, having secured Trish MacFarlane's full testimonies: about the properties, the LSD trips, the 'Uptop way', the allegedly bogus pregnancy. They also had a sense of her great sadness, and the way she seemed to have been both victimised and unceremoniously ripped off. Trish had given Lex de Man a list of 99 adults involved with the cult, providing as much detail as she could about them. Lex told his bosses back in Melbourne that Trish had detailed her 20 years of involvement with The Family, from her first meeting with Anne to Trish's short-lived partnership with John Mackay, and all the alleged misdeeds she knew about with kids and houses. As a result of her testimony and the investigations it sparked, Lex was able to list 11 people who could be charged, including Anne and Bill Hamilton-Byrne, Peter Kibby, Leon Dawes, and Liz and Howard Whitaker.

Lex's bosses heard that, pending legal advice from the Director of Public Prosecutions, Anne could potentially be charged with perjury, creating false birth records, conspiracy to breach adoption laws, false imprisonment, assault, obtaining property by deception, and charges relating to LSD.

While in the United Kingdom, the detectives had met Scotland Yard extradition-squad police to prepare for the possibility that Anne and Bill might be arrested at Broom Farm and would have to be sent back to Australia for trial. No charges had been laid; it was a speculative act by police. Yet the walls were closing in on Anne. The FBI was also briefed about her home in the Catskills and her hideout in Hawaii, should she appear there.

Hurleyville, northwest of New York, in the fabled Catskill Mountains and near Woodstock, is a hamlet within the town of Fallsburg. It's beautiful there; the seasons are distinct and clear, not unlike at Lake Eildon in central Victoria. The colours are the same. Hurleyville's Kiamesha Lake is still and quiet, bordered by trees. It's misty, like Lake Eildon, in the right season. Narrow, shaded roads wind around it.

Here US flags fly from silos and rooftop poles. It was once called the 'Borscht Belt': each year, summer resorts filled with wealthy New York Jews. It has become a Hasidic Jewish area, with cows and hayrolls in the paddocks between dandelions. The bridges are covered, as they are in neighbouring New England. Hurleyville used to be a stop on an old US mail route.

Police knew Anne had a house here, a white-timber, twin-gabled spread with lattice windows, set on 40 hectares.

The property also held two other houses. She bought it in the late 1970s — 1977 or so. Just nearby was Swami Muktananda's East Coast ashram, and she was a regular there. In 1978, she took a collection of cult children from Uptop to visit him, and they all stayed at the Hurleyville house.

The swami, according to former devotee Joan Radha Bridges of New York, was devastatingly charismatic. Joan now publishes online articles as a 'guru-buster', but she was a Muktananda disciple from 1974 until 1982.

'When you were around him, he could just completely suck you in,' she told us. 'And if he looked into your eyes, he could give you experiences. When he would give "an intensive", it was called, people would sit in meditation and he'd go around and swat you with this big peacock-feather wand, which was supposed to be, you know, very magical-powered. And he would awaken the kundalini, which is the spiritual force.'

She joined what was called his 'tour', travelling in a coterie to his ashrams. 'It was completely blissful. Addictive. I wanted to be around him all the time, and so did everyone. And people got nasty about it. If you weren't in the in-crowd and you were new, you were shunned, essentially. As I was around longer and longer, I was allowed to sit up front [with the in-crowd] sometimes.

'The women sat on one side of his meetings and men sat on the other. Which was kind of unusual, but that was supposedly about an energy thing. And also that the men wouldn't get distracted. But it was Muktananda that was getting distracted.'

Muktananda set up an ashram in Melbourne, and, after visiting Santiniketan Lodge in 1975, called it, according to Michael (who was with him), the most peaceful place on earth. This was when he sat on Anne's special chair. 'When Anne came back and sat there again, she said she could still feel his energy,' Michael says.

'His was a more virile energy. Hers was more mythical.'

Muktananda was a constant presence in The Family's life. When Howard Whitaker last saw Anne, for example, after he had agreed to meet his ex-wife Liz outside the Muktananda ashram in Melbourne, Anne was walking a row of children from the cult in the door: 'A troupe of kids dressed in blue with long blonde hair, and they all marched in, in a group,' Whitaker told Lex. 'I guess those are the children that have been referred to.'

But by the time of the 1978 visit to his ashrams in Hawaii and Fallsburg, Anne was said to be trying to bring Muktananda down in a snide power struggle. Although he was someone she professed to adore and in whose teachings she schooled all her children and followers, ultimately she appeared to want his power base. He had thousands, millions, of adherents, including celebrities. It was as if she thought she could be the one true Master, a voice for all the seekers, not only those in Melbourne.

'That was a really interesting thing,' says Sarah. 'She really got herself involved there to the extent where she sponsored Muktananda before he became kind of famous. When he became mega-famous and that organisation Siddha Yoga [which he formed] ... they had lots and lots of money. She really insinuated herself very far into it.'

Sarah had loved Muktananda. She went on several missions with Anne and the other children to visit him. After one trip, she came back to Uptop and built a makeshift shrine to him in the garden, but the Aunties dismantled it. Sarah thought Anne really respected him. But the relationship between the Australian cult leader and the Indian swami was a very strange one. Joan thinks Muktananada never took Anne seriously, and it seems clear to us from the accounts we have heard that Anne, while keen on his spiritual writings, was opportunistic in her pursuit of him and his fanbase.

'The aura of love and compassion and stuff that was around him seemed quite different from the hypocrisy that was around her,' says Sarah. 'I think she solely saw that it was an opportunity for power and money and went for it and managed to cause havoc as usual.'

In all, five Uptop kids travelled to the ashrams. Muktananda got around his ashram compounds in a golf buggy and would give the children rides. 'He loved us children and treated us specially,' says Leeanne, who also went on the trips. One lasted three months.

The swami was getting older and sicker when the children met him and when Anne put him in her sights, and despite allegations of sexual abuse that would later surface in regard to Muktananda, the children felt safe with him and called him Baba. He gave them gifts, they gave him poems and letters; he asked if they wanted to go and live in his ashram in India. But Anne controlled their contact — perhaps because they liked him so much, and felt happy in his company. Sarah was punished for writing a poem to him without Anne's permission.

He offered a sort of sanctuary, even though he would be accused of hideous crimes after his death. 'He offered us a spiritual solace,' Sarah wrote in her book. 'A refuge from the harsh reality of the world in which we lived.'

Anouree went to visit him too, and she loved the chanting. 'It was a very relaxing, calming experience, actually. It was quite a meditative experience. So in a way it worked out quite well for me. It was a good experience to just see a bit more of the world than Eildon had offered.'

The children were given new spiritual names for the duration of their visits: Jahadeva, Mirabai, Barati, Kanti, Luksme. They ate Indian food at the swami's house and went swimming and shopping. They also went sightseeing, like tourists. In the evenings, they would change into clothes Anne had bought in England and listen to Muktananda preach.

One day, after 'bopping' Leeanne with his peacock feather, he told her he had a dream that Anne had been beating her. 'I thought, *Will I tell him or won't I that she does do that?*' She decided against it. 'When I got home, Anne said to me, "Well, what was that all about?" I didn't want to tell her, and to this day I never told her, but because of that she beat me so badly that I could hardly move. I was black and blue all over. She beat me with a stiletto shoe, she beat me with a whip, anything she could get her hands on. She had me on the floor, beating me.'

Joan was there in 1978, in Fallsburg, when Anne began her bitter power struggle with the swami. She was taken aback by Anne — the bewigged Australian 'Master' — and her troupe of odd kids. 'I got this sense that Anne was there to get power from Muktananda, and Muktananda was there to show up Anne. He gave her the name "Ma Yoga Shakti", which means "the great mother Shakti". It was like he was making a joke out of her.'

Anne looked wealthy, like the kind of person who would never get her hands dirty, says Joan. 'Muktananda was trying to impress all of the kids. In a way, probably trying to pull them away from Anne.' However, it was Anne who was often given the prized reward of being allowed to sit at Muktananda's feet during his sermons.

At the ashram, Anne was allowed to set up a clinic, dispensing homeopathic medicines and, according to Sarah, LSD. 'I think Anne's design for being with Muktananda was to figure out how he did what he did,' Joan told us. 'But she just had a few followers. And I think that Anne was jealous. I mean, she wanted to be — you know, she was the messiah, she should be followed by all these beautiful people. Because everybody was always dressed to the nines, especially in the meditation hall. And that would be right up her alley, to be followed by all these beautiful people that were willing to do all this work for her, or do what she said.'

The turning point came a year or so before Muktananda's death — he died in 1982 — when the first whispers of sexual abuse at the ashram surfaced. Another swami, Abhayananda, whose real name is Stan Trout and who, like Joan, has become a 'guru-buster', left the Muktananda faction and moved into Anne's house in Hurleyville. Trout was the one at the forefront of the allegations against the swami. Joan thinks Anne helped Trout spread the allegations about Muktananda to undermine him.

Joan didn't trust Anne from the start but couldn't put her finger on why. 'I felt a darkness from Anne.' She was into the occult, as was Muktananda: 'I know that Muktananda practised black magic.' Joan believes that Anne wanted to learn about such things from him. 'To be around him, to learn more about it. I mean, she had that kind of vibe about her, like you read about people in the early 1900s when they were doing séances.' Joan didn't know at the time that Anne was considered the earthly reincarnation of Jesus to her followers, but figured out that her teachings were 'a hodgepodge of Christianity, and Hinduism, and black magic'.

Anne acquired a lock of Muktananda's hair at the Catskills ashram to cast occult spells, Joan says. All the while, she was being trailed by a group of children from Uptop. The girls had 'identical, fluffy, ruffly dresses, and they all had blonde hair, of course. And it was all pulled up with giant bows in their hair. So, I mean, when you saw them coming it was hard to miss. I always got this impression that she was, like, this spider with all these little baby spiders. It was one of the strangest things.'

After Muktananda died, the full allegations emerged from former devotees. They were numerous. He was accused of preying on young female students in his Fallsburg ashram and of spying

203

on girls in their ashram dorms. He was also accused of condoning violence and having guns in his ashram. Claims were made that he squirrelled away in Swiss banks the large fees he charged for his services. Later still, *The New Yorker* reported claims that he had raped adult women devotees. Joan Rahda Bridges told us she was raped by Swami Muktananda.

The year Anne was reportedly trying to usurp Muktananda at his own ashram, she married Bill, back in Melbourne. Trish MacFarlane was the matron of honour. They tied the knot in a church in the hills in front of a small crowd — a dozen people, at the most. Leon Dawes was Bill's best man, and John Mackay was said to be there too. No Hamilton-Byrne children were at the ceremony.

Dr Raynor Johnson, Anne's key enabler, entered old age. In 1978, he found he could no longer drive. He was 77. He stopped writing in his diary that year too. His final entries are downbeat and frightened; he was convinced the world would soon end.

In a section of his diary headed 'The Master's Work and the Future', Johnson wrote that 'towards the close of 1978' Anne's progress was in its 'early-middle stages' but might not come to anything. He expressed it in terms of the seasons — 'the seed is being sown and germinating here and there in a few lives. Will it survive a hot parched summer? Will a few ears of corn ripen to provide the seed for future generations to sow and reap a distant harvest?'

He noted again that she worked best in secret: unseen, unheard, unknown.

His final diary entry was apocalyptic. By now he had been studying ecology and extraterrestrial lifeforms for some years. His final written words about the woman who rang his doorbell in 1962 indicate that it was all over, or would be soon, and only Anne, The Master, could be the saviour. 'The immediate years look full of menace,' he wrote. 'It has been indicated to us that time is running out, and that in the absence of a new spirit, based on love and wisdom, this civilisation will close in tragedy with the end of the century. The Master alone holds the strategic master-plan for the remaining years. THE END.'

His old Methodist allies — forged in Leeds and London before he arrived in Australia and met Anne — had long cut him loose. He was considered too esoteric, too strange. 'There were mumblings about whether or not something should be done about him,' says former student Ian Weeks. Weeks' father, an eminent Methodist, reportedly advised Johnson to retire from the University of Melbourne early, before he was charged by the church with heresy.

Not long published was one of Johnson's last scholarly articles — in *Light* magazine. It was about the end of the Age of Pisces wherein Earth did not have enough resources to feed all the people. Presciently, he talked about climate change, nuclear weapons, and terrorism. One of his main points was that nuclear fission — an area in which he had worked, with Ernest Rutherford — was unnatural and therefore wrong. He also talked about anthrax and antibiotic resistance.

Johnson also went on a lecture tour in the United Kingdom, describing himself now as a 'practical mystic' and warning repeatedly of a nuclear error. During the trip, he was taken around his old childhood haunts and thought for a moment or two that he and Mary might change their minds and retire to the English countryside after all, rather than the hills of the Dandenongs.

But he returned to Australia. He wrote another book — *Light of All Life: a study of mysticism in life* — but his publisher declined it, and then a year later, in 1980, he was diagnosed with dementia. Johnson was soon lost in that same corridor of split-second, fleeting images that Anne now finds herself in.

He and Mary got a telegram from the Queen on their 60th wedding anniversary, just before he went into a nursing home in the hills. He died a short time before Uptop was raided and the children he had touted as a future race were freed. He is buried in a tiny cemetery, in the hills.

By 1991, Operation Forest was closer to Anne than ever, but they were also in crisis. The white noise around Victoria Police and their pitched gun battles with armed robbers — which may well have been a factor in siphoning police resources from the very earliest investigations into The Family after the raid — had come back louder and stronger.

Four underworld heavies had been charged with killing two young policemen in Melbourne in 1988, in an apparent payback for police shooting dead a known armed robber named Graeme Jensen, who had popped out to buy a spark plug for his lawnmower as police surrounded his car. He was, allegedly, armed.

The four men were found not guilty of the police shootings in March 1991. Allegations were raised that the police who shot Jensen had planted a weapon in his car to justify killing him. A detective on the scene of the shooting was later found to be a corrupt drug-trafficker. A coroner — the same coroner who looked into the questionable Kevin Storey death at Newhaven — didn't buy it. 'There was suspicion and assertion expressed in the inquest that the sawn-off .22 calibre rifle and two .22 calibre bullets had been planted there by police,' the coroner said. However, 'it is hard to envisage anything like those events unless Jensen had possession of a gun which had been seen by police members.'

A senior ex-homicide and armed robbery squad cop, Detective Senior Sergeant John Hill, was asked to investigate the Jensen shooting. Then, in the winter of 1991, Peter Spence signalled he wanted to leave Operation Forest and go back to his old job. John Hill was appointed his replacement.

Spence had become increasingly frustrated at the scant resources given to his team. But he was also confident by now that the taskforce he led would find Anne and charge her with a suite of serious offences.

Truth be told, when Spence's considered request for a Royal Commission into The Family — which would have brought with it coercive powers over witnesses — was turned down, he started to lose faith. 'I found it to be a most difficult time in my police career, just to actually have that conflict, being close to these great young kids. To actually have that connection, and not be able to do the absolute best for them.'

He was also aware of the emotional toll on the members of the taskforce. They were debriefing in the pub. 'There's no doubt that we used to do that occasionally, and drown our sorrows, get rid of these sorts of things that were creating the black dog, as they say.'

To add to the toll, one of Peter Kibby's sons had committed suicide after his father was arrested and charged. Both the Kibby boys were at Uptop for a time. 'Anne said, "I'll take care of your children," and she did — she took them,' says Barbara Kibby. 'She sent me away, she sent me over to England, and I was there for a year or so and then I came back and I had the children back. By the time I got the children back, they were both very damaged. It was catastrophic.' One had trouble speaking. 'David has no memory now of anything that happened to him before he was seven. Nothing.' His brother attempted suicide at 16 and succeeded at 20: an inconsolable sadness for Barbara and one that she still knows was largely because of the cult and Uptop.

Spence knew the taskforce was in good hands with Lex de Man and the other detectives, but deep down he felt that an appropriately thorough investigation would be blocked again. By who, he didn't know. 'It was purely and simply a matter of not being able to get the message through, and get approval right up to the top, to conduct an open, public inquiry. They didn't appreciate the gravity of the whole thing, despite having been totally and comprehensively briefed about all of the aspects of this case. I think it was that they had the power to say either yes or no. And they said no, we've got other things that we want to channel our efforts towards.'

The very nature of the investigation — that it was highly emotional and populated by vulnerable ex-cult children — was the common problem for the detectives. Spence broke his golden rule of policing, after all: he took work home, either literally or metaphorically. He, Lex, and others became very close to a number of the children, and still are. They wanted to save them, and then they wanted to show them how seriously they took it.

In the end, Spence simply lost hope. His had been a long police career; he had perhaps seen too much and knew too much. He left the taskforce and wished them well.

When Detective Senior Sergeant John Hill came in, Lex immediately saw Operation Forest hit some trouble internally. Lex had been there since day one, at the school fire, the event that marked the slight but at least encouraging efforts of police command to follow the case. He got Operation Forest set up in the first place. He was upset by the new uncertainty within it, despite the reams of testimony. 'When you worked for Peter, you knew you were working. He's a big gentle giant.'

The question Lex asked himself was, do I betray the code of the police, the brotherhood? 'I had to make a really conscious decision of whether I was prepared to put my career on the line and be, in today's parlance, the whistleblower, to get the taskforce back on track, or whether because of an individual's reputation and seniority, I was to remain silent.'

We asked Lex about Peter Kibby. He had broken the code of The Family. The group was also a brotherhood — this is what it had named itself in the beginning; Michael still calls it The Brotherhood. Codes within groups are what binds them. Kibby's actions were brave, says Lex. 'You've got to remember the motto: "Unseen, unheard, unknown". It was a very closed culture. He broke the code. He broke the code of silence within that sect.'

When Kibby appeared in court charged with falsifying the document that had originally led Lex and Spence to him, Lex appeared with him, to give a character reference. He was impressed with his moral compass and his honesty. 'In many ways, I look at Peter as someone who had the guts to actually stand up and say, "No, what we did was wrong, and I'm also prepared to tell the story, to stop others."'

Perhaps it was Kibby who helped inspire Lex to make his own tough decision. He went to the deputy commissioner of Victoria Police, the second-in-charge of the whole force. The next morning, he was appointed as the senior investigator on Operation Forest. The taskforce's office had been re-arranged.

The first thing he did was order six big whiteboards. 'I think it was half a dozen. I gave each offender a colour, a number; each child a colour; each series of events a number. And so we started to then plot out with the various children and the various offenders what the evidence gap was, to put a number of criminal briefs together. We ended up with — I think it was about 35,000 pages of evidence that we then had to distil into charges relating to Anne and William.'

Fran Parker was almost swallowed up by the cult, but she survived. Her little boy Jamie was gone, in England with his father. She wanted him back. She had studied nursing at Anne's request, hoping to be reunited with her son afterwards, but she was still waiting. Then she had a dream that the two of them were climbing a ladder together, with him sitting on her shoulders in order to be able to reach higher and keep climbing.

She kept talking to John, the boy's father, by phone, and she made one visit to the United Kingdom. John had distanced himself from the cult too, but had still been in thrall to Anne to the extent that he had taken the boy to the United Kingdom when she advised him to. But Fran wasn't sure about Jamie's status, that was the problem. To reclaim him, who was she to go to? Could she even do that? He wasn't her biological child. 'I thought, *I can't just run away and go to England and take him.* I can't be sure that someone else couldn't have a claim. That's why I had to put up with it all. It was like a hostage situation.'

She sat it out, remembering the sense of hope from the dream. Then through the goodwill of her relationship with John — a contrast to the way the cult manipulated children and custody and identity — she was able to go and get him by mutual agreement. 'It's an old-fashioned word, but John's a man of honour, and he didn't, any more than I did, want any unpleasantness or anger or unfairness. No custody battles; we just had to try to work things through, which we did finally, because Jamie really started missing home. Australia was home, and I was there. And John rang me and said, "He'll have to come back to you." So of course I dropped everything. Spent the last cent. And brought him home.

'So it did come through. I got him back.'

Through the Australian winter of 1992, as some in The Family or formerly of it were finding a way to have a life beyond, Anne and Bill were on the run. Operation Forest didn't know where they were. There were thoughts of trying to infiltrate the cult to find out, but surveillance was deemed enough.

'Where was Anne through this whole period?' asks Lex. 'We didn't know. We were told that Anne was in the UK. We were told that Anne was in the United States. We were told that Anne, for example, was in Hawaii.

'I'm sure through that period of the investigation, Anne came back into Australia and back out of Australia with Bill. But the technology in border security in those days was not like it is today. It was all manual. We didn't have the threat levels that you now have when you go through airports. It was a lot easier in those days to go in and out.'

Lex had never met Anne, but he felt like he had. He learned that she knew all about him too; by now she knew that he was running the taskforce. Word of Kibby's grand betrayal — and Trish's — had certainly reached her.

Lex desperately wanted to lay eyes on Anne. He wanted to see the kind of woman who could be responsible for the devotion, the blind love, the adoration she inspired in others, which he'd seen firsthand in the blue rooms. 'I thought: *Jeez, it would be nice to meet Jesus Christ.*'

Then she surfaced. In July 1992, Anne and Bill were monitored entering the United States at Newark, New Jersey, on a Continental flight. They gave their destination as Houghtaling Road: the Hurleyville house. They had visas until the following January. But then a month later they left again, and flew to Gatwick, London, heading for Broom Farm.

In early September, the Tunbridge Wells police got a phone call from Broom Farm's neighbours, saying they heard a child screaming outdoors in the early hours of the morning, 'I want my mummy'. British police went to the farm without a warrant and were refused entry. Anne and Bill were not there, they were told. So the police got a warrant and went back but found no children — although they did find baby food and a pram.

Lex and two detectives went back to Uptop. By now, adults involved with the cult were living on the property, but the key persons of interest were nowhere to be found. Leon Dawes went to America for a month, in August. Christabel Wallace had just also left Melbourne, for the United Kingdom.

Back in Melbourne, the police asked the Office of Public Prosecutions to give them advice on the potential extradition of Anne and Bill and what charges they could face in Victoria. Carolyn Douglas, then a Crown prosecutor but now a County Court judge, was given the brief. The potential charges she looked at included physical and emotional abuse of the children, perjury, providing false birth documents, false property documents, and false adoption documents.

But the perjury and forgery charges, she felt, could not be proven because she would need to rely on witnesses who were either still scared of Anne or would be deemed 'hostile witnesses' in court. 'They are like the Mafia,' says Douglas. 'You just know there are a lot of people involved who are not going to cooperate. They were cunning as all get-out.'

The decision was made to go ahead with charges of conspiracy to defraud the New Zealand authorities, and conspiracy to commit perjury, over the attempt to register the three children, including Sarah, as triplets. Anne had by 1984 registered two of them as twins in New South Wales. They were not twins, let alone triplets. Anne's intention was to use the fake birth certificates to apply for passports for them.

The allegations of 'continuous and very cruel' physical and emotional abuse, says Douglas, would be difficult to prove because there was no evidence available from anyone, except the children, who was there.

The advice from mental health experts was that the children were severely traumatised after being released from Uptop.

They had been housed together rather than being isolated to be interviewed about what they had witnessed and thus, prosecutors felt, lawyers for Anne and Bill could claim their evidence had been 'contaminated'. It was also felt that re-living their trauma in court while being cross-examined could cause them further harm.

Douglas also advised that extradition from the United Kingdom would fail because the charges were not extraditable there. However, if arrest warrants were issued, Interpol would go on high alert and Australian police would find out as soon as they left the United Kingdom — and the charges were extraditable from the United States.

The police would have loved to see Anne and Bill facing more-serious charges. But the risk was that the kids would front court and be called liars. 'We had to make a decision,' says Lex. 'We wanted to make sure these young people were able to progress in their lives, and some of them were going through some tough times, and to ask them to recount these experiences would most likely have done more psychological damage in the long term to these people than securing a conviction on those other charges.'

Where lies the truth? Each child had their version; everyone in this story has their version of the truth. Yet the children were never allowed to formally tell theirs beyond their statements to police.

The drugs charges relating to the LSD flowing from Newhaven — and the alleged administration of it to individuals as young as 14 — were near impossible to prove because police had to catch people in the act of administering it, and also be able to forensically test the drug to prove it was, in fact, LSD.

So the decision, in the end, was this: charge Anne with the crimes that can be proved with documentary evidence. Don't charge her with crimes that require the former children to give testimony. It was a huge compromise. It might amount to even more of a compromise if she had to be extradited, due to the complexities of international law. But the decision was made. And Anne — languishing in beaucolic Hurleyville with Bill, on her farm with up to 100 cats and dogs — was about to make a crucial mistake.

10

WHITE PLAINS

Sarah's phone rang in Melbourne at 8.30 pm. She picked up. It was Anne.

Anne loved the telephone. She had spent so much time in exile, running her group from afar, that it had always been her main means. Landlines crisscrossed between Hawaii, the United Kingdom, Hurleyville, and Melbourne. Sometimes, back in the Uptop days, after ordering punishments be given to particular children by the Aunties, she would allegedly want to hear the beatings being administered, over the phone.

But this call would be her undoing.

It was 27 May 1993 and, where Anne was, in hiding in Hurleyville, it was 6.30 am. Sarah was a medical student at the University of Melbourne — where the cult was galvanised in 1962 — on her way to becoming a doctor.

They chatted amiably. Sarah and Anne had been in infrequent contact since the raid. It was unusual for Sarah to get a call from Anne, but Sarah indulged her, and talked, and listened. They spoke mainly about one of the former Family children, who was by then in Chile teaching English. Anne said some in the cult had turned against her. Bill took the phone from time to time. When Anne said goodbye, she added, 'Tell Marie Mohr I love her.' This was her arrogance on full display, a sarcastic dismissal of one of those pursuing her to find justice for the children Anne had imprisoned.

But during the course of the conversation, Anne had let slip where she was: 'I'm in America, darling.' Anne said she and Bill were off to Broom Farm in two weeks. It seems incredible that Anne would reveal her whereabouts, and it seems to be that arrogance again — a notion that she was above the law — mixed with a simple mistake, a throwaway line, delivered and then forgotten.

Sarah then made a call of her own: to Operation Forest. Now, finally, after the likely near miss with the screaming child at Broom Farm, they knew where she was.

The FBI had been on standby for several months. The communication methods between the FBI and Operation Forest seems archaic now — but this was old-fashioned policing, 1990s-style, before the internet, before email was in such widespread use. Lex and Operation Forest worked the facsimile machines all night to suit the UK and US timezones.

After Anne's mistake, the FBI mobilised special agent Hilda Kogut, who worked for the New York office of the FBI from a satellite station in Orange County, NY. She specialised in violent crime — armed robberies and kidnappings. 'A lot of the cases that I got were strange and off the beaten path. This was normal-weird.'

The key for her was that this case involved children as victims. 'Children are, for the most part, unable to defend themselves, and they trust adults. So when adults violate their trust, it gives you the incentive to really make it right.'

Hilda came up with a cunning plan to see if she could eyeball Anne at the house. She couldn't just knock on the door or try peering through windows in case it put the frighteners up. There had been sightings of Anne walking her dogs through Hurleyville, but not for a while. Hilda decided to go undercover on the mail run. Not only did she want to see Anne and Bill and verify they were living at the house, but she also wanted to see the lie of the land, literally. She knew she would be asked — if they were there — to arrest them, so she wanted to see what the house was like, where to go in, points of exit, potential escape routes, the condition of the roads.

'I introduced myself to the local postmistress, and then I rode in the post office car with the rural letter-carrier. In those types of communities, the postal service usually knows exactly what's goin' on.'

The postie had a beaten-up old car with only one seat. Hilda sat on a box. 'It's a very large, undeveloped county. There's not a lot of industry up there.' Most of the old resorts are closed, and unemployment is high. 'It is very rural where that house was located, on a quiet road, in a very rural setting.

'I rode with her for a good portion of the day. She was very animated as we drove. She described to me two people, two elderly people, who lived in the house.' Anne was 72, Bill a year younger. 'Her descriptions seemed to be pretty close to what I knew Anne and William might look like. So I felt very comfortable knowing that they were actually living in the house.'

There was mail: for Anne, for Bill, and for Megan Dawes, Leon's daughter, who was living there temporarily. The mail van pulled up at the house. It was quiet. There was a Cadillac parked outside, and Hilda took down the number. It was registered under 'Hamilton-Byrne', she would later find.

Often, the postie told Hilda, either Anne or Bill would come out to collect the mail as she pulled up. She had spoken to them numerous times. But this time, no one came out, or not straightaway. The letters were put in the mailbox and the rusty old car pulled away. As they drove off, Hilda saw a young woman — Megan — walk out of the house, towards the mailbox. It was not Anne; she knew that from photographs. But she knew it was Anne's house.

'A home run would've been for one of them to come out and pick up the mail while I was sitting in the van, but that didn't happen. And it's just as well that it didn't, because my guess is if one of them had come out to get the mail, more Anne than her husband, their interest might've been raised by the fact that there was a second person in that vehicle.'

Back in the FBI squadroom, she told her boss there wasn't a problem. Entering the house would be easy and safe. Hilda triple-checked the street address in Houghtaling Road against her records. 'We had no reason to believe that she and William were not there.'

On 4 June 1993, the FBI and New York state troopers descended at dawn. They came in cars and stopped short of the Hamilton-Byrne house to brief all the officers about where they should be and which exits they needed to cover. Then they drove up and parked outside the house. '[It was] early, a cold morning. Enough to put them at a disadvantage almost immediately.'

Hilda Kogut approached the door with backup. Dogs were barking inside. A wind chime hanging from the porch moved in the breeze. '[There was only] a lousy wooden door,' she recalls. As a female police officer on the front line for 20 years, she had learned that she didn't need to scream and shout. Let the men do that — 'I had to kinda be controlled and confident in what I did.' As she pounded on the door, she said, 'FBI! Open the door, we have arrest warrants. Open the door immediately.'

It opened almost straight away.

'I walked in, I showed William the arrest warrants, I asked where Anne was. And she had just come into the living-room area with a robe on. My guess is she had just stepped outta the shower.'

Anne asked for a lawyer. Hilda told her that as soon as she got to the nearest court — at White Plains, in Westchester County — she would have one.

Then the agents told the pair they needed to get dressed, which they would have to do under supervision. Anne fussed over choosing an outfit and wanted to do her full-makeup. She was cooperative, says Hilda, but fussy. 'She was very, very concerned about how she looked before we left that house. I kept telling her, "We have to move, we have to leave. Let's hurry up." But she was really quite meticulous in getting dressed that morning.'

Hilda noticed Anne's hair. In the arrest news pictures, taken later at the court, her hair is long and a light, dulled red, her hairline disconcertingly high on her head after years of facelifts. She told Anne she couldn't wear a wig.

What was failure for Anne, and what was success? She had kept repeating her message of 'walk on' to her followers: follow me into the oneness. Did she perceive this as a failure, or did she see it as just another trial of a spiritual leader? Was she, in her mind, that image of Jesus, betrayed and persecuted by those she thought were the closest?

Anne and Bill were taken to the New York State police barracks, in a nearby town by the name of Liberty, and then onto a court in White Plains. There they waited in custody all day and into the afternoon until, at 4.00 pm, they appeared before a judge. But their state-appointed lawyer couldn't make it, so they were held in the Westchester County jail in a town called Valhalla for three days.

The aim of police was to keep them in custody — no bail — until an extradition was ordered. But any potential extradition from America was going to be conditional. Anne and Bill were only, as the Australian police had decided, charged with one count each of perjury and one count each of conspiracy to defraud. These were paltry charges, but to satisfy extradition clauses, spare the children the task of testifying, and simply get them back into an Australian court, these were the only charges that would work. Part of the legal rules in the United States meant that no further charges could be laid.

Hilda phoned Lex in Melbourne. It was 3.30 am and the Forest office was full. Marie Mohr was there; Sarah was there. Ed Ogden was there. 'We've got the bitch,' said Hilda.

Finally this woman — whom Lex calls the most evil person he has ever encountered — had been arrested. What started at the school fire in the hills had, for him at least, reached a conclusion.

Lex put the phone down and walked into Forest's kitchen, picked up a couple of chairs, and threw them into the wall. It was an incredible emotional release. 'I broke down,' he says. He threw everything off the table — he 'just [had] an emotional outburst of tears and screaming'.

The others let him be; they knew he needed this. 'I was absolutely, totally obsessed, remembering that we'd gone through the change of leadership, remembering that I'd given a commitment, remembering that I said with the right team we'd get a result. And I had that challenge, "you won't find her, you won't charge her, you won't get a conviction" — those words at the back of my mind from the journo [Marie]. Absolutely, I was obsessed.

'Four years of anguish, probably hate, everything that I'd come to understand about what this woman had done to people's lives. How she'd destroyed, how she'd effected the theft of these kids from birth — having spoken to a number of the mothers of these children and the deception that occurred with them, you can't but be human to get emotional and let it out. So anyone that thinks coppers are harsh bastards and shouldn't get involved, they're fooling themselves. It does impact on you.

'That was my release valve, and I was emotionally and physically drained after that. It took me a few days to get back on track.'

Michael quotes the gospels when we ask how he felt when Anne was arrested. Specifically, he quotes Mark 6: 'But Jesus said to them: A prophet is not without honour, but in his own country.'

He was at home in the hills when he saw news photographs of Anne and Bill handcuffed and in chains, being walked to and from court. Yet he says he still felt her guidance even though she was being 'abused'. He felt her light around him. 'I knew that Anne was strong enough to deal with it. And that, in fact, she was in that position in jail, to reach certain people in jail, that she needed to. People in prison are in need of the light, just like any one of us, because we are all in prison.'

Yet, he says, she never dropped her head. She was statuesque and imposing still. 'Anne was terribly disrespected, and terribly treated, and thrown in prison out of blatant lies. Anne never lost faith, lost trust in who she was. She was totally abused, but lots of great people have been in the past.'

David Whitaker has kept a photograph of her in chains — handcuffs and chains. He cut it out of the front page of *The Age*. 'She was looking very dishevelled.' He smiles. 'Which would have bothered her big time.'

Four days after she was arrested, around 50 cult members in Melbourne met at Santiniketan Lodge in an emergency meeting to plan their response. Anne and Bill were in custody. One former child of the cult, who was living in America, visited them in jail.

Another tried to leave Australia and was stopped at the airport in Melbourne. Then began a tense waiting game between Operation Forest, two embassies, and lawyers for both the US government and Anne and Bill, over bail and extradition.

Kerry Lawrence was the American government prosecutor assigned to the case. He was still a young lawyer; this was his first extradition case. He was briefed by police and by the prosecutors in Melbourne. 'I thought these allegations were pretty horrific, of what they had done to these young people and the families that were affected by their abduction and brainwashing. [It was] about as horrible as anything I'd worked on as a prosecutor, including murder cases and gigantic financial frauds and organised crime cases. This was about as bad as it gets.'

Although he knew the horrific backstory, he only had the perjury and conspiracy to defraud charges with which to work. The charges he was dealing with were minor in comparison to what he'd heard about Anne and Bill. 'On the face of it,' he says, 'it didn't seem that serious. But obviously the underlying conduct that led to the charges in Australia was extremely serious, dealing with allegations of brainwashing, and administering of drugs to these young children. [Yet] the only thing we were permitted to do was take whatever charges were filed in the country where they were sought, and then file those with the court and seek their extradition.'

Lex told us, 'I'm not a religious man, but I was praying that the US legal system would not let us down.'

But initially, all did not go as Lex hoped. The US court needed documents sent from Australia via the Australian embassy in Washington. They were supposed to have been couriered to the court. But they didn't arrive in time. 'There was an administrative stuff-up,' says Lex. 'Right at the critical point. We could have lost the whole thing.'

At their first appearance at White Plains court, Anne and Bill were thus given bail, meaning they didn't need to be held in custody. They were ordered to wear electronic bracelets on their ankles.

Anne sent a discourse to her followers, raising the spectre of failure. 'The invisible forces are guiding us and leading us on, my friends. It is also important for you to know that it has been revealed … certain tests in which we had failed. So this has given renewed trust and confidence because it showed a lot of people that despite apparent failure — all this stuff that has gone on with the Hamilton-Byrne kids — by maintaining a steadfast mind and keeping our face turned to that wondrous light.'

She said the cult must fight evil and the 'lower nature' but it was hard and getting harder. She had, she said, been put in jail for no reason. 'Oh yes, it hurts. We have come to the conclusion that the only way victory is possible is turning to the holy spirit, and all those who have been wicked, evil, we want them helped too. We put ourselves on the side of victory. We may fail many times and we may stumble frequently and we may appear to have failed miserably but if we remain steadfast … the enemy finally retires, finished. All these tests are necessary. They form part of our initiation. All the powers of darkness rise up and try to overwhelm us, but it is in a sense a performance. We are divine children on our planet.'

Lex was mortified they were awarded bail, to put it mildly. He had investigated the case for four years and was stymied right at the last possible moments by documents going missing from a courier.

'They [Operation Forest] were in a state of extreme panic,' says Lawrence.

But two days later the documents turned up, and Anne and Bill faced court again, seeking bail once more. Their American defence lawyer, John Tigue Jr, from the New York firm Kostelanetz, Ritholtz, Tigue & Fink, argued there were no grounds to keep the couple in custody because the offences they had been charged with were minor and non-violent and that associates (specifically Don Webb, Christabel Wallace, and Liz Whitaker) had faced similar charges in Australia and got off lightly.

He told the judge that the Australian government had been irresponsible because they sought extradition on minor charges while suggesting a raft of more serious 'sensational' charges, but these suggestions, he argued, were nothing more than speculation. There was talk, too, of the pair's ill health: Anne's apparent heart condition and Bill's kidney stones. They were too sick to fly back to Australia. This was despite their visas expiring five months earlier.

The two were examined by police doctors and deemed in good health.

It was 'just so much nonsense', says Marie Mohr. 'There was nothing wrong with her. She was as healthy as an ox.'

Lawrence had little to do with Anne except legal formalities, but of course he met her in court, which allowed him to form his own judgements. What he noticed most was what he calls Anne's charm: 'A certain strong sense of charm. She did have a captivating persona and seemed like she could charm the pants off of anybody. She clearly had a very magnetic personality.'

In the US court, she presented as impervious and calm, 'as if none of this was really phasing her, and that everything was going to be fine'.

We ask Lawrence if he could see Anne as the spirit she said she was. A holy spirit; Jesus Christ reincarnated. He laughs. 'I don't know that I've ever seen *anyone* as Jesus Christ reincarnated.'

She seemed too relaxed for the situation, he says. 'She seemed so non-stressed about what was going on that I did wonder about her mental health. And I guess part of that could be a very strong, solid personality. And part of it could be some type of manifestation of mental illness.'

This time, the successful bail application was overturned, and Anne and Bill were taken to jail again to wait for an extradition hearing. An Australian reporter described Anne as looking 'tired and bedraggled' in court, in a yellow sweatshirt and khaki trousers. Her hair was waist-length but tied back. Bill wore jeans and a blue patterned sweater, with tortoiseshell glasses.

They continued to fight the extradition order. But a weariness took over, and perhaps a realisation that if they did go home to face what they knew were minor charges they could either get off or be fined only a small amount. Then an inmate at Westchester County jail, who was being held close to Bill, was murdered. At that point, they put their hands up and said, 'Okay. Extradite us.'

Bill told his lawyers that he didn't feel safe in the American jail. 'It created a sense of panic,' says Lawrence.

'Maybe,' says Lex, 'luck and justice were going to be on our side.'

Lex and two other detectives from Forest, plus an Australian police doctor, flew to New York. Lex saw it as a game of wits: if Anne reckoned she was sick, he would take a police doctor to check her out. The female doctor was also on board in case the fugitives claimed ill health again on the long flight home. 'Checkmate,' says Lex. 'Outwit her and outsmart her. When I got over there, I didn't want Anne to play the medical card again.'

She didn't. Lex spent a few days with the extradition team and the FBI tying up the paperwork. Then, on the last day of the assignment, he met Anne for the first time. Under US law, those being extradited need to be accompanied by US Marshalls until the moment of departure. 'We're on the forecourt outside John F. Kennedy airport in New York and this brown van pulls up and a US Marshall gets out and comes around and slides the door open,' he says. 'So for the first time, here are the two people that I had been investigating with my team, the two people that we'd been chasing.

'And here is this frail old little lady, and a gentleman who was frail, and one look at them, you think, *How could this be Anne and Bill Hamilton-Byrne?* But it was. Anne didn't have any make-up on. She didn't have the obligatory trademark, the blonde wig. And I looked at Anne and I said, "Anne Hamilton-Byrne?" She looked at me and said, "You must be Mr de Man. I thought you'd look a lot older."'

Outwardly Lex was all business, but inwardly he was jumping out of his skin. He was proud and excited, but also uneasy. 'It was rather surreal meeting her for the first time when I knew the evil that she had committed. I knew the evil type of person she was. I'd seen her on footage, I'd heard her voice, I'd seen her in photos, but to see her in person was really mixed emotions.' Visions of what he had heard — the stories of abuse and cold manipulation — reeled through his mind. 'I'm thinking to myself, *How could this person I'm looking at be so evil?* But evil she was.'

He had to get Anne and Bill flown across the United States to Los Angeles and change planes to a Qantas long-haul flight to Sydney, and then to Melbourne: around 22 hours all up. On the flights back, the two sat not next to each but in front and behind, at the windows, handcuffed. Detectives were beside them, and followed them into the toilets when they needed to go. The temptation for Lex was to start asking questions — why did you do it? Why did you drug them? Why do you say you are Jesus? — but he didn't. Anne and Bill barely spoke. Bill checked on her occasionally, but that was all.

A couple of hours out of Sydney, cabin crew asked Lex and another detective if they wanted to go up to the cockpit and meet the pilot. 'He said he knew who we had with us and how proud he was as captain of the Qantas jumbo that would be bringing Anne Hamilton-Byrne and her husband back to Australia to face justice. So that was a bit of a poignant moment in the investigation for me. And a pat on the back for the team. We did well and it was noticed. An Aussie saying to another Aussie "well done".'

In Sydney, the team and the captured fugitives got on a humble domestic flight for the hour-long trip to Melbourne. They needed to go straight to a court to get bail conditions set.

After they landed, in the morning on a Tuesday in August 1993, media chased the team from the airport into the city, trying to get photographs of Anne and Bill in a police car. Then at the court, where they arrived around 10.00 am, there was another large group of bustling media. The couple's Australian lawyer, Patrick Tehan, told the court they were not guilty and wanted bail and would go straight to trial at a higher court — the County Court.

They got their bail on the condition they could not leave Victoria, and they had to hand over their passports. Anne and Bill-Hamilton-Byrne, exhausted and weary, were then driven by a cult member back up to the hills that had hidden them for so long.

11

LOVE IS IN THE AIR

Anne and Bill Hamilton-Byrne's trials in the Melbourne courts were remarkable only for their banality. The inquisitions were administrative and brief. It was a false ending — they eventually conceded they were guilty and were not cross-examined. For Anne, this was part of the game. Her voice would not enter the public record, she would not be questioned, and she would stay unheard, and unknown.

No witnesses were required, but that was always the idea; witnesses would be too damaged or too indoctrinated. Mostly the couple sat together in court in silence.

On a Monday morning in mid-November of 1993, they arrived at the County Court immaculately dressed. Anne wore a luxuriant blonde wig and huge dark sunglasses, eyes hidden, neck draped with heavy jewellery. Bill was in a new dark suit and tie with the crispest of white shirts.

Adam was there with them too, in a suit, his hair shaved at the sides and slicked back on top, a gold hoop in his ear. Anne hooked her arms through his and through Bill's and glared defiantly from behind her glasses at the cameras as they pushed through and up the stairs into the courtroom. Her mouth, in court and with police, always seemed pursed into the beginnings of a smirk.

But inside, very little happened. The charges were read: one count each of conspiring to commit perjury and one count each of conspiring to defraud. Not guilty, they said. The judge adjourned the case. Anne and Bill went back to the hills with Adam.

Adam was in the inner circle again, of his own volition. To Adam, Anne was in trouble and needed his help. This was his idea of 'family' — he always came back to the way Anne had constructed hers and included him in it. Family was still the most powerful force in his life, and even though he vacillated between rebellion and compliance, he could not betray her, not now, not at this time.

He would become the contact point for marijuana in the cult. He was selling to his friends, but also to insiders. Adam says this was Anne's idea, and that his mother in the cult, Liz Whitaker, was also involved. 'Aunty Anne said, "Why don't you sell pot to some of the members of The Family?" Some of them needed it. I knew how to get it. And I got it cheap. It always came to the house, and I would divvy it out. If I wasn't home, Mum [Liz] would invite the customers in and give them a cup of tea or coffee and a smoke, and she kept the people entertained while I was maybe doing a delivery or something, and they loved her. All my mates that bought off me loved Mum. They can't say a bad word against her. She wasn't the bitch that she was when I was a kid.'

Cult numbers were plummeting. There was little chance of new recruits now with Anne and Bill arrested and on bail. It was a case of clinging on to the dedicated followers who remained. Leon Dawes' son Geoff was becoming more important to Anne as his father aged and began to withdraw from the group. Don Webb and John Mackay were still central and had supported Anne in court.

Anne was staunch as her empire crumbled. She continued to give lofty discourses at the Lodge. At times she seemed bitter, but not about the Uptop children being freed or about being chased by police for four years and arrested at Hurleyville, but about her now-tiny flock, as if she had been betrayed not only by individuals but also by the group. Where just a few years before she knew she might be speaking to hundreds, now at the lodge she would look up from her little table and lamp up the front and see ten, maybe twenty.

'I have done my best, and I'm still doing it,' she said, in a recorded discourse during this time. 'Those who are devoted to me realise this and they are united with me, and those who are not devoted, they don't know me. Wake up! Wake up! It's worth the effort now, where we are on this planet, for a little time, for a little time. You think about it! You've got enough brains, those of you who are left.

'We are running late again,' Anne continued. 'Yes, it is half-past six, running a wee bit late. There are a lot of things happening around us, as you no doubt know. Channel Nine has been at it again. We are over that stuff, that doesn't worry us too much at all. I just wonder if Geoff Dawes and Christabel [Wallace] would get in touch after class? You can come round, Geoff. Just for a few moments. I'd like to have a wee word with you. A few things to talk about there. We have a very fine lawyer and a very fine man who is about to be a judge talking to me about things. Something must be done. Quite in opposition to the finances we have got to spare on this.'

Adam remembers seeing members of the cult up and leave during this time, but others remained. 'Some people stood by her through thick and thin. She had her diehards. And I guess I could have been one of them. But mine was for my own security, and my own survival. I had to survive. And I couldn't survive without them at that time.' Bill had already promised $50,000 from his will — for loyalty, says Adam. 'The only way I can describe it, your family, you stick by your family.'

As the judge adjourned the County Court appearance, he also was asked to consider a sticky point of law before a potential jury was selected for a future trial. The question was whether the Victorian court had the right to decide a charge of conspiring to defraud authorities in New Zealand.

Lawyers for Anne and Bill were led by a Queen's Counsel, John Winneke. This was one of his last cases as a silk before he was made a Supreme Court judge. Both his father and his grandfather were eminent judges; his father was made solicitor-general for Victoria and knighted. Winneke, who had played AFL football for Hawthorn and was an officer in the Royal Australian Navy, went to the same school as Michael — Scotch College. He was very, very expensive.

His tactic was to get the charges thrown out on the basis that a Victorian court had no right to decide them, arguing the conspiracy to defraud count was not designed to infringe a Victorian law or 'cause mischief' in Victoria. It was for the New Zealand courts to decide the case, he argued. He cited a British House of Lords decision ordering that a British company, which was alleged to have defrauded a German government department, be tried in Germany. But the court heard that the cult's incriminating documents were filed in and signed in Victoria, then sent to New Zealand.

The legal seesawing over this took months in the Supreme Court, which eventually found the charges were indeed inadmissible and could not be heard because they were unknown to Victorian law. Police quickly charged the pair with admissible local Crimes Act offences: one count each of 'conspiring to make a false statement' about the triplets. And so Anne and Bill's criminality — their degree of culpability — was downgraded again.

Lex was in an emotional state. He was frazzled and nervous, so much so that by now his friends outside the police force were worried about him. It had been seven years since the school fire in the hills, and Lex was now the only one remaining from the original police taskforce. Adding to the intense stress was the suicide of Detective Senior Sergeant John Hill, who had replaced Spence in the taskforce. Hill was accused, with other police, of being an accessory after the fact to the murder of gangland enforcer Graeme Jensen, in that he allegedly concealed evidence suggesting the police were criminally liable. He died in 1993 in a Melbourne park just a few months before Anne and Bill had entered the County Court in a flourish that first time. He always maintained his innocence, and the charges were dropped.

More than anything, Lex was scared of failure. The charges had been diminished, and diminished again. The top lawyers on Anne and Bill's side were looming over the case. 'I was obsessed,' he says. 'I would have felt failure. I would have felt a total failure to those kids. A total failure to Peter Kibby. A total failure to the profession of policing.'

The trials came almost a year later, in September 1994, in two sittings a few days apart. Anne and Bill had changed their minds and now decided to plead guilty to a single charge each. Winneke, the QC, argued they were quiet, unassuming people who were known to be compassionate and caring. He told the court that Operation Forest had ended in a whimper, with only these minor charges, and asked the judge to not record convictions. The judge told the court he wasn't ready to make a ruling on this yet — but he probably wouldn't send the pair to jail.

The day after the guilty pleas, and just before Anne and Bill were finally sentenced, journalist David Elias, who had been following the case longer than police, wrote in *The Age* that since the raid 'not one adult has been brought to account by authorities for the ill-treatment of the children', despite government and police investigations.

He also revealed that in 1985 Australia's Department of Foreign Affairs was given evidence of faked passports of Uptop children by Dick Wordley, the crusading 'missing children' journalist from Adelaide, and an Adelaide parliamentarian, Ralph Jacobi. Jacobi asked the then foreign affairs minister, Bill Hayden, to have a look, which he did, writing back to Jacobi that while the allegations were 'substantially' correct, nothing was wrong with the passports. Hayden became the governor-general of Australia shortly after, and still held that position when Anne and Bill faced court in 1994.

David Elias spoke to Sarah, who told him the former children of Uptop were resigned to the fact that nobody would be charged over the regime of starvation and beatings, the physical and mental torture, that had occurred there. No one. 'The system has let us down persistently,' she told him. 'We just ask, what was the point of it all?'

Then, on 26 September, Anne and Bill were sentenced. The law does only what it can. It cannot take into account stories a court has not heard and of which it has not tested the veracity. Judge David Jones was at pains to explain that only one charge each had been presented to him and so that was all they could be sentenced for — 'not for other actions that might have been thought to have taken place'. Convictions were recorded. The judge noted that the pair had already spent three months in jail in America, and were elderly (Anne was nearly 73; Bill, 72), so he would not order further jail time. Each was fined $AU5,000.

Sarah was in court to hear the sentencing. The miniscule fines she saw dished out, after a quarter of a century of torment and deception, was a deflating experience. The cult's arrogance, even at that moment, angered her. Members of The Family were in court too — 'glaring and saying nasty things about us children. It all ended up a farce. She got off.'

And she did; she got away with it. There was no justice. There was no acknowledgement that the children had been mistreated. The children saw the Aunties go to jail for fiddling the social security 'but they didn't go to jail for beating us nearly every single day and starving us for three days at a time,' says Sarah. 'No one got in trouble for that.'

Sarah said she saw Anne's grand performance change during these times, in that she feigned poverty and played up the idea that she was being persecuted. But she also lost her trademark steely control. 'There was less money coming in, and she was getting older and forgetting where the money was stashed. She'd get people to do certain things with money, but it was a spiderweb. People die or leave or lose memories. She wasn't able to manage her cult as a business anymore. Better to hunker down and deal with remaining members as she had to, and say the rest was the persecution of Jesus.'

Michael maintains that Anne was persecuted: oppressed, he says, on religious grounds. He says human thought is always adversarial and thus Anne's adversaries lined up to take her down: too much right and wrong, he says, cops and robbers, black and white, bad and good.

To Marie Mohr, opting for minor charges in order to get a quick extradition was a mistake. 'I was bitterly disappointed. There was no justice. It hurt the kids, and so it should. How could you justify to them, how could you explain to them? They'd all given hearts and souls and statements and worked so closely with the police and others to try and get the community to understand what had happened to them. Then we shut the door and [said] "nothing we could do". I think it was wrong. I understand why they made the decision, but I think they made the wrong decision.'

She says the children could have fronted court. They had survived much more in their lives than cross-examination. 'I think it underestimated them and I think it let them down.'

Lex was also unsatisfied with the outcome. The maximum penalty for the offence Anne and Bill were charged with was a $AU60,000 fine and five years' jail, and it wasn't even near that. But he got Anne charged, and he got to show what he believed were her true colours rather than the gaudy apparition with heavy make-up she presented when recruiting for The Family. 'We were able to show that she was no one special. She was basically a very cunning crook. I can argue about the penalty — but the penalty was the penalty the judge at the time could provide. But we got her before the court. She will never be able to think that she got away with it. She is the most evil person with the most evil set of crimes that I have ever investigated in my 18-year career with Victoria Police. If you want to know the definition of evil, you look at Anne Hamilton-Byrne.'

Two weeks after being convicted and fined $AU5,000, Anne and Bill — and Don Webb — went on ABC Radio, the national public broadcaster. It was a long interview with broadcaster Ranald Macdonald, who had been managing director of *The Age*.

During the interview, Webb called the children 'cabbages'. 'They were write-offs,' he said, 'they were cabbages. They were destined for institutions.'

Anne's version of her group's story here, in the fullest explanation of her actions she has ever given, was that while she was teaching yoga and working at Newhaven in the very early 1960s, 'some rather important people' approached new Newhaven matron Joan Vilimek with a bunch of handicapped children that needed adopting. Anne arranged the adoptions among her yoga students.

She denied taking money and denied any LSD dosings, but conceded that the drug was used widely inside Newhaven. She denied ever telling anyone she was Jesus — 'I've never heard such bosh.' She admitted to using fse passports for children because it was easier to get through airport customs that way.

In fact, Anne talked so much that Bill and Don Webb barely got a word in. In contrast to her quiet behaviour in court, she sounded chirpy and conversational. When Bill spoke, he was more flippant; in answering a question about how many children they had, he said: 'When we got married, it was almost like *Cheaper by the Dozen*.' While talking about one child, Anne interrupted to remind him that the child was 'dumb'.

Anne said she was not a religious teacher: 'I do teach yoga. I have a Master.'

'It's yoga,' she continued. 'My mother was very into it, my father was Buddhistic, Buddhism. I heard lots of religious arguments in our house! It just came. I met the Teacher, of course, when I was about 15. He was literally all around the world. It wasn't until my husband died in 1955 that I would do what he said I would do. I went through this death experience, this terrible thing. I was three months' pregnant at the time. By 1956 I was into it, as well as nursing. I taught meditation. Then I started — in 1962, I started publicly teaching hatha yoga, which was most successful. I did eight classes a day for eight years. When the children came — when gradually the children came — we found ourselves with more and more responsibility. I'd already trained quite a number of people for seven years that would take over if ever I wasn't there.'

When asked whether she dyed the children's hair to make them look like one family, Anne said yes, that was why. 'Of course it was. I wanted them to look like brothers and sisters. We never told them that they weren't ours. We didn't do that. I only know wherever we went, people said to us what beautiful children they were, what lovely manners they had. They're wonderful at everything. I wanted them to achieve so that they could achieve to the very highest that they could. Some of them were in music, some of them were in languages. Just being ordinary good men and women, but not to be laughed at.'

Macdonald asked Anne whom she blamed for the cult's troubles. He put it to her that her experiment had failed. 'Your plan, your family, has dissipated, hasn't it,' he said.

'Yes,' answered Bill. 'But why?'

Anne said she couldn't blame anyone. She couldn't blame herself; she couldn't blame Sarah or Leeanne or any of the children from Uptop.

'I just think it's very sad,' she said. 'We were told that the children would never be normal. I did everything I could. We all thought, not just myself, we had the best advice from psychologists and welfare workers to let them feel that they were part of our home. That was the only way they were going to feel, one day, to be able to support themselves — knowing they belong to something.'

She ended the interview by saying she had plans for the future: to take in a group of mentally handicapped children.

Just a few months later, in early 1995, Macdonald did another ABC broadcast with Leon Dawes' daughter, Megan Dawes. Megan was 26, and said she was a nurse working in Hawaii. During the interview, she said her parents split up when she was five and were unable to look after her and her brother Geoff, so they put them into Uptop. She spoke at length about how good

The Family was, and is — she used the present tense — and how the children who alleged imprisonment and abuse were led into false memory syndrome by psychologists after the raid; that is, prompted to recollect things that Megan said never happened.

Her line was that the children became greedy and duplicitous after the raid. It is a line that many members of the group, especially Michael, maintain. 'I notice how incredibly successful these abused children have turned out to be,' she told the interviewer. 'You think, *My God, you've gotta be joking*, with some of the stuff they carry on with.'

Megan denied that any drug use took place at Uptop. The punishments were smackings, not beatings. She also said there was no indoctrination of any sort. Instead, she likened the way Anne and Bill took in children to the way they took in dogs. 'Anne and Bill have a place in America — it's in New York in the hills, in the Catskills — and people dump animals, and basically when they saw a starving animal they couldn't leave it there so they took it. And they've got to the stage they have 40 dogs they are looking after.'''

Meanwhile, Leeanne had met a young man named Ollie. She met him through Geoff Dawes, who invited her to a Gilbert and Sullivan performance Ollie was in, although Ollie was not involved with The Family, and they wanted to get married. Since Anne and Bill had been extradited and convicted, Leeanne had been to see them, not in the spirit of forgiveness, but as a kind of offering. She was the first to escape Uptop but also the first of that core group to extend any kind of hand to them, beyond Sarah's occasional contact. But it was vexed and horribly mixed up in the mess of Bill's betrayal of Leeanne, his favourite make-believe daughter. She was 'Daddy's girl', but she now knew he was not her daddy.

Bill wanted to be involved at the wedding: because he considered himself Leeanne's father, he felt that — despite all that had happened — he should walk her down the aisle. 'He was all excited. I thought, *I can give that to him, as an adult.* So I did.' They had spoken of this together when Leeanne was younger.

He also wanted to give the father-of-the-bride speech, but this was one step too far for Leeanne. She figured that walking her down the aisle was all right because all he had to do was hold onto her and walk. A speech would mean speaking, and speaking would mean lies and yet more denial of the monumental lie of the children's upbringing at Uptop. She asked Marie Mohr, who had become something of a sister figure, to give the speech instead. 'Bill was devastated that I didn't ask him to speak,' Leeanne said. 'And Anne and Bill let me know about it afterwards.'

Although many of the group's members were not invited, most of one side of the church were members of The Family, either from the inner circle or from the fringes. Leeanne asked Ollie's parents to essentially chaperone Anne and Bill on the day. 'They said they'd look after them for me and make sure they didn't cause any problems and no one would cause problems for them.'

Leeanne had been reunited with her real parents after the raid. But it was complicated on many levels: she found she had a stepfather as well as a birth father. Plus Bill — 'the father I grew up with'. She initially found it difficult to gel with her birth mother, even though each had been looking for the other. Her brother knew he had a sister somewhere, Leeanne's mother told her, and that 'something was missing'.

'I try and put myself in that situation as a parent,' says Leeanne, 'but I can't because I would never give up a child under any circumstances. I find that very, very difficult. I also found it very confronting at the time when my daughter was born. My mother wanted the baby that she gave up. But she didn't want or didn't know how to deal with an 18-year-old who had gone through a horrific childhood. That would have been very confronting for her, knowing what I had gone through. She tried to mollycoddle me and wrap me up in cotton wool, and I'm too independent for that. I used to fight her and argue and it never worked. I found it very difficult, and even to this day we have difficulties because I don't believe she understands me.'

Marie Mohr's speech was another remarkable episode in the postscript of this cult: the journalist who pursued Anne to Hawaii and confronted her there, and who worked closely with police and befriended the children the cult abused, speaking for one of those children in front of her captors. In her speech, she said:

> I have known Leeanne for almost ten years now. It's a relationship that has built slowly from the beginning, one which took us time to trust each other and get to know each other and to open up to each other. And of course once we got through a few barriers in the early days, what I found, which I think anyone who knows Leeanne has found, is a woman with an enormous heart, with enormous energy, with courage, determination — some may say stubbornness, some may say outspokenness, some may say a lot of things — but what I would say is I have seen her blossom into a very caring, very sharing woman, who I know will give you all the love in the world, Ollie, because that's her personality.
>
> There is not one bitter bone in Leeanne's body. She is always looking forward and not backwards. I think that's one of her survival mechanisms and one of the reasons I am very proud of her — because she has never felt sorry for herself. She has always held her head up and her shoulders back and got on with life.

Leeanne and Bill danced together to 'Love is in the Air'. Anne stood back on the edge of the dance floor, clapping to the music. She wore ivory. When the song finished, she grabbed Bill and danced with him, awkwardly, to 'I Got You Babe'.

Ben was at the wedding and spoke to Anne. She came over to talk to him and, over the course of their conversation, tried to draw him back into the fold. Ben says it was surreal, but he was able to erect a wall because he had long ago figured out that Anne wasn't who she purported to be. He was, he says, able to 'cut her off'. 'She had her take and her view of the world and continued to try and impose that upon me. There's no emotional tie, there's no physical tie, and there's no spiritual tie, and those three ties were things she very much tried to have, and I was able to very much separate from all three of those.'

Leeanne's life with her own children became loving and stable, despite a divorce from Ollie. Her children are now adults. She talks about trust a lot. Marie mentioned that in the wedding speech too — that she had to earn Leeanne's trust. Leeanne remembers the family in the hills with the daughters from the Kenlaurel dancing school: she trusted them, and they trusted her. Cathy and her mother, Erica, helped Leeanne and listened to her. Leeanne found, as she grew into life outside The Family, that she stuck close to those she trusted.

Leeanne continued to see Anne and Bill after she was married, as part of that offering she felt she needed to give to them. 'I felt invincible. Life had moved on. I thought that I could deal with her, but I really couldn't.'

On one visit, Megan Dawes, who was still very close to Anne, was at Anne and Bill's house in the hills. Megan and Leeanne bickered, and Leeanne confronted Anne's authority once again, as she had done at Uptop before she escaped. They were arguing about the truth of what had happened there beside the lake.

'Megan didn't want to face reality,' Leeanne says.

Anne was sitting in the same room, listening. She asked Leeanne: 'Who do you blame?'

'I said, "I blame you. I blame you for everything that you put us through. You were our mother."'

Anne was downcast, and Leeanne saw her, for the first time, in a new light. 'I thought, *You are a very sad, despicable woman. You're really going to end up a very lonely woman in life.* Guess what, she's a very lonely woman in a nursing home. She's got no children around her. She has sect members, but they're not family.'

Peter Kibby, the cult's great Judas, was by now a Melbourne taxi driver. In 1999, he went to court to try and keep his part-ownership of Santiniketan Lodge in the hills, administered now by a cult entity called the Santiniketan Park Association, which was registered as Anne and Bill were being charged in America. Geoff Dawes is the secretary.

When the cult bought the prime hills land in 1968, Anne appointed directors, including Raynor Johnson; his daughter, Beryl Hubble (aka Christine Fleming); Anne's daughter, Natasha; and Peter Kibby. In 1973, Kibby paid $AU14,000 to a cult member as a loan towards renovations, and in 1999, in court, he won his case — the judge found that the association claiming total ownership were 'nothing more than a fluctuating group of individuals'.

In 2015, as Anne lay in the nursing home, the association (fighting Kibby's widow, Barbara, and Anne's daughter, Natasha, for the right to own it) used a legal method called 'adverse possession', where primary users or occupiers of a property can try to claim it after 15 years. The case continues. 'We have spent 15 years paying the rates to get ownership,' says Michael, also an association member, 'so it has taken time. It's very slow-moving, the law.'

One day, we spoke with Michael about Anne dying. We were trying to talk to him about her physical death and explain that she would, to us, cease to be. What happens then? The light of Michael's life will surely die.

'To go beyond fear,' he says, 'is a pathway worth following. And in that way you then have the courage and the strength to be a sacred warrior. That is our teaching.'

'Are you a sacred warrior?' we asked him.

He laughs. 'It's a job in progress. As is all of creation. It's an ongoing thing. But I did stand up to defend Anne against the arrows, didn't I? Lots of other people didn't, but I did.'

We asked: Does that mean you are her successor?

'I'm not to say anything,' Michael says. 'I don't know. All I know is the next step on the path for me. The next challenge. That's all I want to know. If anything else is further, it'll be shown to me. The mills of God grind slow. And eventually you become aware of your destiny. I'm waiting for that sign, just like you are. We're all waiting for the sign, aren't we?'

Michael was fudging. But, we asked him, are you willing?

'Are you? Are you willing? Willingness is to do with awareness. And I'm waiting for the awareness. The next moment. Because it's not necessarily a booming voice from the Heavens. It can be a moment of incredible stillness that only you know. It's the light in people's eyes. Anne would always say to us, "Never put out the light in another person's eyes."'

In fact, the scenario for after Anne's death is complex, and mired in the web of betrayals and loyalties she has lived her life among. Money and property still play a large part in dictating the terms.

In 2000, Anne was still named in 20 company and trust documents, all in Melbourne, all shareholdings or directorships. Some were ghost companies, others not. Now, most have been rolled into a registered Australian charity called Life For All Creatures. It is also registered in the United States.

Office holders in Life For All Creatures include Geoff Dawes, John Mackay's son Tim Mackay, and a woman named Helen McCoy, who says she has never been a member of The Family but runs the charity as an animal shelter in the hills, where she lives.

McCoy and Dawes have power of attorney over Anne's legal and financial affairs. McCoy positions herself as a friend of Anne's rather than a follower. She has got closer to Anne as Anne has got older. During the early 1990s, Anne's worth was estimated at as much as $AU150,000,000 in properties, land, and cash. Now, as she lies in a nursing home, her estate is valued at $AU10,000,000. Significantly less, but still considerable.

Life For All Creatures was largely born out of a company called Hamilton-Byrne Ltd, in 2001. It recently changed its registered address away from Helen McCoy's home in the hills to Crowther House, Anne's one-time home, which we hear is now occupied by Tim Mackay, aged in his 50s, and a 73-year-old cult member called David Munroe.

The main former cult companies, now deregistered, were called Saffete and Faffete. Anne or her proxies — some using her name or versions of it — can be linked to at least 13 other active companies, all based in Australia. One of them owns a sheep station in central Victoria, north of Melbourne.

Helen McCoy is nearly 70. She recently retired as the principal of a Melbourne special school for disabled children. Cult documents were alleged to have been destroyed when her former house in the hills burnt down during a bushfire. She has since moved elsewhere, still in the hills.

In 2012, the state government reportedly launched an inquiry into how member of The Family and an architect, who has since died, came to be awarded $8,000,000 in contracts for work at McCoy's school, an association she said she declared when the tenders went in. The school has also been reported to the state's Equal Opportunity and Human Rights Commission — by parents — after allegedly restraining disabled children.

McCoy told Melbourne's *Sunday Herald-Sun* in 2014 that decades ago she learnt meditation from Anne and went to a meditation group she held, where the two became friends. Her association with Anne, she said, has not involved any children.

She would not talk to us.

We ask Michael about her, but he just shrugs and smiles and says he knows little. 'It is not my business to know. What she does with animals is just saintly.' He ceased to be a director of Life For All Creatures in June 2014, not long after Tim Mackay was appointed.

Michael is what you might call Anne's aide, even though he does not have any legal or financial powers over her significant estate. He has always distanced himself from the murky, abusive end of the cult. Michael says that he visits Anne in the nursing home every day even though others around him, and supposedly around her, do not. He makes her cups of tea and sits in silence with the woman he says inhabits the Christ consciousness and does not have dementia.

Michael gushes over her physical state. She fell over and injured her pelvis in early 2016, but has since recovered. She eats very little; when we were there, we watched as she squirted a boxed protein milk, through a straw, into a cup of tea. Despite being very thin and deep in the throes of the fatal brain disease that not only erases memory but also weakens immunity, she seems to be very strong.

'The people who think she is demented don't understand where she is coming from,' says Michael. 'They come in occasionally, when their diary allows them, and Anne doesn't want them there or doesn't want to speak to them, or she withdraws into an inner world where she doesn't communicate.

'They think it's dementia but it is not. It's another dimension. I can't understand why some people want to turn her into something negative.'

He tells us without blinking or missing a beat that she once turned back the tide. This was in Hawaii in the 1980s, he says. She and Bill had walked along a beach but were in danger of being caught by the incoming ocean on the way back, so she stopped the tide. Also, he told us, she could prototype herself: she could make a duplicate image of herself to be in two places at once. One time she did it, he says, and one version of her was in a dog's cage in the hills, sitting with the dogs.

Bill died of liver cancer in 2001. He was 79 and had also developed dementia. We hear that he was physically worn by being on the run and arrested, jailed, extradited, and charged. And we also hear rumours that his enthusiasm for Anne and for the cult was waning as he aged.

Members of the group had two reiki masters treat him as he became sicker and bedbound, at Crowther House. His sister flew out from the United Kingdom in Bill's final months and, according to former cult members, persuaded him to re-write his will so that his estate — he owned a lot of property near Melbourne — should go to his real children, from his first marriage.

On his deathbed, Bill reaffirmed his Catholic faith. His life, in death, reversed to where it had come from prior to meeting Anne.

Bill once told an interviewer: 'There was no intent for evil whatsoever. It was only for good.'

His body was kept at Crowther House for several days. At the funeral, in the same Catholic church in the hills that he and Anne were married in, and attended by 200 people and monitored by security guards, Bill's daughter Melanie argued with a cult member and we are told tried to throw herself into his grave. Bill's former family had always resented Anne's treatment of him and the way they say she turned him against them.

Anne was at the service but did not make a speech.

Adam thinks that Bill, though sick, was poisoned — because he had lost ultimate faith in the cult and intended to sign over his estate to his blood family. 'I think there was something not quite right,' Adam says of Bill's death.

Anne's likeliest cause of death will be the physical effects of dementia as she becomes incontinent and can no longer eat, as her body packs up and parts of her brain die off and she can no longer fight anymore. On our visit with Michael to see her in the nursing home, where she is surrounded by photographs of Bill and the children, and photographs of herself, she falls asleep in her chair. This is not unusual. She wakes and sleeps, wakes and sleeps. Then she wakes fully and those piercing, dangerous eyes dart around the room. There are blue crystals on a table, along with a folded newspaper. Our eyes follow hers to both.

She will die. We all will die. But what Michael thinks he has learned from Anne and The Family is that some things are beyond human, and death need not be the end. 'People will say, "Your guru is dead," and that will be true,' he says. 'But the lineage doesn't cut out. There will always be a Great White Brotherhood on this planet. Always.'

12

THE KINGDOM

David Whitaker wanted revenge. The cowshit he had posted to a cult member was just the start. He didn't want to hurt anyone. He just wanted to tell the truth, and use the truth as a weapon.

His mother, Elizabeth Whitaker, died in 2010. He helped his sister Judith organise a funeral. David tells us that Liz always said she never wanted a funeral, so his sister began organising one for her, to spite her.

When Liz was dying, David's brother went to see her and they reconciled, to a degree. 'I think it was very, very good for him,' says David. 'I chose not to.'

When the day of the funeral approached, he still wasn't sure if he would actually go. His siblings told him they couldn't do it without him.

David decided that a eulogy would be his weapon. The church was full of cult members, but Anne was not there; she had just been diagnosed with the earliest stages of dementia. His eulogy was like a king-hit. He ambushed them. 'Anne gathered a group of children together, mostly by stealing, and installed them in a house at Eildon. Those children were to be brought up to lead the world to salvation after the holocaust. Elizabeth was one of the Aunties who reared these children. I know this sounds a little fanciful, but Elizabeth did not doubt any of this, for a second. She truly believed that by living the way she did, she would not only save her soul but that of the whole of humanity. A lot of this is denied now, but I was there, I heard it all, and I can assure you, it was exactly what was said and what was believed.

'So the stakes were very high, and this justified any means,' he continued. 'Elizabeth gave up her relatives and her children. She never knew her grandchildren, was convicted of fraud and went to jail, and reared children in circumstances that would now be considered child abuse in the pursuit of this divine, cosmic goal of saving humanity.

'Drugging children and brainwashing them — a technique she learned from my father — was also part of this process,' he said. 'So is there any point to me bringing all this up now? I think there is. The only way to make any sense of Elizabeth's life is to see it from her point of view, through her beliefs, because absolutely nothing else mattered to her. She stuck to her beliefs and died with them intact. But there is a lesson here for the living: if we are going to stick to our set of beliefs and values to the end, it's probably wise to pull them out from time to time and have a cold, hard look at them to ensure that they are logical and that they don't hurt anyone else. Because there was a fair bit of collateral damage to Elizabeth's beliefs.

'I know that Mum would want me to say the mantra over her ashes, but like her I must stick to my beliefs, and just say goodbye.'

Michael was at the funeral. He was angry, and accosted David about the eulogy after the service, saying it was one-sided and wrong. 'He thought that it really wasn't as bad as that, and that I hadn't got over the fact that my parents were divorced,' says David. 'And I said to him, "No, Michael, it was that bad, and it was that bad then and it's bad now and it'll always be bad." And I told him that if he or anyone still believed in it, it was weak-minded, and invited him to go away before I said something really unpleasant to him. And he did.'

Michael's view is that David and his brother were 'terribly traumatised' — 'You don't want to get David going,' he says. 'He is rather brusque. I was friendly, but he wanted to argue. The thing is, they were devastated by their mother and father splitting up. It always goes back to that: the destruction of the father who was the godhead for the children. Their mother was crucified for that by them.'

Liz was, of course, also Adam's cult mother. He stayed loyal to her with unbelievable rigour, nursing her through her dying years at her home in the hills — which he has inherited and lives in. His mental health plummeted when she died; by 2012 he was, he says, 'suicidal, not eating or caring. Why live on a planet where no one cares about you?'

The talk within the cult was he had brought on his own suffering and would lose the house, but he didn't, and he managed to summon the energy to pull himself up and seek counselling. His counsellor helped him find his real family, which cemented his already growing self-esteem.

Adam found his birth mother had died in 2000 in Tasmania, but he has connected with his mother's sister and her family and is starting to spend a lot of time with them. He has met his real sister, and an uncle who lives in Queensland. His reconciliation is a work in progress. He is not in constant contact with his birth family and has found that if he doesn't call them for a while, they understand. He feels he has moved on from The Family and is happier and more confident. Yet still, there is always the slightest of hooks pulling him backwards. 'It's been hard to digest everything. It's very hard for me to actually show my true, true emotion, which is ecstatic. But there's a part of me that's still holding back a little bit. Got the barriers up because it's all new.'

He deeply regrets never meeting his real mother, even though he knows that he might not have grown up beside her because of her mental illness. In fact, Adam is still torn. Sometimes he even thinks he might have actually been better off raised in the cult. 'Probably I had more opportunities, even though it had its really, really bad downfalls, but whatever family you are in there's going to be the good, the bad, and the ugly.'

This is his loyalty speaking. What is family? A group of people who live together, a group of people who share the same values, a group of people from the same blood? A group of people forced together and who survive hardship together? Any or all of those things. Adam doesn't really know the right answer, although he has begun to call his blood family his 'real' family and refer to himself as the newest family member.

He loves Anne fiercely. He calls it a 'very deep' love. He is drawn to her, but knows enough to keep a certain distance. 'I can still see it, still feel it,' he says. 'The revering or the adoration or whatever it is. She was a very powerful woman. When she'd walk into a room, the whole room would stop and she didn't have to say anything. It still feels that she has that power — [there is] that sense of being with the Queen, or Captain Janeway. There is a sense of strength still in her. But at the same time, I think she needs to be held accountable for the atrocities. The buck stops with her.'

He suspects she is over-egging her dementia. After one visit to see her, in 2015, Adam felt strongly that she was playing a game and is much more aware of her surroundings than claimed. 'When she looked at me, she knew who I was, and just the way that we were able to slip into our bond that we had. She and I had a special bond. There's a sense that I knew what she was thinking and she knew what I was. I could see she was watching very, very intuitively and carefully. I could see that she was watching her words — a demented person wouldn't be able to do that. There's still part of her that's fully wide awake.'

Barbara Kibby was swallowed up into The Family for a long time. She married into it by marrying Peter; she lost a son. But she survived too, and she recognises that Anne picked on specific vulnerabilities in those she targeted. For Barbara, it was the lack of attachment to her own mother. 'She was able to tap into something that's there within every one of us. If you had a childhood lacking something, you carry that into adulthood. It's like a hole that's there, and if you meet someone who you think fills that hole, you absolutely crawl to it like a moth to a flame. If you have the lack of a mother figure, you're always drawn to somebody who is like a mother.'

By the time Liz Whitaker died in 2010, four of The Family's victims had successfully sued Anne. Two were children at Uptop, and each were paid compensation for aggravated damages. The third was the son of a cult member and the fourth an adult member who sued Anne over an unpaid debt of more than $AU400,000 from two 1980s property deals in the hills. It couldn't happen now; Anne's advanced dementia prevents anyone claiming anything from her ever again. In the eyes of the law, dementia is equivalent to death, and you can't sue the dead.

Anouree was one of those who sued. Her successful claim was based on testimony of starvation and beatings: of being hit with a bat, the metre-long ruler, and wooden canes. She said that she was tranquilised and raised in isolation without a proper education or social interactions, and suffered from ongoing psychological problems as a result.

Anouree had suffered severe depression between 2000 and 2002, to the point where, she says, she was 'dysfunctional'. She had been teaching English in Japan in the late 1990s and came back very ill, not eating properly and vomiting. The law changed slightly in 2003 to give people more time to begin historical claims for damages, and Anouree says that she was approached by law firms in Melbourne, who had researched other cases against Anne, in 2005. She decided that legal action was a good idea, not only for the money but also to validate these terrible things that she knew happened to her but existed in a kind of vacuum. 'I felt very relieved at the end of it. It was a wonderful result, and it gave me some understanding about myself, that I indeed had been damaged.'

She is now married with her own family and lives in the countryside near Melbourne. She is an optimistic person and has realised that her Uptop years were only part of her life. There are other parts now, good parts, stable parts. Certainly a lot of the spiritual teachings she was forced into in her formative years were about equanimity and 'all things must pass', and it seems true within Anouree; she is positive, despite everything. 'I would consider my experience at Eildon as a somewhat isolated incident. I find that the people I now know, and the people I've met along the way from my journey away from Eildon, demonstrate to me that most of the time, human nature's pretty good and pretty cool.'

Anouree has two children and initially found it hard to get close to them, especially as babies. 'The essential link of closeness,' she says. When she gave birth to both, she couldn't hold them straightaway. She was frightened of contact, and wary of a baby's innocence because her innocence had been ruptured. 'That was so hard for me. I had to make contact with my two babies physically. I was determined to do so, because I knew that would be an investment for the rest of my nurturing for these two children.'

The postscripts for the Uptop children are all, like Anouree's story, about recovery and degrees of redemption. How to survive damage, how to find redemption, how to live on and walk on. We ask Anouree how she will feel when Anne dies. 'I will definitely feel relieved. But she might as well be dead now.'

Ben found his redemption in Jesus Christ — the Biblical one. He is born again and heavily involved with a Christian church in Western Australia. But it was a long road. He was reunited with his three half-brothers (from his mother Joy's first marriage — the cult Aunty he never knew, as a child, was his mother) not long after the Uptop raid, and in the 1990s married and had two children. He also began seeing his grandmother, his mother's mother.

Joy was still deep within the cult and had been since Anne had, she believed, cured her with a miracle right back in the 1960s. She had obeyed Anne and not contacted her son. But one day, while visiting his grandmother in a nursing home in Melbourne, Joy was there.

'Providence had allowed us both to connect,' Ben says. 'Which was incredible. The conversation I had with her was surreal, it was just like meeting anyone from the street. "Ben, how are you?" "Good, here's my kids, here's my wife; meet Joy."'

Joy was living in the United Kingdom, but she agreed to meet Ben again while in Melbourne. She told Ben who his real father was (he had died) and admitted that if she had her time again and had better information to hand she would not do the things she had done. 'That's probably as close as we're ever going to get to her saying, "I stuffed up and I'm sorry,"' says Ben. 'You can't go back and fix the past, but it would be a travesty of justice to destroy the future for her. Everyone deserves the chance at redemption.'

So Ben set about restoring his relationship with her. 'My kids, at least,' Ben says, 'should have the option of having a grandmother, and if I can see that she's not going to damage them, she's not going to fill them with poison, then it's safe.'

Trust grew between the two. She had given him up as a baby, believing that she had handed him to Jesus, and then she had become an Aunty for a time, overseeing not only him but also a bunch of other kids. So in a sense what she had done was not just give him up but also distance herself from him further by not acknowledging him to be her son. 'I have a relationship with my mother that is to the level where she will allow it to go, with a level of honesty that she wants, and it's very painful for her.'

Ben took Joy and his children to Uptop once. The lakehouse at that point was uninhabited, but it is a traumascape for a returning cult child: a haunted place. 'I showed my kids around. I had always told them what had happened. I was able to do it in a manner where they were able to see it for what it was, able to ask the questions, understand.'

He came to the Christian God through Anne, in a sense, but also because he saw what he calls the 'intelligent design' of Him through nature. In simple terms, he was looking for the light after the dark, and this was where he found it. He recognises the 'beauty' of Lake Eildon's landscape and countryside, in a literal and a symbolic sense. He figured there was a divine power looking over him through the years when another elaborately maintained divine power — Anne — held sway. 'I'd always had a belief there had to be something there, a God in the sky who did have some level of control.' The fact that he survived Uptop only made this belief surer in his mind.

Ben met some Christians, and they told him they knew this God and He was benevolent, which, for Ben, made a change. '[Their God was] a gentleman who wouldn't force himself upon me. Powerful, and who would interject in life, which the Bible spoke about as miracles.'

Ben has experienced miracles directly, he says. He has persisted in looking for meaning. His cult story began with Anne performing a miracle on his mother; she got out of bed and walked. And what is a cult if not a collection of people looking for meaning under the direction of a charismatic leader? Ben has retained elements of the cult's supernaturalism about him, but only in the benign, benevolent sense, and in them he has found redemption. He says that he tested God's power by asking Him to stop rain falling and dogs barking, and God showed him. 'And then it became clear that, *Hang on, there is, wow, this, there is something, there is!* There is a power there that is willing to listen to me. I know God spoke to me and said, "You know I'm real, stop testing me. I've proven myself, now I want you to get to know me."'

Ben's analogy is simple: he found the way from darkness to light. He calls both places 'kingdoms'. Where darkness lived, darkness was spoken of, he says. 'Where the truth is hidden, things go on that damage people, constant fear. The end effect on people is one of being bound, and it's destructive, and it's not healthy. So it was coming out of the kingdom of darkness into the light and then into an environment where you're able to be healed and to move on and create a good future. Believing there can be a future, knowing there will be struggles, and knowing there will be a power to overcome all critical things.'

He knows the Uptop discipline was horribly out of proportion: 'not designed for restoration of relationship and genuine character being built for the better of that person'. With his own children, he is careful to implement 'loving discipline'. This means that if one of his kids needs to be disciplined — with a talking-to or punishments within the home — he makes sure the child is reassured afterward and the loving relationship is restored. 'You are saying the love is still there, I still care, this is done out of love. That's redemptive, that's restoring, this is necessary to shape character.'

Ben learned the difference between right and wrong beside the lake. He knew, when he was old enough, that what was happening was wrong. His view is that Anne wanted to be a guru much more than she wanted to be a mother. 'The truth is, we weren't their [Anne and Bill's] children. She had to transition us into seeing her as a guru, seeing her as someone who had complete control. You don't want a mother bond. She had to have people incapable of forming relationships with other people, that craved her affection and her approval, that feared her and respected her. You're dependent upon her, and she can control. That's what she had to create.'

For Leeanne, her children are the centre of her belief system. She is confronted by the idea that children could be harmed individually or systematically and, more so, that children could be given up or given away.

Like Anouree, Leeanne's experience of labour and birth were profound and showed her how strong powers of goodness can be. One of her births was long and difficult, and it illustrated to her that a pure bond is the truest thing imaginable. 'How could you do that and then give up that child and not even see her? There is no way in the world that anybody would make me do that to my children ever, under any circumstances. I don't care how bad the circumstances are, that's my child and that child has been inside me.' Giving birth triggered strong feelings about her birth mother and ideas around separation. 'I really hated my mother at that point. I could never come to terms with the fact that she thought it was right to give me up.'

Leeanne is angry that her childhood disappeared to the point where if she had died, she reckons, no one outside the cult would know. Hidden away and abused, given a fake name, the apple of her Master's eye and Daddy's Girl. She's angry that the police investigation didn't nail Anne or Bill on serious charges: 'It's appalling they were never punished for what they put us through as children.' She's angry, too, that the safety net for them when they were freed was minimal. 'Every one of us has been affected in some way, we all have mental scarring.' But Leeanne says all the Uptop children took one thing from their horrific experience together beside the lake — survival. 'That's all we did, we just survived, and we're lucky we survived. Now as adults with children of our own, we're still all trying to survive. We're still all trying to live in the world that we never grew up in.'

In 2016, as this book and the associated documentary film *The Family* were being finished, Sarah Moore died. She had spoken to us at length over a period of four years but suffered extremely poor physical and mental health, which she always attributed to the cult.

She lived by herself in a unit in suburban Melbourne, near the hills but not in the hills. She was in contact with a close circle of blood family, friends and helpers, but was found dead in the unit. Police said the cause of death was heart failure. She was 46.

Sarah was the Uptop kids' fulcrum. To them, she was the smartest and the boldest; the others largely followed her lead. After Leeanne escaped, Sarah rebelled one last time and was excommunicated to 'die in the gutter'. Her outspokenness made her the children's spokesperson in the media after the raid, and she developed a close relationship with Marie Mohr (whom she lived with for a time) and David Elias of *The Age*.

She was initially closest to Anne. Sarah found that she could get in Anne's ear and used that channel to advocate on behalf of the children, as they got older, to try and get them better treatment. Anne would listen to Sarah and take her views on board. 'I did feel a bit special compared to some of the other kids.

She didn't dye my hair and she gave me that extra time.'

Sarah was initiated into the cult, and rejected the spiritual advances of Swami Muktananda in favour of Anne's spiritual teachings, but then, as she became a teenager, she rejected Anne. 'Once I betrayed her, I had fulfilled the role of Judas. Every messiah has to have a Judas, I guess. I agreed to talk to the police, even though I knew that was betraying her. Everything that happened from then on was my fault, whether I was involved with it or not.'

Sarah received death threats from cult members and said her flat was broken into numerous times. Sarah was seen as the person who fed all the lies about abuse at Uptop to the other children after the raid: the ringleader, the provoker. The cult's line was that she brainwashed them and instilled a victim mentality. Sarah's telling and re-telling of the Uptop story — including in her own book, published in 1995 — became the established narrative around the cult: the blonde hair, the beatings, the buckets.

'They keep bringing it up,' Michael told us, after Sarah's death and funeral, not talking in cosmic riddles anymore but plainly spoken. 'Like regurgitating a foul smell from their stomachs. They are on a victim-fuelled rocket to nowhere.'

Sarah's life, and death, were tragic. After being freed from the cult she met her own birth mother and remained in touch with her, but all those years ago, beside the lake, when Anne wasn't there, Sarah assumed she would come back to rescue her and the children. When told Anne was overseas, Sarah would look out over the lake and see the other side and think, *That's where she is. Overseas.*

'We didn't realise that she had set it up. We thought we were in this hell-hole and she'd get us out of it. We'd rock ourselves to sleep at night and get punished for the rocking. Calling out

259

"Mummy, Daddy." Thinking that they were just over the lake. We'd be calling out for them to come and save us from the beatings and stop the abuse.'

A year after the raid she helped instigate, Sarah enrolled at the University of Melbourne to study medicine, but she found it difficult to proceed calmly with the façade of a normal life. She knew Anne had said she had placed a curse on her, and Anne had also spread the lie — through the lodge — that Sarah had cancer and would suffer horribly for her betrayal.

In fact, Sarah was diagnosed with glandular fever and endometriosis, and was in severe pain a lot of the time. In her first year at university, she attempted suicide and was put into a psychiatric hospital. Then she moved in with Marie, re-started her studies, and in 1993 went on her first elective posting into Asia as a student doctor, working for the American Refugee Committee on the border of Myanmar and Thailand with the displaced Karen Burmese minority.

'Medicine is about pain and suffering and people sometimes dying, no matter what you do,' she wrote. 'It's about blood and sweat — some of it your own — and about hopelessness and tears and feeling like giving up occasionally. But it is also about smiles and gratitude and love and finding peace and courage and wisdom from other people, no matter what language they speak. Being in the camps taught me about myself. It helped me on the journey to finding out who I am. Sometimes all you could be was a human being.'

The following year she set out again, to India, into the slums of Kolkata with an NGO called Calcutta Rescue. She also worked with the medical unit attached to a Hindu mission. She wrote her book *Unseen, Unheard, Unknown*, finished her degree, and worked as a doctor at clinics and hospitals in Melbourne. She also studied psychoanalysis at university.

But Sarah's mental health suffered, and combined with her poor physical health, took an acute toll. 'That whole combination of having endometriosis and actual real pain combined with stuff that I had repressed from the cult combined into a more or less lethal cocktail.'

In 2004, she began forging prescriptions to get the opiate pethidine for her own use. She was charged by police and went to court and pleaded guilty. The court heard she had bipolar disorder and post-traumatic stress disorder. She was not able to practise as a doctor anymore, and in 2008 she attempted suicide again, by injection in her leg, but she made a mistake and injected air. Her lower leg had to be amputated and she spent the rest of her life in a wheelchair.

Sarah maintained that she was poorly treated by police over the pethidine charges and then poorly treated in the hospital over her leg. She always said that it didn't need to be amputated, but it was. 'Bit of a let down by society — I hadn't done anything much more than try and service (society) to the best of my capacity since I left the cult.'

Then in 2009 Sarah got herself involved in a perhaps ill-advised media stunt — with Melbourne's *Herald-Sun* tabloid and Channel Nine's *Sixty Minutes* — to have a reunion with Anne. Her motive, as she saw it, was to try and make at least some peace. She was by now a Buddhist. The television journalist Karl Stefanovic asked Anne if she was 'evil' or 'a monster', as she denied the beatings and dunkings and drugs and claimed, once again, to be Sarah's natural mother. Anne called stories of abuse 'absolute bullshit'.

Michael sat in on the interview, out of shot, but imposed himself upon it by accusing Sarah of lying about Uptop. He pointed at her and raised himself in his seat in defence of his Master — Anne was wearing a wig and dark glasses, with pink lipstick and pearls, but was slouched in her chair — and said to Sarah: 'You are living a fantasy of pain and deprivation.'

Anne chuckled.

At Sarah's funeral, friends, including Ben, Leeanne, and Anouree, denounced Anne by reminding those present what Sarah had been through as a child and as a young woman and also reminding them, despite it all, of Sarah's compassion towards others, drive to help others, and positivity.

But while she was still alive, Sarah wondered why it was that her Uptop brothers and sisters could not adapt well to the outside world, and why the pain would never go away. 'Self-loathing, feelings of worthlessness and shame, and irrational guilt were our legacy,' she wrote. Sarah told us before she died that the Australian government should launch a full inquiry into The Family with a view to compensating victims further. She drew upon a case from New Zealand where a large, communal cult called Centrepoint was broken up by authorities after charismatic leader Bert Potter, a vacuum-cleaner salesman with big supplies of LSD and ecstasy, was jailed for indecently assaulting children. Assets belonging to his cult were seized by the New Zealand government and given to victims, upon application, for counselling, education, or poverty relief.

Sarah's funeral had a Buddhist theme. Lex de Man and Peter Spence were there, Marie Mohr was there, saying farewell, goodbye, along with Leeanne, Ben, and Anouree. To their horror, Michael arrived — 'because Sarah insisted I be here,' he said. It was a stormy Melbourne winter day; Michael told us later that the storm was Sarah's 'angst' gathering once and for all and dispersing to the winds to be gone.

Michael walked away from the funeral before it had finished. He said this was because it was dishonest — the lies about the abuse, the attacks on Anne. Blame the Aunties, he said, if anyone.

Anne never did anything wrong. 'She has been betrayed,' he said. His final word. 'But she is inscrutable. She walks on. And that does not mean she will not seek vengeance.'

Anne lives on. Just before Sarah's funeral, Lex told us: 'Unjustly, she dies while the cult leader continues to live.' Dementia renders Anne unable to communicate meaningfully, or to remember. She cannot speak for herself anymore. But she still has thoughts and feelings. What is in her thoughts, and what does she feel? Did she ever feel any better than sitting in her purple chair at the front of the lodge, the place silent in the hills, hundreds of followers wrapped in blankets against the cold, her word as the law? What does she think now of Raynor, of Howard, of Trish, and of Liz? Did you, Anne, ever tell a lie? Did your mother ever take you in her arms? What, in the end, did you want?

We think of that room of Anne's in the nursing home, in the shadow of Melbourne's hills — the small, overheated room full of photographs. Photographs of The Family, the kids with white hair, Bill tanned and handsome; Anne looking at herself in a mirror in her spectacular prime, doomed and statuesque, glamour heavily applied. These are haunted objects, and she sits among them and she lies among them.

Anne's extraordinary haunting remains as well in her buildings and streets: the cult's grove in Ferny Creek, still largely under her spell in both the real and metaphysical sense — the big houses up there, Winbirra and Crowther House, with their heavy curtains and ornate drawing rooms. Uptop, of course, hidden by the lake with the submerged, wounded trees. The Santiniketan Lodge, fallen in disrepair. Newhaven. Hurleyville. Broom Farm.

Even if Anne wanted to talk or confess or wonder about her choices, as she reaches 100 years old — born in 1921 in a tiny, backroads place — perhaps she can't. But what we have learned about her is that she wanted to claw her way out of there so desperately, she constructed an entirely new identity. She wanted to surround herself with what she thought was love — the love of adults, children, and the universe. But it was fake, an illusion, a terrible dream.

She invented a religion from a kitbag of delusions and known theosophical tropes at the perfect time in the perfect place, and she appointed herself in charge. She gave herself magical powers. She drove Jaguars and Daimlers and wore sophisticated red dresses and high heels. She plied people with LSD to make them believe her. She said her own spiritual guru could walk through time, that she was Jesus, and that aliens flew flying saucers through Earth's skies in spring.

Keep close, she told them all, protect me. 'They want me dead.'

ABOUT THE FILM

An incendiary, heartbreaking investigation into one of Australia's most notorious cults, and the scars its victims still bear today.

Anne Hamilton-Byrne was beautiful, charismatic, and, many say, incredibly dangerous. Convinced she was a living god, Hamilton-Byrne headed an apocalyptic sect dubbed The Family. With her husband, Bill, she acquired numerous children — some through adoption scams, some born to cult members — and raised them as her own. Isolated from the outside world, the children were dressed in matching outfits, had dyed blonde hair, and were allegedly beaten, starved, and injected

265

with LSD. Taught that Hamilton-Byrne was both their mother and the messiah, the children were eventually rescued during a police raid in 1987, but their trauma had only just begun.

Melbourne director Rosie Jones (*The Triangle Wars*) and producer Anna Grieve (*Croker Island Exodus*) have spent years digging into the disturbing mysteries of The Family. With survivors and current members of The Family telling their stories on camera, alongside the Australian and international police who worked the case, this confronting documentary exposes not only what happened within the still-operating sect but also within the conservative Melbourne community that allowed The Family to flourish.

The Family had its world premiere at the Melbourne International Film Festival July 2016 and will screen theatrically in 2017.

'Plenty of style and lots of emotional heft' **THE AGE**

'A damning, absorbing portrait of one of the most insidious groups in Australian history ... an engrossing study not just of a specific situation, but of the psychology behind it.' **SCREEN DAILY**

'Jones' movie is a triumph. Bleak, terrifying, and heart-breaking, it is a powerful cautionary tale and an affirmation of the strength and resilience that people can be capable of, even in the worst of circumstances.'
AUDIENCES EVERYWHERE

'Evil and abuse masked under by the cloth of goodness and (non-official) religion flourishes everywhere in the world.' **FILM IRELAND**

Developed and produced by Big Stories Co. in association with

**For the latest theatrical release details,
visit www.thefamilysect.com**

NOTES ON SOURCES

We have made every effort to ensure the accuracy of the information within this book was correct at time of publication. Where we have relied on others' firsthand accounts of events, we have quoted their words as recorded for the feature documentary *The Family* or additional interviews with them. Where we have quoted from letters, transcripts, and case files, we have reproduced the text as it appeared in the original.

First-person accounts in *The Family* are drawn from interviews with 18 participants filmed for the feature documentary *The Family* as well as separate interviews with some over four years of research. Six of these interviews were with former cult children, two with former Australian policemen, and one with a former FBI agent in the United States. Two more were with journalists who had covered the cult's story. One series of interviews was with a current cult member, and several more were with former cult members.

Further material is from files gathered for the Victoria Police taskforce Operation Forest, the library of *The Age*, and police and legal sources. We also interviewed numerous other people who had dealings with the cult or had family connections to it, but never joined.

We have used ABC radio interviews with Anne and Bill Hamilton-Byrne, Donald Webb, and Megan Dawes by Ranald MacDonald from 25 October 1994 and 3 May 1995.

Material on the earliest formations of The Family is drawn from Dr Raynor Johnson's unpublished diary, covering the years 1962 to 1978.

We drew on Dr Sarah Moore's book *Unseen, Unheard, Unknown* (Penguin Australia, 1995; published under the name Sarah Hamilton-Byrne) for her descriptions of LSD use in the cult.

In the chapter 'The Seekers', we have drawn on *Raynor Johnson: a biographical memoir* by Alan Moore (Lakeland Publications, 2007), *Lift Up Your Eyes* by Ambrose Pratt (Robertson and Mullens, 1935), and *The Light and the Gate* by Raynor Johnson (Hodder and Stoughton, 1964). We also referred to *The Light and the Gate* in 'Blue Rooms', regarding The Venerable Sumangalo.

In 'Uptop', we have referred to Dr Sarah Moore's book *Unseen, Unheard, Unknown*, in particular her descriptions of self-harming while at Uptop. We have also drawn from her book in 'The Hole' (descriptions of the food at Uptop and attending Kenlaurel dancing school), 'The Sound of Music' (hair bleaching), 'Hurleyville' (Swami Muktananda), and 'The Kingdom' (her medical career).

In 'The Hole', we have drawn on '"Mother" Tells: I illegally took 28 children', *The Herald*, 5 November 1987.

In 'Fires', we have referred to Marie Mohr's report for Channel Nine News, 30 October 1985.

In 'Sacred Manna', we have quoted from Dr L. Howard Whitaker's paper on therapeutic use of LSD from 'Lysergic Acid

Diethylamide in Psychotherapy', parts I and II, in *The Medical Journal of Australia* 51: 5–8, 11 January 1964. We have also used material from one of Marie Mohr's reports, 'The Family Part 3', featuring Marie Mohr in Hawaii with Anne and Bill Hamilton-Byrne, *A Current Affair*, Channel Nine, 30 April 1990, and have quoted from the Daily Hansard, Parliament of Victoria, Parliamentary Debates, Legislative Assembly, 51st Parliament, First Session, Tuesday 15 May – Wednesday 16 May 1990.

In 'Santiniketan', we referred to *Raynor Johnson: a biographical memoir* by Alan Moore to help understand Johnson's last days. In the text we have referred to an interview with Johnson, 'Secret Society Part One', *Dateline*, Channel ATV-0, circa June/July 1971. We have also quoted from the letter David Whitaker wrote (with his brother) to members of The Family, of which he provided us a copy.

In 'Love is in the Air', we have quoted from the speech that Marie Mohr gave at Leeanne's wedding in 1995, courtesy of Leeanne and Marie Mohr.

In 'Blue Rooms', we have used extracts from Anthony Leigh's manuscript, 'Now I Can Get My New Tattoo', courtesy of Anthony Leigh.

In 'Hurleyville', we have referenced Raynor Johnson's article in *Light*, College of Psychic Studies, volume 95, number 3, 1975.

In 'The Kingdom', we have quoted from the eulogy David Whitaker wrote for his mother, of which he provided us a copy. We have also quoted from Karl Stefanovic's story 'The Family', *Sixty Minutes*, Channel Nine, 2 October 2009, and drawn from Stephen Drill's article 'Authorities Launch Review After Links Between Notorious Cult "The Family" and Melbourne School', *The Sunday Herald Sun*, 27 July 2014.

FURTHER READING

Brunton, Paul, *The Secret Path*, E.P. Dutton and Company, 1935.

Furst, Peter T., *Hallucinogens and Culture*, Chandler and Sharp, 1976.

Hamilton-Byrne, Sarah, *Unseen, Unheard, Unknown*, Penguin Books, 1995.

Horne, Donald, *Time of Hope: Australia 1966–72*, Angus and
    Robertson, 1980.

Huxley, Aldous, *Island*, Harper and Brothers, 1962.

Johnson, Raynor, *The Imprisoned Splendour: an approach to reality,
    based upon the significance of data drawn from the fields of
    natural science, psychical research, and mystical experience*,
    Hodder & Stoughton, 1953.

Moore, Alan, *Raynor Johnson: a biographical memoir*, Lakeland
    Publications, 2007.

Storr, Anthony, *Feet of Clay: a study of gurus*, Harper Collins, 1997.

Wordley, Dick, *Cathy's Child*, Gazelle Publications, 1979 (first
    published as *A Piece of Paper*, Tempo Books, 1973).

ACKNOWLEDGEMENTS

We are indebted to many people for their assistance with this book.

It would not have been written without the extraordinary help of former Detective Senior Sergeant Lex de Man AFSM, whose dedication to the pursuit of justice for those caught in The Family continues. His vivid memories, and those of his colleague, former Detective Senior Sergeant Peter Spence, helped us to get inside the Victoria Police taskforce Operation Forest, which brought charges against Anne Hamilton-Byrne. Thanks also to Victoria Police for their assistance.

Our special thanks go to the brave people whose interviews for the feature documentary *The Family* are a major part of this book: Barbara Kibby, Fran Parker, Anthony Leigh, Michael, Bryan Cussen, Rob Maclellan, Ian Weeks, Philippe de Montignie, Hilda Kogut, Kerry Lawrence, Joan Radha Bridges, and Marie Mohr. And especially to the former children of the cult, Adam, Sarah, Leeanne, Anouree, Ben, and David.

Thanks also to Kay Scott, Alana Balfour, Jenny Dawson, Syd and Christine Savage, Chris and Kaye Rigg, Judge Carolyn

Douglas, John Helmer, and the Citizens Commission on Human Rights, as well as those who so generously assisted in the research but prefer to remain anonymous.

Many thanks to John Thomson, Angus Thomson, and Peter Tapp. At *The Age*, thanks to Jason Steger, Michael Bachelard, Michelle Stillman, and Maria Paget, and thanks also to David Elias and Gerard Ryle for their dogged reporting on The Family in the 1980s. Big thanks to Benjamin Law, Alex Adsett, Peter Bain-Hogg, Linda Klejus, Penny Stephens, and Tom and Kit Johnston.

Very special thanks to film producer Anna Grieve, for her dedication and unwavering commitment to the telling of this story. She has wisely commented on the many drafts. Her advice has been invaluable.

Lastly, special thanks to Julia Carlomagno and Henry Rosenbloom at Scribe for their expert guidance.